Selected Essays
in Kaleckian Economics

Koinon:
Sozialwissenschaftliche interdisziplinäre Studien

Herausgegeben von Savvas A. Katsikides

Band 11

PETER LANG

Evangelos N. Charos/
Savvas Katsikides (eds.)

Selected Essays in Kaleckian Economics

A Collection of Essays on Profits and Investment

PETER LANG

Bibliographic Information published by the Deutsche Nationalbibliothek
The Deutsche Nationalbibliothek lists this publication in the Deutsche Nationalbibliografie; detailed bibliographic data is available in the internet at http://dnb.d-nb.de.

Library of Congress Cataloging-in-Publication Data
A CIP catalog record for this book has been applied for at the Library of Congress.

Cover Design:
© Olaf Gloeckler, Atelier Platen, Friedberg

ISSN 1434-274X
ISBN 978-3-631-67886-2 (Print)
E-ISBN 978-3-653-07025-5 (E-PDF)
E-ISBN 978-3-631-70240-6 (EPUB)
E-ISBN 978-3-631-70241-3 (MOBI)
DOI 10.3726/978-3-653-07025-5

Peter Lang – Berlin · Bern · Bruxelles · New York · Oxford · Wien · Warszawa

www.peterlang.com

Contents

Preface

This collection of essays mainly represents the collaborative efforts of Douglas Mair, Professor Emeritus of Heriot-Watt University in Edinburgh, Scotland and Anthony Laramie, Professor of Economics at Merrimack College in North Andover, Massachusetts. Other co-authors, over the last decade or so, include Jerry Courvisanos, Associate Professor of Innovation and Entrepreneurship at the University of Ballarat, in Victoria, Australia, Hossein S. Kazemi, Professor of Economics at Stonehill College, in North Eastern Massachusetts, and the editor of this volume, Evangelos Charos, Professor of Economics, also at Merrimack College. This collection covers a variety of works, some previously published, and some not, that span a twenty-year period.

The first chapter, "Full Employment: Gift Horse or Trojan Horse?" by Mair and Laramie, was originally published in the Review of Social Economy, Volume LX, No. 4, in 2002, and was presented at Kalecki's Centenary Conference at the Warsaw School of Economics in 1999. This article recognizes Kalecki's 1943 essay "Political Aspects of Business Cycles" as a seminal work on political business cycle theory. Mair and Laramie interpret, as Kalecki puts it, business leaders' opposition to full employment policies as a form of rent seeking, that these oppositions were anticipated in Olsons's theory of distributional coalitions, and that these distributional coalitions provide the transmission mechanisms (missing in Kalecki's work) and tensions that generate the political business cycle.

The second chapter, by Mair and Laramie, was first published in the *International Review of Applied Economics*, Vol. 10, No. 2, in 1996. In this article, Mair and Laramie discuss, using a Kaleckian framework, "The Macroeconomic Effects of Taxation in a Federal Europe." In this paper, Mair and Laramie explain how fiscal policy—in particular changes in the composition of taxation—could be used to promote full employment in the context of the constraints imposed by Maastricht Treaty, and explain how the economic incidence and effects of taxation vary between national and regional political authorities.

The third chapter, authored by Mair, examines the role of fiscal policy in an independent Scotland. In this chapter, the historical context of fiscal autonomy for Scotland is discussed and the focus is on Scottish control over the corporation income tax. Mair reviews neoclassical tax theory and finds it deficient for the standard assumptions of microfoundations, the market-clearing full employment assumptions, and discusses various strains of the Kaleckian/Post Keynesian alternatives to the problem of understanding the economic incidence of profits taxes.

Mair concludes that the Scottish government's attempts to reduce the capital tax to accelerate economic growth would likely be frustrated by increases in the income tax rate, and that, given the increased income inequality and rising "financialisation" of income, the relevant fiscal option is capital taxation.

The fourth chapter, "Regional Tax Differentials: A Kaleckian Approach," by Laramie and Mair, was originally published in ***Regional Studies***, Volume 39, No. 3, in 2005. This article extends the work of Kalecki (1971/1937) and Laramie and Mair (2000) to consider how regional taxation has both local and macroeconomic effects. The various elements of Kaleckian tax incidence and effects are specified. Local tax policies, for example at the state level in the U.S., have macroeconomic effects (including excess burden effects), and these macroeconomic effects are transmitted back to "economic regions" depending upon the disaggregation of (static) distribution factors. As an example, the effects of an increase in the income tax levied by the Scottish Parliament are illustrated. In this paper, "beggar thy neighbor" effects are discussed where local jurisdictions have the incentives to be fiscally conservative, while encouraging "neighbors" to be fiscally liberal, to capture the spillover effects of fiscal stimuli. Two policy implications emerge: First, a federation of independent fiscal authorities will likely race to the bottom and provide an inadequate level of fiscal policy (in the Musgravian sense of inadequate allocative, redistributive and stabilization functions). Second, a federal fiscal authority is needed to account for and prevent this race to the bottom.

Chapter 5, "The Effects of Taxation in a Kaleckian Growth Model," by Laramie and Mair, was originally published in ***Metroeconomica***, Volume 54, Nos. 2 & 3, in 2003. This article extends Kalecki's (1971/1968) long-run theory of economic growth to consider the effects of taxation, and is based off an extended version (where the gearing ratio and capacity utilization matter) of Kalecki's third and final attempt to explain, and, therefore, fine-tune his theory of "economic dynamics." In particular, Kalecki, as is well known, understood the long-period as consisting of a series of short-periods. In the short-period, investment determines profits, but, through lags, the profits affect investment. The result is both a trend and a cyclical pattern of investment that is co-dependent. The effects of wage and profits taxation on the long-run trend rate of growth depends on a set of empirical questions related to the government budget stance, and the tax shifting assumptions/the distributional effects of taxation. For example, given a balanced budget constraint, an un-shifted profits tax increase: a) accelerates the depreciation of existing capital; b) has no effect on business profits (if workers do not save any of the additional income generated through the balance budget effect); and c) increases the trend level of investment.

Chapter 6, by Courvisanos, Laramie and Mair, "Tax Policy and Innovation: A Search for Common Ground," was originally published in ***Intervention***, Volume 6, No. 2, in 2009. In this article, the mainstream and Kaleckian approaches to fiscal policy are contrasted, the role of taxation in affecting economic growth is revisited, the role of taxes on greenhouse emissions, in our Kaleckian approach, is used to illustrate the effects of taxes on the rate of innovations, and we illustrate how taxes interact with a "political innovations cycle" where businesses hold back "best practice" (innovations) capital goods, depending upon relative costs and profit conditions. The article identifies the three fears that capitalists have with respect to innovations (which parallel the fears with respect to full employment): a) loss of economic control, as new entrants into markets are encouraged by innovations; b) loss of policy control, as innovations become distributed through public institutions; and c) loss of workforce control, where innovations are intended to maintain "high union membership structures."

Chapter 7, "Accounting for Corporate Profits: 1991–2014," by Laramie and Mair, illustrates how the national income and product accounts, following recent changes to the definitions in the U.S., can be used to "operationalize" Kalecki's theory of profits. In particular, corporate profits are shown to be largely defined as the sum of gross domestic investment, the government budget deficit, the current account surplus and corporate dividends less the sum of the consumption of fixed capital and personal savings. The behavior of profits and their components is described following the recessions of 1991, 2001 and 2007–2009. The economic expansions of corporate profits following the 1991 and 2001 recessions were largely investment driven (corporate increased almost pro tanto with gross domestic investment). In addition, the government budget deficit acted as a stabilizer on corporate profits. During this time period, no apparent relationship between government budget deficit and the current account deficit is found.

Chapter 8, "Kalecki and Fisher: Income and Capital Taxation," by Laramie and Mair, is a history of thought exercise. Both Kalecki and Fisher published seminal works in 1937: Fisher – "The Nature of Capital and Income"; Kalecki – "A Theory of Commodity, Income and Capital Taxation". Fisher and Kalecki both explore the origins of income from capital. Fisher considers the various charges and credits that generate net income flows, and he concludes that income from capital is psychical—like consumer and producer surplus. Fisher concludes that psychical income is best approximated as consumption (in the true theoretical sense of the word), and then considers the advantages of a consumption tax over other taxes, such as income and capital gains taxes, while implicitly assuming that the economic and legal incidences of taxes are identical. Kalecki, on the other hand, saw the origins of income to capital as business investment and capitalist consumption decisions, while explicitly assuming that the legal and economic incidences (as a "consequence of Mr. Keynes's General Theory") could be quite different. Unfortunately for the field of public finance, the Fisherian approach to taxation has dominated public policy discussions, and the dual tax system (where income from capital receives preferential tax treatment) has evolved, contributing to the rise in income inequality, low wages, and excess capacity.

Chapters 9 and 10 are empirical investigations of Kalecki's theory of investment as modified by Courvisanos (1996). These chapters are co-authored by Charos, Kazemi, Laramie and Mair (CKLM). Courvisanos (1996) incorporated into Kalecki's theory of investment some of the behavioral elements of Keynes (like the capacity utilization rate, the interest rate, the gearing (leverage) ratio), and he termed the resulting theory of the business cycle the "susceptibility cycle." Both chapters build upon the idea that new orders have a set of behavioral elements, and that new orders, subject to lags and shocks, determine actual investment expenditures. In Chapter 9, CKLM use the U.S. census data to explain New Orders of Non-Defense Capital Goods in the U.S. in the period 1992 and 2013, using net corporate cash flows, the capacity utilization rate, a sales accelerator, an interest rate spread, a gearing/leverage ratio, the wage share, and national defense's share of GDP as explanatory variables. The estimated coefficients have anticipated sign and are statistically significant except for the the wage share and the gearing ratio coefficients. In Chapter 10, we repeat the study in Chapter 9, but then use our model to understand the relationship between orders of capital goods and shipments of (expenditures on) capital goods. In understanding the relationship between new orders and shipments of capital goods, we find that shipments and new orders are cointegrated and that new orders and the debt-to-equity ratio are cointegrated. The cointegration of these variables allows us to use a vector error correction model where we show, using quarterly and monthly data, how changes in the debt-to-equity ratio affect changes in the relationship between new orders and shipments of capital goods.

We thank Evangelos Charos, our editor, the editors at P. D. Lang, the various publishers who gave us permission to reprint previously published articles, especially Michelle Dickson, at Routledge, Taylor and Francis.

A. Laramie

References

Courvisanos, J. 1996. *Investment Cycles in Capitalist Economies: A Kaleckian Behavioural Contribution*, Cheltenham, Edward Elgar.

Fisher, Irving (1937). "Income in Theory and Income Taxation in Practice." *Econometrica*, 5, 1, 1–55.

Kalecki, Michal (1937). "A Theory of Commodity, Income and Capital Taxation." *The Economic Journal*, 47, 187, 444–450.

Laramie, Anthony J., and Mair, Douglas (2000). *A Dynamic Theory of Taxation.* Edward Elgar.

Kalecki, M. (1971/1943), "Political aspects of full employment." *Political Quarterly*, in *Selected Essays on the Dynamics of the Capitalist Economy*, Cambridge, Cambridge University Press.

Kalecki, M. (1971/1968), "Trend and business cycles reconsidered," *Economic Journal*, 78, 263–276, in *Selected Essays on the Dynamics of the Capitalist Economy*, Cambridge, Cambridge University Press.

Anthony J. Laramie, Merrimack College, MA, USA
Douglas Mair, Heriot-Watt University, Edinburgh, UK

Chapter 1: Full Employment: Gift Horse or Trojan Horse?*

Abstract: Kalecki's 1943 essay *Political Aspects of Full Employment (PAFE)* is widely recognised as a seminal essay in the theory of the political business cycle. The paper argues that *PAFE* may also be interpreted as an early recognition by Kalecki of the phenomenon of rent seeking. Kalecki's discussion of the rent-seeking behaviour of businessmen is shown to have anticipated Olson's subsequent theory of distributional coalitions. A Kalecki-Olson analysis provides an explanation for the movement in income shares in the UK since 1975.

1. Introduction

Kalecki's paper *Political Aspects of Full Employment* (1943) is held in high esteem in the literature on political business cycles – 'a brilliant essay (Boddy and Crotty (1975)), 'a classic article' (Henley (1988), 'a brilliant and perceptive piece' (Feiwel (1974). Nordhaus (1975) acknowledges that the 'only serious [early] theory [of the political causes of the business cycle] is that of M. Kalecki'. Henley (1988) notes that *PAFE* is still extensively cited in the economics, political science and sociology literatures and reports that the Social Science Citation Index recorded over 50 citings between 1980 and 1988. But, despite this acclaim, *PAFE* is essentially incomplete.

Mitchell, for example, while confirming Kalecki's originality as the progenitor of political business cycle analysis, argues that *PAFE* is deficient in at least one key respect.

> "According to Kalecki, inflation and unemployment are not simply manifestations of capitalism but tools of control for the manipulation of workers. But Kalecki went far beyond traditional Marxism; Kalecki was, in fact, the originator of the political business cycle analysis. In his theory, however, business interests prevail over the political institutions; it is not so much the politicians who initiate and manipulate the electoral cycle as it is the capitalist class which manipulates the economy and politicians. Unemployment is the major means of disciplining the workers. Kalecki was not entirely wrong; unemployment

* Mair, Douglas and Laramie, Anthony, Gift Horse or Trojan Horse, Review of Social Economy, Vol. LX, No. 4, December, 2002, pp. 567–593. Reprinted by permission of the publisher Taylor and Francis, Ltd, http://www.tanfonline.com

> does place a powerful constraint on union demands. Unfortunately, Kalecki, like most Marxists, never spelled out the political mechanism by which capitalists are able to implement their economic policies. But they did not need to do so in a society with a small political sector; they could act directly over the economy by their own investment decisions' (Mitchell, 1988, pp. 94–94).

Similarly, Sawyer (1999, pp 487–488) has two principal criticisms of *PAFE*. The essence of *PAFE* is Kalecki's thesis that the conflict of interest between capitalists and workers will prevent the attainment and maintenance of full employment. Like Mitchell, Sawyer observes that what Kalecki did not identify was the actual transmission mechanism between the interests of these two classes on the one hand and the political and institutional systems of parliamentary democracies on the other. However, as Mitchell has argued above, in the context in which Kalecki was writing, which was of pre-war democratic economies with relatively small public sectors and economically impotent politicians, there was no need for him to do so. But this is not convincing because in *PAFE* Kalecki was anticipating a situation in which governments would have learned the 'trick' of achieving full employment by their own spending decisions. It, therefore, behoved him to be more explicit about the transmission mechanisms through which businessmen would register their opposition to full employment in a democratic society.

Sawyer's second reservation is that in a democratic society with intervals of 4 to 5 years (or perhaps less) between elections, there is insufficient time for the feedbacks between capitalists and workers over the political and social tensions of full employment to work themselves through. This suggests that Kalecki's concept of a 'political business cycle' should more properly be thought of as a 'political trend'. This is the view, for example, of Steindl (1979).

In *PAFE,* Kalecki did indeed provide early, though incomplete, insights into the role of political institutions as they affect the business cycle. Our purpose in this paper is not to look for the missing pieces that would complete *PAFE*. Instead, we wish to present a rather different interpretation of *PAFE* as an early contribution to the theory of rent seeking. Traditionally, economists have defined economic rent as income in excess of opportunity cost and rent seeking as any behaviour, political or otherwise, intended to increase that excess. Although Kalecki more or less ignored the tools of orthodox economics in his writings, we find in *PAFE* arguments that conventional economists would recognise as statements of rent seeking.

In order to evaluate the political business cycle and rent-seeking aspects of *PAFE,* we first consider Kalecki's investment model. Next, we identify the rent-seeking motives in *PAFE*. We then link our rent-seeking interpretation of *PAFE* to Olson's (1965, 1982) ideas on collective action and distributional coalitions and appraise the process of rent seeking and its implications for the business cycle in a Kalecki-Olson framework. We conclude that Kalecki provides an alternative approach for Olson to explain how the process of collective action comes to bear on aggregate economic performance and present evidence of how it has influenced post-war income shares in the UK.

2. Investment and the Political Business Cycle

Kalecki, like Keynes, viewed investment as the primary source of cyclical fluctuations in the capitalist economy. Kalecki (1954) developed an 'automatic' business cycle theory in which businessmen's investment decisions were argued to depend on their capital, on the savings of firms and their controllers and on changes in the rates of profits. The extent to which savings are reinvested into firms is limited by increasing risk as reflected in the savings coefficient in Kalecki's investment equation. The reinvestment of savings will also be affected by changes in firms' economic conditions, as reflected by changes in their rates of profits, and by how firms react to these changes as reflected in the rates of profits' coefficients. Kalecki rejected Keynes's marginal efficiency of capital (MEC) theory of investment because the MEC is unstable with respect to changes in investment. He showed instead that aggregate investment determines profits with a certain definite time lag and, consequently, that the profitability of investment varies with the level of investment. Kalecki's analysis captures a number of the elements of the investment decision. Even though the core of Keynes's investment theory can be rejected, elements of both theories, Kalecki's with its emphasis on entrepreneurial capital and the rates of profit and Keynes's with its emphasis on uncertainty, can be combined to develop a theory of investment and the political business cycle.

Such a model can be found in Courvisanos's (1996) idea of a susceptibility cycle in which he combines Kalecki's original investment model with a number of Kaleckian/Keynesian behavioral elements. While there are a large number of models that provide strong theoretical and empirical support for the existence of a Kaleckian-based investment cycle pattern, they all lack an underlying behavioral explanation of investment instability. By taking into account technological, economic and institutional factors that are recognised in the literature on behavioral and institutional economics, Courvisanos has developed a behavioral version of Kalecki's investment model which explains investment in the context of institutions and uncertainty. The objective Kaleckian manifestations of businesss confidence identified by Courvisanos are profits, the rate of change of profits, financial gearing and capacity utilisation.

In *PAFE*, Kalecki argued that the level of employment under *laissez-faire* capitalism depends heavily on businessmen's 'state of confidence', in other words on those factors which Courvisanos argues constitute the susceptibility cycle. He wrote:

> "...the social function of the doctrine of 'sound finance' is to make the level of employment dependent on the 'state of confidence'" (Kalecki, 1943/1971, p. 139).

The crux of the problem occurs when a government is prepared to use public expenditure to ensure full employment. That is when the power of businessmen to control investment, and through investment to control employment is threatened. Thus, the maintenance of *full employment* would:

> "....cause social and political changes which would give new impetus to the opposition of business leaders. Under a regime of permanent full employment, the 'sack' would cease to play its role as a disciplinary measure. The social position of the boss would be undermined and the self assurance and class consciousness of the working class would grow......In the slump, either under the pressure of the masses, or even without it, public investment, financed by borrowing, will be undertaken to prevent large scale unemployment. But if attempts are made to apply this method in order to maintain the high level of employment reached in the subsequent boom a strong opposition of 'business leaders' is likely to be encountered" (Kalecki, 1943/1971, pp. 140–144).

3. Kalecki and rent-seeking behaviour

But Kalecki leaves us guessing as to how the 'strong opposition of business leaders' will actually translate into effective political action, apart from enlisting the support of some tame economists to proclaim that maintaining a situation of full employment through government spending is manifestly unsound! In order to address this point and get at what we think is the real essence of *PAFE*, it is important to be clear just what Kalecki was really trying to explain. In his own words, what was of 'paramount importance' were:

> "the misgivings of big business about the maintenance of full employment by government spending. The consistent opposition by big business to experiments for increasing employment by government spending in all countries except Nazi Germany is not easy to explain. It is this difficult and fascinating question with which we intend to deal in this article" (Kalecki, 1943/1971, p. 138).

He defined three categories of reason for the opposition of 'industrial leaders' to full employment achieved by loan-financed Government spending (Kalecki 1943/1971, p. 139). These were:

- dislike of Government interference in the problem of employment as such
- dislike of the direction of Government spending (public investment and subsidising consumption)
- dislike of the social and political changes resulting from the *maintenance* of full employment (Kalecki's emphasis).

Taking them in turn, dislike of the first was due to a fear of a *loss of control* over government policy that businessmen would experience 'once Government learns the trick of increasing employment by its own purchases' (Kalecki 1943/1971, p. 139). Dislike of the public spending dimension of the second was again due a fear of a *loss of [policy] control* as government extended its influence into areas such as transport or public utilities which had previously been the domain of private business. Dislike of the consumption-subsidising dimension of the second was *ethical* rather than economic.

> "For here a 'moral' principle of the highest importance is at stake. The fundamentals of capitalist ethics require that 'You shall earn your bread in sweat' – unless you happen to have private means" (Kalecki 1943/1971, p. 140).

Dislike of the third was again due to a fear of a *loss of control,* this time in the workplace.

> "....under a regime of full employment, 'the sack' would cease to play its role as a disciplinary measure. The social position of the boss would be undermined and the self assurance and class consciousness of the working class would grow" (Kalecki 1943/1971, pp. 140–141).

He asserted that businessmen would be prepared to forego the higher profits they would enjoy under full employment because they value 'discipline in the factories' and 'political stability' more highly than profits. To confuse metaphors horribly, what it seems to us Kalecki is saying is that when businessmen look the 'gift horse' of full employment in the mouth they observe therein a 'Trojan horse'. By a *reductio ad absurdum* approach, he argues that stimulating *private* investment by cutting income tax or interest rates or by subsidy, however attractive this might be to businessmen, would not suffice to maintain full employment.

> "....if it were attempted to *maintain* full employment by stimulating private investment.... the rate of interest and income tax would have to be reduced continuously....in not too remote a time the rate of interest would have to be negative and income tax would have to be replaced by an income subsidy" (emphasis in original) (Kalecki 1943/1971, p. 143).

Willynilly, businessmen would have to accept a growing extension of loan-financed government spending if full employment were to be maintained. So, how can they make their opposition felt? At this point, Kalecki uses what at first sight may seem rather unusual terminology. Instead of referring specifically to 'businessmen' when talking about opposition to full employment, he refers instead to 'business leaders' or 'leaders of industry' either on their own (Kalecki 1943/1971, pp. 139, 141, 142, 144) or on several occasions to 'business leaders and their experts' (Kalecki 1943/1971, pp. 140, 144). Is this purely a semantic point or did he have something else in mind? Another argument he uses may provide a clue. He talks of the emergence of a coalition between businessmen and 'boom –tired' *rentiers*, big and small:

> "….a powerful block is likely to be formed between big business and the *rentier* interests, and they would probably find more than one economist to declare that the situation was manifestly unsound. The pressure of all these forces would most probably induce the Government to return to the orthodox policy of cutting down the budget deficit" (Kalecki 1943/1971, p. 144).

The issue here is the one that has bedeviled Kalecki, namely the failure of his critics to appreciate that there are two quite distinct strands to his theory of profits. First, there is the macroeconomic strand in which he argues that the *level* of profits is determined by the investment decisions of capitalists as expressed in his well known aphorism 'Capitalists earn what they spend while workers spend what they earn'. Second, there is the microeconomic strand in which he argues that the *share* of profits in national income is determined by the 'degree of monopoly'. Combining these two elements results in a theory in which national income is pushed up until it reaches the level determined by the 'distribution factors' i.e. the determining the income shares of wages and profits.

What businessmen have to achieve is a delicate balancing trick. On the one hand, through the autonomy they exercise over their investment decisions, they exercise control over politicians and the level of employment and also their own incomes. However, if the level of employment falls too low, political pressure increases for 'something to be done' and this becomes a credible threat once governments 'learn the trick' of influencing the level of employment by their own spending decisions. If the level of employment rises too high, then businessmen face the threat of a 'loss of discipline in the workplace' which manifests itself in a declining share of profits in national income due to a falling degree of monopoly brought about by increased levels of organised worker power.

A falling rate of profit as the economy approaches full employment will be due to either or both of two factors. First, businessmen may already have started cutting back on investment at an earlier stage in the upswing of the business cycle as a result of the increasing susceptibility identified by Courvisanos. This will result in a fall in the *level* of profits and will be accompanied by a falling *share* of profits as the degree of monopoly falls. In the absence of government intervention, these effects will be transitory. The economy will peak briefly at the level of full employment and will then embark on the downswing of the next cycle. If, however, the government intervenes to maintain the economy at the level of full employment, business susceptibility will receive a positive boost, thereby increasing investment and the level of profits. A declining *rate* of profit at full employment can only come about through a declining profit *share*, i. e. a declining degree of monopoly. The tradeoff faced by businessmen is between higher future *levels* of profit, accompanied by (i) declining control over politicians and their workforces, and (ii) a falling income *share* for profits, or lower future *levels* of profit, accompanied by (iii) higher levels of control over politicians and their workforces, and (iv) an increasing income *share* for profits. Their opposition to full employment indicates a preference for the latter.

This leads us to conclude that *PAFE* may be thought of at least as much as an essay on rent seeking as on the political business cycle. Basically, Kalecki is arguing that what concerns businessmen about the *maintenance* of full employment is their loss of control both over governments and their workforces and the demise of the capitalist work ethic. This will manifest itself in a falling income share. Retention of that control and that ethic, with its concomitant higher income share, is deemed to be worth more than the higher level of profits that would accompany full employment.

The distinction between businessmen's concerns over the *level* of profits and their concerns over the *share* of profits is important. Kalecki does not make this distinction explicit in *PAFE* although it is central to his theory of income distribution. We find evidence in *PAFE* to support this interpretation. Now, while businessmen may be prepared to accept a lower *level* of profits than would have been the case under full employment, we have to ask what prompted their opposition to increased government spending in the first place? It is clear from *PAFE* that it is their concern over a falling profit *share*. Underlying businessmen's fears is the recognition that there must inevitably follow a reduction in profit's *share* of national income.

> "The economic principles of Government intervention require that public investment should be confined to objects that do not compete with the equipment of private business, e. g. hospitals, schools, highways etc. *Otherwise the profitability of private investment might be impaired*....there is a danger that the Government, in pursuing this policy [of extending the scope of public investment] may eventually be tempted to nationalise transport or public utilities so as to gain a new sphere in which to carry out investment (Kalecki 1943/1971, pp. 139–140) (emphasis added).

Extension of Government intervention would either result in lower profits as a consequence of competition from public sector operators or the complete loss of private sector profits as a consequence of nationalisation. Either way, the outcome will be a fall in profits' income *share*. Businessmen's concerns over the erosion of capitalist ethics is not inspired by some high moral stance but by a fear that it will result in a reduction in profit's income share as the *raison d'être* of capitalism is challenged. The growth in the self-assurance and class consciousness of the working class brought about by full employment would result in strikes for wage increases and improvements in working conditions. Whatever political tensions these might create, they would result in an erosion of profit's income share as Kalecki (1954) was to argue in his discussion of the factors influencing the degree of monopoly.

4. The UK Political-Business Nexus

Kalecki's *PAFE* thesis is that the emergence and persistence of full employment will result in a concerted campaign on the part of business and *rentier* interests to persuade politicians that full employment is socially, economically and politically undesirable. For that to be the case, there needs to exist, we think, evidence of a systematic and coordinated channel of interaction between businessmen and politicians. This does not, however, appear to have been the case in the UK, at least for the past thirty years or so. For example, Grant (1987, p. 8) argues that despite increasing concentration of economic power, traditionally British business has been politically weak, making it difficult for government to enter into a partnership relationship with business even if it wanted to. Turner (1984, p. 3) characterises the historical relationship between business and the state in Britain as one of 'bargaining between two weak entities which often did not know their own minds'.

Grant (1987, pp. 165–169) recognises that the relationships between business interests and business, whether organised or not, have been a relatively neglected area of political science research in Britain. The relationship between business and political parties is often difficult and awkward but even the Conservative Party cannot be relied upon to act as the authentic spokesman of business. While the majority of businessmen may be Conservative supporters their support, Grant claims, is generally passive rather than active and they often have considerable reservations about the policies of the party. Equally, Conservative Party leaders have often felt badly let down by business. Edward Heath, for example, was apparently frustrated by the failure of British business to invest once, as he saw it, his government had created the economic conditions in which investment could take place.

While there are obviously a wide range of channels through which business and government communicate and interact, it does not seem to us that British experience over the past thirty years or so supports the proposition that there has been a coherent, systematic, class-oriented symbiosis between business and government. That is not to say that governments, particularly since 1979, have not introduced policies that were in the interests of business, but these do not appear to have been the result of a consciously orchestrated strategy.

This appears to have been the practice of Conservative governments under Mrs. Thatcher after 1979. An important element of Conservative policy from 1979 was a programme of reduction of the trade union powers. Five trade union reform acts of 1980, 1982, 1984, 1988 and 1990 extensively reduced the legal immunities that the trade unions had previously enjoyed. Supporters of the reforms claim that they effectively brought the trade unions back within the scope of the law. By the mid-1970s British trade unions had significantly enhanced their political and economic powers as a result of further extension to their legal privileges and immunities. Five principal trade union reform acts of the period 1980–1990 had the effect of removing many of the privileges – closed shops, secondary picketing, demarcation disputes, threat of dismissal for non-membership of a trade union – which had previously been benefits of trade union membership.

Was this industrial relations legislation the conscious and deliberate act of a 'capitalist' government consciously acting on behalf of business in order to 'restore discipline in the workplace'? Again, the evidence does not support this conclusion. Hanson (1991, pp. 15–16) identifies four main principles underlying the Conservatives' post-1979 approach to trade union reform. For our purposes, the two most relevant are:

- the process had to be step by step, with the next step being taken only when the previous one had proved its worth
- apart from the first step, the policy had to be pragmatic: it had to be worked out in the context of prevailing needs and circumstances.

Thus, Hanson concludes that these principles have meant that the Conservative approach to trade union reform since 1979 was pragmatic rather than strategic or even, he adds cynically, *ad hoc*. To a significant extent, the personalities and interests of the successive Secretaries of State for Employment under Mrs. Thatcher had a marked effect on the progress of the legislative programme.

Pragmatic or not, the effect on trade unions and labour relations was dramatic. Membership of closed shops fell from 5 million in 1979 to zero in 1993. Trade union membership fell by over 4 million in less than a decade and the proportion of workplaces recognising trade unions fell to less than 50 per cent. The proportion of the workforce paid under collective bargaining arrangements fell from around three quarters in 1979 to less than half by 1993. Strikes per worker in Britain in the 1980s fell more rapidly than in any other country and regained levels not experienced since the 1930s. Riddell notes:

> "A report produced in September 1988 for the Confederation of British Industry by Professor William Brown of Cambridge University noted that, while trade union recognition had survived the upheavals of the 1980s to a remarkable degree, individual employers were exercising greater control as the influence of joint national deals diminished. 'If employers continue to acquiesce in managing their labour with the assistance of a trade union they are doing so in a tighter, more controlled way'" (Riddell, 1989, p. 59).

5. The Logic of Collective Action

In the absence of evidence to support an overt rent-seeking relationship between business and government in the UK, it is necessary to consider how businessmen do actually achieve their desired political and economic ends within a Kaleckian framework. A central issue in *PAFE* is Kalecki's implicit recognition of the Prisoners' Dilemma problem of the conflict of interest between the private interests of individual businessmen and their collective interest as a class. This can be inferred from his references to the role of 'businessmen and their leaders' to which we refer above. Individually, businessmen will welcome full employment with its concomitant higher profits. Collectively, they see it as a threat to their hegemony over politicians and their workforces. While it is not in the interests of any one businessman to forego the higher profits of full employment, collectively it is in their interest to do so. But how will this be achieved under the institutions of the *normal* capitalist system?

This Prisoners' Dilemma problem of the conflict of interest between private and collective action was addressed some twenty years after *PAFE* by Mancur Olson in *The Logic of Collective Action* (Olson, 1965) and its sequel, *The Rise and Decline of Nations* (Olson, 1982). According to Olson (1982, p. 21), the paradox is resolved if organisations are fortunate enough to find a *selective incentive* that may be either positive or negative. For business interests, positive selective incentives, for example, may take the form of fiscal, legal or other trading advantages. However, selective incentives have little applicability to large groups except where the large groups can be federations of small groups capable of interaction (Olson, 1982, p. 24). But, the segment of society that has the largest number of lobbies working on its behalf is the business community.

> *"The high degree of organisation of business interests, and the power of these business interests, must be due in large part to the fact that the business community is divided into a series of (generally oligopolistic) 'industries' each of which contains only a fairly small number of firms"* (Olson, 1965, p. 143) (emphasis in original).

From this, Olson (1965, p. 143) concludes that, because the number of firms in each industry is often no more than would comprise what he calls a 'privileged' group, these industries will normally be small enough to organise themselves into an active lobby with the political power that 'naturally and necessarily' flows to those who control the business and property of the country. This contrasts with the position of workers who are normally members of large latent groups that can only organise and act effectively when their latent power is crystallised by some organisation that provides political power as a by-product.

> "The multitude of workers….are organised only in special circumstances, but business interests are organised as a general rule" (Olson, 1965, p. 143).

Olson's general thesis (1982, p. 34) is that groups that have access to selective incentives will be more likely to act collectively to obtain collective goods than those that do not and that smaller groups will have a greater likelihood of engaging in collective action than larger ones. From this general proposition, Olson then derives a number of implications of which, for our purposes, the most important are (Olson, 1982, p. 74):

- there will be no countries that attain symmetrical organisation of all groups with a common interest and thereby attain optimal outcomes through comprehensive bargaining
- members of small groups have disproportionate organisational power for collective societies and this disproportion diminishes but does not disappear over time in stable societies
- on balance, special-interest organisations and collusions reduce efficiency and aggregate income in the societies in which they operate and make political life more divisive
- distributional coalitions slow down a society's capacity to adopt new technologies and to reallocate resources in response to changing conditions, and thereby reduce the rate of economic growth.

A 'distributional coalition' is an organisation that engages in 'rent-seeking' behaviour (Olson, 1982, p. 44). Such a coalition can best serve the interests of its members by striving to seize a larger share of society's output on their behalf. Olson draws the strong conclusion

> *"There is for practical purposes no constraint on the social cost such an organisation will find it expedient to impose on the society in the course of obtaining a larger share of the social output for itself"* (Olson, 1982, p. 44) (emphasis in original).

6. Collective Action and Macroeconomic Theory

Having developed his thesis that distributional coalitions can have significant long-term adverse effects on a country's economic performance, Olson then runs into difficulty when he attempts to integrate his argument into contemporary macroeconomic theory. He identifies certain criteria that an acceptable macroeconomic theory must satisfy (Olson, 1982, pp. 194–196):

- it must at no point violate any valid microeconomic theory
- it must explain *involuntary* as well as voluntary unemployment
- it must accommodate both equilibrium and disequilibrium
- it must be consistent with booms as well as busts
- it should be able to explain the really dramatic differences across societies and historical periods in the nature of the economic problem.

He evaluates Keynesian, monetarist, 'disequilibrium' and rational-expectations 'equilibrium' models and finds them all unsatisfactory for a common reason, namely, a lack of congruity with their microeconomic foundations. Olson's preference is for what he considers 'an important but inadequately appreciated insight of Robert Clower's' (Olson, 1982, pp. 207–210). The details of the Clower insight do not concern us here. What is important is that what Olson calls the 'Clower-Olson' approach provides an explanation of frequent fluctuations in the level of real output or business cycles in societies with a significant degree of institutional sclerosis which is at no point inconsistent with any valid economic theory (Olson, 1982, p. 210). Had he chosen to consider it, Olson would have found that Kalecki's model also meets his requirement. Kriesler observes:

> "....the way in which micro and macro theories are interrelated in Kalecki's analysis is similar to the classical approach.....In particular, for Kalecki, neither theory dominates nor forms a constraint on the other. Rather than any form of hierarchical relationship, the two theories lie side by side (so to speak), and both give information which the other cannot give, while the interrelation of the two yields further information not obtainable from either in isolation" (Kriesler, 1996, p. 56)

All Olson's essential desiderata are in Kalecki, particularly explanations for the persistence of involuntary unemployment in cyclically fluctuating capitalist economies. Of particular relevance is the emphasis in Kalecki of the *product* market rather than the *labour* market as the principal arena in which real wages and income shares are determined.

7. Linking Kalecki and Olson

If Kaleckian theory is to provide an alternative vehicle for Olson's theory of coalitions, we must demonstrate how the two can be reconciled. The key, we think, is to be found in a passage from Olson where he expresses essentially the same problem that had bothered Kalecki in *PAFE* forty years earlier:

> "For the economist, it is natural to ask who in government *or elsewhere* might have an interest in blocking the mutually advantageous transactions with the involuntary unemployed...political parties would not have any *direct interest ....and the business community as a whole would want the extra employment for the extra demand it would bring to business in general*" (Olson, 1982, p. 201) (emphasis added).

But there might be exceptions to this general desire to reduce involuntary unemployment. There is the possibility that 'insiders' with the same or competitive skills would have an incentive to block the employment of similarly qualified 'outsiders'. But also:

> "The only *other group that could have such an interest would be a monopsonistic (or buyers') cartel or lobby of employers; it would need to block mutually advantageous transactions between individual employers and workers to keep wages below competitive levels.* No model of involuntary unemployment or theory of macroeconomics that ignores the motive that makes unemployment occur can be satisfactory" (Olson, 1982, pp. 201–202) (emphasis in original).

In order to link Kalecki and Olson we must identify the *selective incentive(s)* in Kalecki that reconcile individual and collective action. The link, we argue, is that Olson's 'selective incentives' are embodied in Kalecki's 'degree of monopoly' Businessmen will always prefer a higher to a lower 'degree of monopoly'. This is not the same thing as arguing that firms will always seek to maximise profits. As Kalecki (1954, p. 12) recognised, the uncertainties faced by firms in the process of price fixing meant that it cannot be assumed that firms will attempt to maximise profits in any precise sort of way.

What Kalecki meant by the 'degree of monopoly' has been the source of much confusion. It does not have the interpretation given to it by Lerner (1934) as simply the reciprocal of the elasticity of demand. Rather, following Reynolds (1984), we argue that the degree of monopoly may be thought of as reflecting the institutional or environmental influences within which firms are operating. In this sense, we argue that Kalecki is advancing a behavioural theory of pricing (Courvisanos,

1996). Firms are not assumed to be maximising profits or sales or growth of output. The pricing behaviour captured by Kalecki's equation (1) below is consistent with a model in which firms aim to maximise profits in the long period where it is recognised that "….the long period is but a slowly changing component of a chain of short-period situations" (Kalecki, 1954). One reason, apart from uncertainty, why firms do not maximise profits in the short period may be because they recognise that demand in subsequent periods is influenced by current and previous prices. Thus, it seems to us justifiable to think of Kalecki's theory as relating to the behaviour of firms, rather than to their objectives.

Now, while it is possible to interpret Kalecki's concept of the degree of monopoly within a static Structure-Conduct-Performance framework, there is much more to it than that. Kalecki recognised that during a recession there may or may not be a rise in profit margins. This will depend on whether the squeeze on profits causes competitive pressures to intensify or whether there will be tacit agreement among firms to maintain or increase profit margins. Thus, there is more to the degree of monopoly than just industrial structure which is just one of a number of factors affecting the intensity of competition. The legal framework, affecting firms' propensity to collude is one; the height of trade barriers or the level of the exchange rate and their effects on the intensity of competition in domestic or overseas markets areothers. Firms' expectations about the future and the direction of government policy, the psychology of decision makers, the internal organisation of the firm are all further important influences on how firms respond to external circumstances such as fluctuations in costs or demand. It is the sum total of these and other factors that, we argue, constitute the 'degree of monopoly'.

This wider behavioural interpretation of Kalecki's degree of monopoly accords with with Olson's assessment of the purposes and achievements of business groups:

> "The judgment that the 'special interests' – the individual industry groups – have disproportionate power, though the business community as a whole does not, is apparently consistent with the general trend of current affairs. For it seems that the particular interests do win tax loopholes, favourable tariffs, special tax rulings, generous regulatory policies and the like" (Olson, 1965, p. 148).

What is the purpose of the exercise of this disproportionate political power other than to reduce or eliminate unwelcome competitive pressures? And what is that other than increasing the 'degree of monopoly' of the firm or the industry?

8. Kalecki's Degree of Monopoly Theory of Income Distribution

In Kalecki's degree of monopoly theory of income distribution, the relative share of wages in the value added of an industry, w, is given as:

(1) $w = 1/(1 + (k - 1)(j + 1)$

where k is the ratio of industry proceeds to prime costs (wages plus materials) and j is the ratio of the cost of materials to the wage bill. Thus, the relative share of wages in the value added of an industry is determined by the degree of monopoly and by the ratio of the materials bill to the wage bill. Then, substituting for k and j appropriately adjusted ratios k' and j', the relative wage share, w', for the manufacturing sector as a whole can be written as:

(2) $w' = 1/1 + (k' - 1)(j' + 1)$

What will cause the degree of monopoly to change in a capitalist economy? Kalecki identified a number of possible causes. These he offered as 'for instances' rather than as an exhaustive list of all the possible factors determining the degree of monopoly. But the fact that he identified both endogenous and exogenous factors supports our argument that the 'degree of monopoly' is a concept that should be interpreted broadly.

> "First and foremost the process of concentration in industry leading to the formation of giant corporations should be considered. The influence of the emergence of firms representing a substantial share of the output of an industry can be readily understood in the light of the above considerations. Such a firm knows that its price *p* influences appreciably the average price *p-bar* and that, moreover, the other firms will be pushed in the same direction because their price formation depends on the average price *p-bar*. Thus, the firm can fix its price at a level higher than would otherwise be the case. *The same game is played by the other big firms and the degree of monopoly increases substantially. This state of affairs can be reinforced by tacit agreement…Tacit agreement, in turn, may develop into a more or less formal cartel agreement which is equivalent to full scale monopoly restrained merely by the fear of new entrants*" (Kalecki, 1954, p. 17) (emphasis added).

This passage supports our interpretation of the 'degree of monopoly' as a 'selective incentive'. Even in the absence of a formal cartel, there is a strong incentive for the firms in an oligopolistic industry all to play 'the same game' of increasing the degree of monopoly. Given Olson's argument above concerning the general ability of businesses to organise themselves effectively, then pursuit of this 'selective incentive' is not only desirable but feasible.

Kalecki's second factor operating on the degree of monopoly is:

> "….the development of sales promotion through advertising, selling agents etc. Thus, price competition is replaced by competition in advertising campaigns etc. *These practices also will obviously cause a rise in the degree of monopoly*" (Kalecki, 1954, p. 17) (emphasis added).

In the contemporary literature on rent seeking, advertising is seen as a major contributory factor to the ability of firms to acquire and maintain monopoly rents (Cowling and Mueller, 1980). This approach, however, focuses on the *allocational* implications of advertising and does not, as Kalecki did, recognise the *distributional* implications. In an empirical study in the spirit of Kalecki's degree of monopoly, Laramie *et. al.* (Laramie, Mair, Miller and Reynolds, 1999) have found evidence of a strong positive relationship for a sample of UK manufacturing industries between the mark up, *k*, and the intensity of advertising as measured by the ratio of advertising expenditures to sales.

Next:

> "In addition to the above, two other factors must be considered: (*a*) the influence of changes in the level of overheads in relation to prime costs upon the degree of monopoly, and (*b*) the significance of the power of trade unions. If the level of overheads should rise considerably in relation to prime costs, there will necessarily follow a 'squeeze of profits' unless the ratio of proceeds to prime costs is permitted to rise. *As a result, there may arise a tacit agreement among the firms of an industry to 'protect' profits and consequently to increase prices in relation to unit prime costs. For instance, the increase in capital costs per unit of output as a result of the introduction of techniques which increase capital intensity may tend to raise the degree of monopoly in this way. The factor of 'protection' of profits is especially apt to appear during periods of depression….there is a tendency for the degree of monopoly to rise in the slump, a tendency which is reversed in the boom* (Kalecki, 1954, pp. 17–18) (emphasis added).

In this passage, Kalecki is again focusing on the importance of the degree of monopoly as a 'selective incentive', this time in a way that is entirely consistent with Olson's requirement that an acceptable macroeconomic theory must be consistent with booms as well as busts.

Finally:

> "The existence of powerful trade unions may tend to reduce profit margins for the following reasons. A high ratio of profits to wages strengthens the bargaining position of trade unions in their demands for wage increases since higher wages are then compatible with 'reasonable' profits at existing price levels. If after such increases are granted prices should be raised, this would call forth new demands for wage increases. It follows that a high ratio of profits to wages cannot be maintained without creating a tendency towards rising costs. This adverse effect upon the competitive position of a firm or an industry encourages the adoption of a policy of lower profit margins. *Thus, the degree of monopoly*

> *will be kept down to some extent by the activity of trade unions, and this the more the stronger the trade unions are* (Kalecki, 1954, p. 18) (emphasis added).

It is important to recognise the qualifications that Kalecki makes with respect to the influence of trade unions. The degree of monopoly is kept down only 'to some extent' by the trade unions. This is consistent with Olson's view that the organisational ability of trade unions is generally much weaker than that of businesses with consequential effects on their political and economic power. Kalecki is much too astute to fall into the trap of arguing that any increase in wages will result in an equivalent fall in profits. In *Class Struggle and the Distribution of National Income* (Kalecki, 1971/1991) he recognises that trade union power does have some restraining influence on mark-ups, but:

> "...only by ....penetrating the world of imperfect competition and oligopolies are we able to arrive at any reasonable conclusion on the impact of [trade union] bargaining for wages on the distribution of income...such shifts [in the distribution of income] that occur are: (*a*) connected with widespread imperfect competition and oligopoly in the capitalist system; and (*b*) they are contained in fairly narrow limits (Kalecki, 1971/1991, p. 159–163).

Here again, we find further evidence of compatibility between Kalecki and Olson. Olson rejects macroeconomic 'disequilibrium' theories on the grounds that they seek to find the source of 'disequilibrium' solely in the *labour* market. In Kalecki, events in the labour market are of secondary importance. The real action is in the imperfectly competitive and oligopolistic *product* markets of the capitalist system although he does recognise that:

> "the-day-by-day bargaining process is an important co-determinant of the distribution of national income" (Kalecki, 1971/1991, pp. 163–164).

The macroeconomic element of Kalecki's theory of income distribution derives from his theory of the determination of profits (Kalecki, 1942, 1954). Profits can be defined simply as the sum of investment and capitalist consumption. Kalecki posed the question – what is the significance of this national income identity? Does it mean that profits in a given time period determine capitalists' consumption and investment or vice versa? The answer, he argued depends on which of these elements is subject to the decision of capitalists. Now, capitalists may decide to consume and invest more in a given period than in the preceding one but they cannot decide to earn more. It is, therefore, the consumption and spending decisions of capitalists that determine profits and not vice versa. Capitalists' consumption is in two parts, one is what Kalecki considered would be a small and stable part of profits and the other an autonomous element that would only change slowly over time. By far the greater part of capitalists' income will go to fund investment.

9. Kalecki-Olson and Post War Income Distribution in the UK

We now seek evidence to support our contention that Olson's thesis can be accommodated within a Kaleckian framework. This, we think, can be found from an examination of the economic performance of the United Kingdom in recent years. Both Olsonian and Kaleckian interpretations have been advanced to explain British economic performance over the last thirty years or so. Riddell (1989, pp. 6–7) claims that Olson's argument did indeed have considerable influence on Mrs. Thatcher and Conservative government policy after 1979. The Olson thesis, developed in *The Rise and Decline of Nations,* is that societies decline because of the growth of vested interests – of producers, trade unions and state bureaucracies – which over time impede change and reduce economic efficiency. To the extent that societies become inflexible, increasingly slow to adapt and lose competitiveness, this leads to the development of 'distributional coalitions'.

> "Mrs. Thatcher and her allies….have implicitly accepted the Olson thesis….As Professor Olson has himself more recently argued, the Conservatives during the 1980s have challenged this sclerosis in Britain by seeking to weaken the trade unions, nationalized industries and establishment attitudes and values" (Riddell, 1989, pp. 6–7).

We now consider the feature of the post-war UK economy that we think is central to the Kalecki-Olson thesis. In Figure 1 below, we show for the period 1948–1997 the shares of GDP of employee compensation (for convenience of expression, we call this 'wage share' w) and of gross operating surplus of companies (for ease of expression we call this 'profit share' p.) To highlight their movements, we also plot x, the difference between w and p. A falling x indicates a rising profit share and vice versa. Figure 1 shows that from 1948 to 1973, the income shares of wages and profits in the UK were more or less unchanged. w was virtually constant at 60 per cent, as was p at just over 20 per cent. Accordingly, x was steady at just under 40 per cent.

However, between 1973 and 1975, the situation changed significantly. In two years, w rose by over 10 per cent to 66 per cent and π fell by a fifth from 22 per cent to 18 cent. This is shown most dramatically in the sharp rise in x of nearly a quarter from 38 per cent to 48 per cent between 1973 and 1975. There then followed a sharp reversal and by 1978,

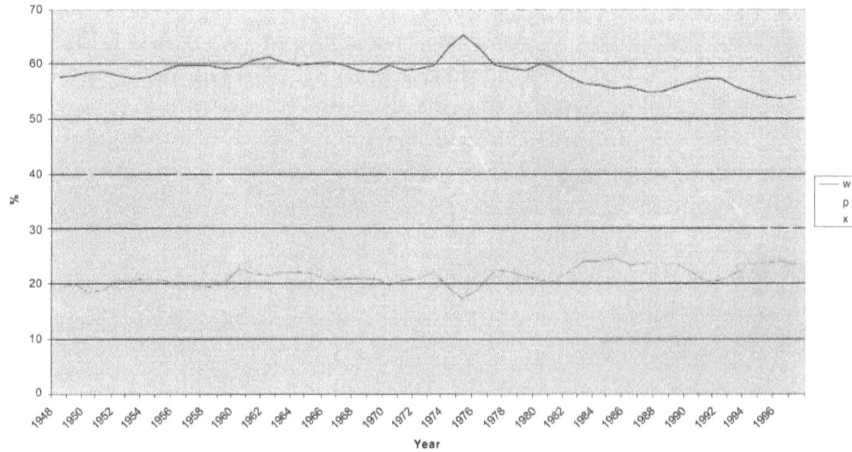

Figure 1: Income Shares UK 1948–1997

income shares had regained their 1973 relativities. However, the post-war pattern of stable income shares did not re-establish itself. Since 1978, *w* has declined steadily and by 1997 had fallen by a fifth from its 1975 peak to 54 per cent. There has been a corresponding upward movement in *p*. Again, *x* shows this change in income share most dramatically, falling by nearly 20 percentage points from nearly 50 per cent in 1975 to 30 per cent in the mid 1990s. The average value of *w* over the period 1948–1975 was 59.6 per cent and this has fallen to an average of 56.9 per cent from 1976–1997. The average value of *p* from 1948 to 1975 was 20.5 per cent and this has risen to 22.5 per cent over the period 1976–1997.[1]

Two other approaches provide supporting evidence of the changing pattern of income distribution. First, we look at the behaviour of *k* (gross output/(material + wage costs)) for the manufacturing (production industries) sector of the UK economy. Recall from equation (2) above that wage share *w* is inversely related to *k* and to *j* the ratio of materials to wage costs. Assuming, that *j* remains constant, then *w* and *k* will move in opposite directions, the movements in *k* reflecting changes in the institutional or environmental conditions in which firms set prices (the 'degree of monopoly). We plot in Figure 2 below the move-

1 Regression of *x* against time with a dummy variable to distinguish the period 1948–1976 from the period 1977–1997 confirms a structural break in 1976 (x = 37.6224 Dummy (20.5141) + 0.8086Time (30.2066) – 0.7074TimeDummy (-6.6289), (t-ratio in parenthesis)).

ments in *k* from 1963–1995. It stood at 1.48 in 1963 and was little changed at 1.50 in 1968. Annual data for *k* become available from 1970 onwards. In 1970, *k* stood at 1.48: by 1974–1976, it had fallen to 1.38–1.40, i.e. there was a rise in wages' income share. From a low of 1.38 in 1976, *k* rose to 1.46 in 1980, i.e. there was a recovery in profits' income share. Since 1980, *k* has risen more or less continuously to stand at around 1.58 by the early 1990s, confirming the rise in profits' income share.

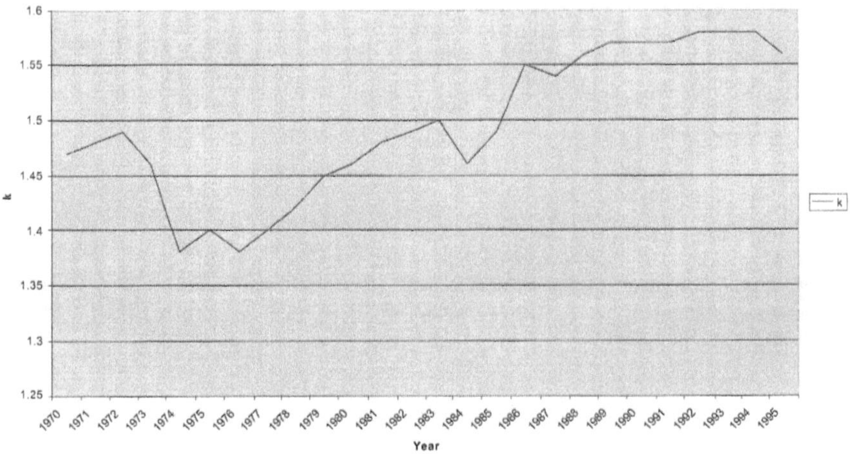

Figure 2: k UK 1970–1997

Further evidence of the pattern of changing income distribution is provided by Laramie, Mair and Toporowski (2000). By means of Weintraub's consumption coefficient, they show that in the UK over the period 1972–1995 the ratio of ratio of non-employment ('capitalist') income to ('worker') income from private sector employment rose from 0.38 to 0.51, i.e. a rise of a third in 'capitalists'' income share. At the same time, the average propensity to consume out of 'capitalist' income rose by over a quarter from 0.48 in 1972 to 0.64 in 1975. This suggests that the increase in profits' (capitalists') income share since the 1970s has gone to fund higher consumption rather than higher investment.

The period of turbulence in income shares in the UK coincided almost exactly with the ending of post-war full employment. Between 1950 and 1975, unemployment in the UK averaged 2 per cent and never rose above 4 per cent. It rose to over 5 per cent in 1976 and has averaged over 9 per cent since then. There has been a similar pattern of change in the behaviour of the growth rate of GDP. This averaged 2.76 per cent over the period 1948–1975, but fell to an average of 2.29 per cent over the period 1976–1997.

With the restoration of 'discipline in the workplace' and the removal of one of the most visible causes of sclerosis, should not the UK then have manifested a significant recovery in its economic performance? From a Kalecki-Olson perspective, the answer is 'no'. What the trade union reforms of the 1980s enabled was the restoration of the collective political and distributional powers of business interests in the UK that had been blunted, but not buried, during the postwar period of full employment and consensus politics. One 'distributional coalition', the trade unions, had taken advantage of an *abnormal* set of capitalist institutional and environmental conditions – Keynesian demand management economic policy, full employment, preferential legal immunities – to behave in ways that Kalecki had predicted in *PAFE*. By its intemperate behaviour, this 'distributional coalition' forfeited many of the 'selective incentives' that had made it politically and economically effective. Its demise during the 1980s and 1990s provided the opportunity for the most effective 'distributional coalition' of *normal* capitalism, the business interest, to reassert itself. But this reassertion, operating principally through the product market, is much more insidious and pervasive than the gladiatorial confrontations of the labour market.

10. Conclusion

In this paper we have considered the traditional view of Kalecki's 1943 *PAFE* paper as a seminal essay in the literature on political business cycles. In one sense, we find *PAFE* to be a rather unsatisfying essay. Whilst Kalecki may have set *PAFE* in the context of a cyclically fluctuating economy, he does not identify any form of political mechanism through which the class interests of business might manifest themselves in order to persuade a democratically elected government of the dangers of full employment. This is what we have attempted to do in this paper.

Although the concepts of 'Prisoners' Dilemma' and 'rent-seeking' did not formally enter the realm of economics until after the publication of *PAFE*, it is clear to us that Kalecki's central concern was to try to resolve the paradox of the conflict between the individual and collective interest of businessmen. His view of the state as the lackey of the capitalist class, which is implicit in *PAFE*, led him to conclude that there would be an unquestioned willingness on the part of politicians to forego the political advantages that control over the level of employment in the economy would enable. This interpretation does not appear to us to square with contemporary interpretations of the relationship between government and business in the UK. Rather, the relationship seems to be uncoordinated and often one of mutual suspicion.

Bottom line, it seems to us that *PAFE* is an essay on income shares. Businessmen perceive the threat from full employment to their ability to control their share of national income, they will no longer be 'masters of their own destiny'. What they are prepared to contemplate, as Kalecki clearly states in *PAFE*, is a more slowly growing national income in which their income *share* is safeguarded, or even enhanced, by a level of unemployment above that of full employment. To maintain their income *share*, businessmen will engage in 'rent-seeking' behaviour. Kalecki hints at such behaviour in *PAFE* when he talks of businessmen and ' boom – weary' *rentiers* forming a coalition to press the case for the abandonment of full employment and also of businessmen finding 'more than one economist' to preach the doctrine of sound public finance. But he does not discuss how effective he thinks such rent-seeking behaviour is likely to be.

Kalecki already had the seeds of the answer to the 'Prisoners' Dilemma' in his 'degree of monopoly' theory of income distribution which he had articulated in *Economica* as early as 1938. There is no discussion in the 1938 paper of the factors likely to influence the level of the 'degree of monopoly', for example, the power of trade unions. This followed in Kalecki (1954). But it is abundantly clear that Kalecki had recognised that it is at the disaggregated level of the firm or the industry that the distribution of income is determined. This is confirmed by his repeated attempts in the 1938 paper to take into account the effects of changes in industrial composition on his estimates of aggregate wage shares in the USA and the UK.

There is in *PAFE* a hint at the 'degree of monopoly' and the role of the trade unions in determining the distribution of income, but only insofar as *rentier* interests are concerned.

> "It is true that profits would be higher under a regime of full employment than they are under *laisser-faire:* and even the rise in wage rates resulting from the stronger bargaining power of the workers is less likely to reduce profits than to increase prices, and thus affects adversely only the *rentier* interests" (Kalecki, 1943/1971, p. 141).

The allusions in *PAFE* to 'Prisoners' Dilemma' and 'rent seeking' are unmistakably there although they have to be rather teased out. This is hardly surprising when one considers how far ahead of his time Kalecki was in thinking in these terms. It seems to us that there are mutual synergies in linking Kalecki with Olson. Kalecki gives Olson an alternative micro-macro framework. Olson's ideas of 'selective incentives' and 'distributional coalitions' give wider meaning and application to Kalecki's 'degree of monopoly'.

A Kalecki-Olson framework provides an explanation for the behaviour of income shares in the UK over the past 25 years. A combination of major circumstances in the mid 1970s transformed within a very short period of time the environmental and institutional framework within which the 'degree of monopoly' had established itself since the end of World War 2. The 'selective incentives' or influence of trade unions on the 'degree of monopoly waxed and waned within a three or four year period. The Conservative trade union reforms of the 1980s may have facilitated, but did not initiate, the significant redistribution of income in favour of profits that has taken place in the UK over the past quarter century. In the last 50 years or so, the UK economy has manifested two quite distinct phases – the one from 1948–1975 of *abnormal* capitalism of low inflation, relatively rapid growth, full employment and stable income shares; and the second from 1975–1997 of *normal* capitalism of high inflation, relatively slow growth, high unemployment and changing income shares. It is, unfortunately, this latter phase that the Kalecki-Olson framework suggests is *normal* capitalism.

There remains the final question of how to interpret *PAFE* in the context of Kalecki's later work. One might argue, for example, that *Theory of Economic Dynamics*, in which Kalecki brought together much of his earlier work on business cycles, is wholly apolitical. Although he recognises that in the long run there will be a general tendency for the degree of monopoly to rise, and thus to decrease the relative share of wages in national income, Kalecki makes no explicit reference to any politico-economic nexus through which this tendency might be facilitated (Kalecki, 1954, p. 30). Three of the factors that he thought would influence the degree of monopoly – changes in the level of overhead costs to prime costs, the ratio of material costs to wage costs and changes in industrial composition – are not obviously amenable to political manipulation. The two factors that could be – the increase in industrial concentration, whether explicit or tacit, and the growth in trade union power – have offsetting effects on the degree of monopoly. In any case, competition policy is likely to have had as big a negative effect on the degree of monopoly as anti-trade union legislation. Nor does Kalecki draw any implications in *Theory of Economic Dynamics* for future levels of investment or rates of growth from his conclusion concerning the long-run upward trend in the degree of monopoly.

However, in our view, this is too simplistic an interpretation as it fails to recognise the inherent paradox of *PAFE*. We think that *PAFE* occupies a special role in Kalecki's work because he shows that the purposes of economic policy will be turned upside down. As we have argued above, the microeconomic foundations of

Kalecki's degree of monopoly theory of income distribution are implicit in *PAFE.* This is a critical element of the microfoundations of Kalecki's macroeconomics. The macroeconomic implication of *PAFE* is that the quest for a higher profit share depresses economic activity and is one of the major obstacles in the road to full employment. Kalecki does not say this explicitly in *PAFE* but again it is implied in *Theory of Economic Dynamics.* What we hope this paper helps to make clear is that this implication provides the link between *PAFE* and *Theory of Economic Dynamics.* As students of Kalecki are well aware, he emphasised different things at different stages of his work. In *PAFE,* Kalecki dealt with the political aspects of full employment. In *Theory of Economic Dynamics* and other later work, he had other fish to fry. The 'political' fish had already been caught and eaten, so why serve it again? This is fully in line with Kalecki's general parsimonious and laconic approach. There is nothing in any of his arguments that is not directly germane to the issue under discussion. In our opinion, *PAFE* resonates with *Theory of Economic Dynamics. PAFE* does not stand outside Kalecki's core model, it is just that in the core model Kalecki chose not to emphasise it.

References

Boddy, R. and Crotty, J. (1975): "Class Conflict and Macro-Policy: The Political Business Cycle", *Review of Radical Political Economics,* 7, 1, 1–19.

Clower, R. W. (1965): "The Keynesian Counterrevolution: A Theoretical Appraisal", in Hahn, F. H. and Brechling F. P. R. (eds) *The Theory of Interest Rates,* London, Macmillan.

Cowling, K. and Mueller, D. C. (1980): "The Social Costs of Monopoly Power", in Buchanan, J. M., Tollison, R. D. and Tullock, G. (eds), *Towards a Theory of the Rent-Seeking Society,* College Station, Texas A & M University.

Courvisanos, J.(1996): *Investment Cycles in Capitalist Economies,* Cheltenham, Edward Elgar.

Feiwel, G. R. (1974): "Reflections on Kalecki's Theory of the Political Business Cycle", *Kyklos,* XXVII, (1), 21–47.

Grant, W. (1987): *Business and Politics in Britain,* London, Macmillan.

Hanson, C. G. (1991): *Taming the Trade Unions,* London, Macmillan

Henley, A. (1988): "Political Aspects of Full Employment: A Reassessment of Kalecki", *Political Quarterly,* 59, (4), 437–450.

Kalecki, M. (1933/1971): "An Outline of a Theory of the Business Cycle", *Selected Essays on the Dynamics of the Capitalist Economy, 1933–1970,* Cambridge, Cambridge University Press.

Kalecki, M. (1937): "A Theory of Commodity, Income and Capital Taxation", *Economic Journal,* 44, 444–450.

Kalecki, M. (1938/1991): "The Determinants of the Distribution of National Income" in Osiatynski, J. (ed) *Collected Works of Michal Kalecki, Volume II,* Oxford, Clarendon Press, Kalecki, M. (1971/1968): *Selected Essays in the Dynamics of the Capitalist Economy, 1933–1970,* Cambridge, Cambridge University Press.

Kalecki, M. (1942): "A Theory of Profits", *Economic Journal,* 52.

Kalecki, M. (1943): "Political Aspects of Full Employment", *The Political Quarterly*

Kalecki, M. (1954): *Theory of Economic Dynamics,* London, Unwin University Books.

Kalecki, M. (1971/1991): "Class Struggle and the Distribution of National Income", in Osiatynski, J. (ed) *Collected Works of Michal Kalecki, Volume II,* Oxford, Clarendon Press.

Kriesler, P. (1996): " Microfoundations: a Kaleckian Perspective" in King, J. E. (ed) *An Alternative Economic Theory: The Kaleckian Model and Post-Keynesian Economics,* Boston, Kluwer Academic Publishers.

Laramie, A. J., Mair, D., Miller, A. G. and Reynolds, P. (1999): "An Empirical Analysis of the Degree of Monopoly in the Spirit of Kalecki", mimeo, University of Staffordshire.

Laramie, A. J., Mair, D. and Toporowski, J. (2000): "Weintraub's Consumption Coefficient: Some Economic Implications and Evidence for the UK", *Cambridge Journal of Economics,* 24, 2, 225–236.

Lerner, A. (1934): "The Concept of Monopoly and the Measurement of Monopoly Power", *Review of Economic Studies,* Vol. 1.

Mitchell W. C (1988): "Inflation and Politics: Six Theories in Search of Reality" in Willett, T. D. (ed.) *Political Business Cycles,* Durham, Duke University Press.

Nordhaus, W. (1975): "The Political Business Cycle", *Review of Economic Studies,* XLII, 169–190.

Olson, M. (1965): *The Logic of Collective Action,* Cambridge, Ma., Harvard University Press.

Olson, M. (1982): *The Rise and Decline of Nations,* New Haven, Yale University Press.

Reynolds, P. J. (1984): "An Empirical Analysis of the Degree of Monopoly Theory of Income Distribution", *Bulletin of Economic Research,* 36.

Riddell P (1989): *The Thatcher Decade,* Oxford, Basil Blackwell.

Sawyer, M. C. (1999): *The Legacy of Michal Kalecki, Vol. 1*, Cheltenham, Edward Elgar.

Steindl, J. (1979): "Stagnation Theory and Stagnation Policy", *Cambridge Journal of Economics*, 3, 1, 1–14.

Turner, J. (1984): "The Politics of Business" in Turner, J. (ed.) *Businessmen and Politics*, London, Heinemann.

Douglas Mair, Heriot-Watt University, Edinburgh, UK
Anthony J. Laramie, Merrimack College, MA, USA

Chapter 2: The Macroeconomic Effects of Taxation in a Federal Europe*

Abstract: The signing of the Maastricht Treaty in 1992 has created a dilemma for fiscal policy at both a theoretical and a policy level. The conflict between the increasingly important stabilising role for fiscal policy post-Maastricht and the pursuit of fiscal harmonisation requires a re-examination of the theoretical framework within which policy discussion should take place. Orthodox tax incidence theory cannot adequately analyse the macroeconomic effects of taxation and the paper proposes an alternative post-Keynesian approach based on the tax and business cycle theories of Kalecki. To illustrate the applicability of a Kaleckian approach to taxation in a Federal system, the paper presents a discussion of the macroeconomic effects of state and local taxation in the US. It ή also shown to be necessary to study the structure of state government receipts, the expenditure functions of state governments, the state government budget stance and the nature of intergovernmental relations in order to identify macroeconomic effects.

1. Introduction

The signing at Maastricht on 7 February 1992 of the Treaty on European Union (hereafter the Treaty) has brought back into focus the importance of fiscal policy as a means of achieving the convergence conditions necessary for the successful achievement of the Treaty's objectives. Two sets of factors will determine the success or failure of fiscal policy post-Maastricht: (i) the seriousness of the commitment of the governments of the member states to the implementation of the fiscal policies necessary to achieve the objectives of the Treaty; and (ii) the robustness of the theoretical reference model used to analyse the relationships between the convergence targets and the fiscal variables (Roberti & Visaggio, 1994).

A number of commentators, for example Eichengreen (1990, 1992a, b, 1993, 1994), Bayoumi & Eichengreen (1994), Buiter et al. (1993), Sala-i-Martin & Sachs (1992) have all investigated aspects of fiscal policy in a post-Maastricht context,

---

* Mair, Douglas and Larmie, Anthony, "The Macroeconomic Effects of Taxes in a Federal Europe," The International Review of Applied Economics, Volume 10, No. 1, 1996, pp. 7–22. Reprinted by permission of the publisher Taylor and Francis, Ltd, http://www.tanfonline.com

in several cases using US experience to illustrate the fiscal issues which arise. Implicitly, these studies have used conventional mainstream theories of public finance as their paradigm.

In this paper, our principal objective is to argue the case for post-Keynesian/ Kaleckian (PKK) theory in the debate over the role of fiscal policy in a post-Maastricht European Union (EU). We outline a PKK macroeconomic theory of tax incidence, in which the micro and macro elements that determine the incidence of taxes are fully integrated, and show how it can be used to identify the incidence and macroeconomic effects of state and local taxes within the federal constitution of the US. We offer the US evidence as an example of the potential of a PKK model for the EU in exploring the macroeconomic effects of fiscal policy at member state level within a federal context.

2. The Maastricht Convergence

CriteriaArticle 109j of the Treaty establishes four convergence criteria for the adoption of a single currency and admission to the Economic and Monetary Union (EMU). These criteria relate to (i) price stability; (ii) exchange rate stability; (iii) convergence of long-term nominal interest rates; and (iv) sustainability of a country's public finance situation. Briefly, the criteria are specified as follows.

(i) *Price stability.* This shall mean that a member state has a price performance that is sustainable and an average rate of inflation, observed over a period of one year before examination for suitability for admission to EMU, which does not exceed that of at most the three best performing member states in terms of price stability by more than one and a half percentage points.

(ii) *Exchange rate stability.* This shall mean that a member state has respected the normal fluctuation margins provided for the Exchange Rate Mechanism of the European Monetary System (EMS) without severe tensions for at least two years before examination. In particular, the member state should not have devalued its currency's bilateral central rate against any other member state currency on its own initiative for the same period.

(iii) *Long term nominal interest rate convergence.* This shall mean that, observed over a period of a year before examination, a member state has an average nominal long term interest rate that does not exceed that of at most the three best performing member states in terms of price stability by more than two percentage points.

(iv) *Sustainability of public finance situation.* There are two quantitative requirements in terms of the budgetary discipline for membership in terms of, first, the budget deficit and, second, nominal gross public debt.
   (a) In terms of the budget deficit requirements, a member state should have ensured that the ratio of the planned or actual deficit to GDP at market prices does not exceed the target of 3%.
   (b) In terms of the public debt requirement, the member state should have ensured that the ratio of public debt to GDP does not exceed the target[1] of 60%.

Two further constraints that the Treaty imposes on member states are as follows:

(v) *Prohibition of monetary financing.* The central bank of a member state shall be prohibited from purchasing debt instruments directly from the central (federal) government.

(vi) *Indirect tax harmonisation.* The provisions for harmonisation of legislation concerning most indirect taxes will be adopted to the extent that such harmonisation is necessary to ensure the establishment and the functioning of the internal market within the time limit laid down in the Treaty.

3. Conflicts in the Maastricht Treaty

The conditions summarised above are an attempt by the authors of the Treaty to reconcile two conflicting issues. On the one hand, the creation of the European System of Central Banks and the introduction of a single European currency will result in a loss of monetary autonomy which needs to be compensated by greater fiscal flexibility (Kenen, 1969; Eichengreen, 1993). With the loss of independent monetary policy, the ability of a member state to take stabilising fiscal action becomes all the more important. On the other hand, the whole thrust of Community fiscal policy since the earliest days of the EEC has been to move towards fiscal harmonisation and to restrain fiscal policy in order to facilitate the attainment of the EMU.

The Treaty contains two classes of fiscal provisions: (i) articles concerning fiscal policy during both the transition to monetary union (Stage Two) and monetary union itself (Stage Three); and (ii) articles that apply only to Stage Three. Stage Two began on 1 January 1994. Member states are to abolish all restrictions on capital movements and to adopt multiyear programmes designed to ensure the international convergence of their public finances. They are to begin strengthening the independence of their central banks. They are to avoid 'excessive deficits' and the accumulation of 'excessive debts' as defined above. Not later than 31 December

1996, the European Council must decide, by qualified majority vote, whether a majority of member states satisfies all the preconditions defined above in order to participate in the monetary union. If they do, the Council may set a starting date for Stage Three. If the date for inaugurating Stage Three has not been set by the end of 1997, it will begin automatically on 1 January 1999, as long as even a minority of member states satisfies the conditions.

These conditions reflect the continuing priority the Council attaches to the objective of fiscal harmonization. Eichengreen (1994, p. 170) challenged the rationale for this supervision and asked why the member states cannot be relied upon to manage their fiscal affairs themselves? A concern that has featured prominently in the background papers to the Delors Report and the Treaty has been for the international macroeconomic spillovers of national fiscal policies, which may be magnified as a consequence of economic and monetary integration. However, Eichengreen cited the empirical studies of international fiscal transmission of Oudiz & Sachs (1983) and Bryant et al. (1990) as evidence that such effects may be small and unlikely to be significantly magnified by further economic and monetary integration.

Eichengreen (1994, pp. 170–171) concluded that whether one believes that closer integration within the EU will create a bias towards excessive deficits, monetisation of public debt and inflation depend on the institutional setting and market structure one has in mind. He cited approvingly the model of Canzoneri & Diba (1991) as an approach to the problem. Essentially, this is an application of the Ramsey-Phelps optimal taxation problem to be solved by an optimising central bank. The model is predicated on increasing international capital mobility and the corresponding adjustments to domestic and foreign interest rates induced by capital mobility. This, in turn, will lead to higher taxes by domestic and foreign governments in order to pay the higher interest charges on outstanding debt.

4. Mainstream Theory of Tax Incidence

The framework, briefly summarised above, within which the analysis to date of the role of fiscal policy in a post-Maastricht Europe has been carried out, marks the critical nature of the difference between orthodox mainstream theory and PKK analysis. The mainstream analysis seeks primarily to study the macroeconomic effects of relative price changes. This is the approach that has dominated the mainstream since Harberger's (1962) two-sector general equilibrium model of corporate tax incidence in which the emphasis is on the response of factor flows to tax-induced changes in factor incomes.

The mainstream views on tax incidence are reflected in the neoclassical theories of income distribution (Kotlikoff & Summers, 1987). Whether taxes are levied on commodities, incomes or wealth (property), taxes ultimately affect the demand for and supply of factors and factor returns. A comparison of factor incomes before and after the imposition of a tax is used to determine the incidence of the tax. Within this family of models, the economic incidence of taxes may be less than, equal to or greater than the legal incidence, and this incidence is independent of who pays the tax, whether producer or consumer, or to which level of government the tax is paid, federal, state or local.

The neoclassical models of tax incidence range from standard partial equilibrium to general equilibrium to dynamic. These models are all supported by a core set of assumptions, i.e. market clearing and the marginal product theory of income distribution. Moreover, when considering the effects of taxation in a general equilibrium framework, factors of production are assumed to be in fixed supply, highly mobile and aggregate demand effects of tax changes are assumed to be nullified (Mieszkowski, 1972). This dependence on the marginal productivity theory of income distribution means that neoclassical theory can only consider situations of continual full employment.

5. PKK Macroeconomic Theory of Tax Incidence

PKK macroeconomic tax incidence can be distinguished from the mainstream neoclassical general equilibrium approach on two grounds: (i) in the PKK paradigm, macroeconomic foundations are present in the incidence of various taxes; and (ii) neoclassical notions of market clearing and full employment are replaced with PKK institutional pricing and underemployment.

We begin with Kalecki's degree of monopoly theory of income distribution. This is expressed in the relationship $\omega = 1/1 + (k - 1)(j + 1)$ where ω is manual labour's share of value added, k is the ratio of aggregate proceeds to aggregate prime costs (i.e. the mark-up) and j is the ratio of expenditures on raw materials to expenditures on manual labour. Changes in the degree of monopoly factors affect k and thus lead to changes in ω. Reynolds (1984) has produced evidence in support of Kalecki's theory and this has been further confirmed in more recent work by Laramie et al. (1994).

Following Kalecki ([1937] 1971), Asimakopulos & Burbidge (1974) and Laramie (1991), we drop the assumptions of perfect competition, market clearing and fixed factor supplies; we allow for aggregate demand effects by assuming a non-homogeneous marginal propensity to consume; we replace the marginal product theory of income distribution with Kalecki's degree of monopoly theory of income distribution; and we recognise that the long run is made up of and dependent upon what has happened in many short periods. As a consequence, many of the standard neoclassical conclusions are reversed.

Kriesler (1989) argued that micro and macro foundations stand side by side in Kalecki's analysis of capitalist economies. The micro- and macroeconomic foundations feed into each other and both are present in the analysis of tax incidence. At the macro level, aggregate spending flows determine the level of profits. At the micro level, market power, as measured by the degree of monopoly, determines the distribution of income. Tax policies can affect the aggregate flow of spending and profits, but pricing decisions, as reflected in business mark-ups, determine the intra/inter-industry and class distributions of income. Ultimately, the confluence of these factors determines the short period incidence of taxes and this short-period incidence, insofar as it impacts on business investment, generates a long-period effect. Thus, a dynamic Kaleckian theory of tax incidence identifies, in particular, the effects of taxation on depreciation and on the aggregate level of profits.

5.1 Kalecki's Contribution

Kaleckian tax incidence theory is concerned with the macroeconomic impact of taxation and demonstrates that the legal incidence and the economic incidence of taxes differ in both the short and long run. He analysed the effects of taxation on both the level and the distribution of income on the basis of a number of typically Kaleckian assumptions: a closed economic system operating with surplus labour and capacity; a balanced state budget with all state expenditure financed by taxation; any increase in taxation spent on officials' salaries or doles for the unemployed; investment determined prior to the period under consideration; a fixed capitalists' marginal propensity to consume, insensitive to changes in expectations of income; workers' savings equal to zero; and a perfectly elastic money supply.

Under these assumptions, Kalecki showed that an increase in the consumption tax rate, *ad valorem,* on wage goods does not affect the level of gross profits. The tax on wage goods represents a new type of prime cost. When this tax increases, prime costs and the value of sales increase, leaving gross profits and national income unchanged but reducing workers' real wage rate. An income tax on capitalists' incomes, which is not part of prime costs, increases gross profits by the amount of the income tax and leaves unaffected the part of gross profits received by capitalists. This increase in gross profits also leaves unaffected the expected profitability of investment and increases unemployment, while the effect on real wages is uncertain. Finally, the introduction of a tax on capital increases gross profits by the amount of the tax. In the short run, the portion of profits going to capitalists remains constant, but the expected profitability of investment increases, thus increasing future profits and employment.

From this analysis, Kalecki concluded that capital taxation is the best way to stimulate business and reduce unemployment as it has all the merits of financing state expenditure by borrowing but is distinguished from borrowing by the advantage of the state not becoming indebted. But he doubted whether any government would have the political will to introduce it on any significant scale. It is perhaps for this reason that Kalecki's theory of tax incidence has lain neglected for over 50 years.

Kalecki's original formulation and its subsequent extension by Asimakopulos & Burbidge (1974) are short-period equilibrium models in which it is implicitly assumed that prices are set in some unspecified way by price leaders and that the aggregate supply curve is perfectly elastic. Damania & Mair (1992) have rectified this shortcoming of the Kaleckian short-period model by means of supergame analysis of non-competitive behaviour. By introducing informational uncertainty and a trigger pricing strategy to punish deviant behaviour, Damania and Mair demonstrated how Kalecki's short-period model can be made dynamic in a way entirely consistent with Kalecki's expectations of the timing of price wars over the business cycle.

5.2 Dynamic Kaleckian Theory of Tax Incidence

Laramie & Mair (1996) have developed a dynamic Kaleckian model of tax incidence by integrating Kalecki's theory of tax incidence with his theory of the business cycle. The model builds on Laramie (1991) where he integrated the tax structure into Kalecki's ([1968] 1971) theories of the distribution and determination of income and showed that taxation of wages and salaries and profits, even with a balanced budget constraint, can impact on profits.

Taxation and government spending can be integrated into Kalecki's trade cycle theory in the following way. Kalecki ([1968] 1971, p. 171 *et seq.*) considered three determinants of new investment decisions: (i) entrepreneurial savings; (ii) the prerequisites for their investment; and (iii) an innovation factor. Whether entrepreneurial savings, *E*, are reinvested depends on the relationship between the actual level of investment, /, and the level of investment that generates the standard ('normal') rate of profits, $I(\pi)$. The extent to which the difference between investment that generates the standard rate of profits and actual investment impacts on investment decisions depends on r, the intensity of the reaction of entrepreneurs. To these are added innovations-induced investment decisions, *Bit),* a semi-autonomous slowly changing function that depends on past economic, social and technological developments.

Fixed investment decisions, *D*, can be written as

$$D = E + r(I((\pi) - I) + B(t) \quad (1)$$

Entrepreneurial savings can be written as a fraction of post-tax profits, *P*. Thus

$$E = \lambda P \quad (2)$$

On the assumption of ample unused productive capacities, investment that generates the standard rate of profits will capture only a portion, *n*, of the new real profits generated, ΔP, augmented by productivity increases from new investment. These productivity increases will increase the real costs of using existing equipment and result in a shift of production and profits from old to new equipment. This transfer of profits is assumed to be proportional to real costs, the difference between national income, *Y*, and profits, *P*, i.e. $\omega(Y - P)$.

The profits generated by new equipment are $nAP + \omega(Y - P)$ and the rate of profits on new equipment is $\pi = [n\Delta P + \omega(Y - P)]/\Delta K$, where ΔK is the change in capital stock. Investment that generates the standard rate of profits can be written as

$$I(\pi) = [n\Delta P + \omega(Y - P)]/\pi \quad (3)$$

Equation (3) can be rewritten by finding an expression for national income as a function of profits. Given markup pricing, profits are largely determined by capitalists' spending decisions independently of their pricing decisions. The latter, however, determine the wage share of national income. Given capitalists' spending and the resulting level of profits, the level of national income is determined by the wage bill that is generated by the wages' share of national income. Recognising that total taxes are a function of both the pre-tax wage bill and profits, national income can be written as

$$Y = P\,(1 - t_w)/\,(1 - t_\pi)\,(1 - t_w - a) \quad (4)$$

Where t_w = tax rate on wages; t_π = tax rate on profits; and a = the wage share.

Equation (4) shows that the tax system influences the relationship between profits and national income directly through the impact of taxation on wages and profits and indirectly through the wage share.

By substituting (4) into (3), the level of investment generating the standard rate of profit can be rewritten as

$$I(\pi) = [n\Delta P + \delta P]/\pi \quad (5)$$

where δ is the rate of depreciation in the sense that it represents the rate at which profits are lost to existing capital as the result of technical progress; it is expressed as

$$\boldsymbol{\delta = \omega[\alpha + t_\pi(1 - t_w - \alpha)]/(1 - t_\pi)(1 - t_w - \alpha)} \quad \textbf{(6)}$$

Recognising that investment decisions in period r, (D_t), are translated into investment expenditures in period $t + \tau$, ($I_{t+\tau}$), so that $D_t = I_{t+\tau}$, Equation (1) can be rewritten as

$$I_{t+\tau} = \lambda P_\tau + r(\{ [n\Delta P_t + \delta P_t]/\pi\} - I_t) + B_t \quad (1')$$

As can be seen from (T), the tax system impacts on investment through the level of profits and the rate of depreciation. The impact of taxation on depreciation is through the real tax bill associated with old equipment. Technical progress will raise the costs and reduce the profits of old equipment and accelerate its obsolescence. The extent to which changes in the tax rates on wages and profits impact on the rate of depreciation depends on the extent to which either tax is shifted through an adjustment to business mark-ups. Laramie & Mair (1996) show that on certain shifting assumptions, changes in the taxation of wages and or profits will affect the rate of depreciation, which, in turn, will impact on the level of investment and alter the structure of the business cycle.

The mechanism through which changes in taxes affect the level of profits is as follows. Kalecki ([1968] 1971) showed that aggregate profits, P, as measured by the difference between aggregate sales and prime costs can be represented as the sum of gross private investment, the government budget deficit ($G - T$), the trade surplus and the difference between capitalist consumption and worker savings. We derive Kalecki's profit function by using a variant of Weintraub's consumption coefficient, a (Laramie, 1991). Thus the level of profits is expressed as

$$P = I + (G - T) + V(a - 1) \quad (7)$$

Since the wage bill, V, is dependent on national income, Y, and assuming a balanced budget constraint ($G = T$) and a zero trade balance, the profit function can be written as

$$P = [1/(1 - \alpha a)]\ [I(1 - \alpha) + aG(a - 1)] \quad (8)$$

The impact of taxation on the level of profits can be determined by differentiating (8) with respect to changes in the tax rates on wages and profits. Thus, with a balanced budget constraint, taxation impacts on the level of profits through changes in government purchases and the wage share. As with the depreciation effect, the impact of a tax change depends on the shifting assumptions but there are tax changes that will have positive or negative effects on the level of profits.

Thus, taxation has an impact on profits through two channels: (i) the rate of depreciation, and (ii) the level of profits. These taxation effects can be integrated into Kalecki's business cycle theory by differencing the profit function, Equation (8) and then substituting the profit function and its difference form into the investment Equation (T). From this, it can be deduced that the impact of taxation on investment over the cycle depends on the following: (i) the cyclical variation in investment; (ii) the change in the cyclical variation in investment; (iii) a depreciation effect; (iv) a distributional effect, operating through changes in the wage share; and (v) a tax shifting effect, operating through changes in the mark-up.

With a balanced budget constraint, changes in the structure of taxation as between wages and profits, under certain shifting conditions, will have the effect of dampening or attenuating the business cycle. The important considerations to take into account are: (i) the stage of the cycle at which the economy happens to be; (ii) the long-run trend of investment; (iii) the direction of tax policy; and (iv) the process and degree of tax shifting (see Laramie & Mair, 1996).

The most significant conclusion to emerge from the above analysis is that, with a balanced budget constraint, taxation has an impact on investment only in the presence of a non-zero trend. Under these circumstances, an unshifted change in the tax on wages is inversely related to the trend level of investment and a change in the profits tax has an indeterminate effect on the trend level of investment, depending on the relative strengths of the depreciation and profits effects. Structural government budget deficits, therefore, act as a stimulus, and not as a deterrent, to investment.

To summarise: we have presented a Kaleckian macroeconomic theory of tax incidence that has identified the channels through which changes in the structure of taxation will impact on the aggregate level of activity. This stands in contrast to the standard Keynesian balanced budget effect and/or various crowding out effects. The model has highlighted the importance of fiscal incidence; that is, that the mix of government expenditures and tax receipts is important in determining macroeconomic effects. We proceed next to show how a PKK model of the macroeconomic incidence and effects of state taxes within a federal structure can be developed. We illustrate this model by reference to the US system of federal and state and local taxation as a starting point for the debate in Europe on the role of fiscal policy in Stages Two and Three of Maastricht.

6. PKK Macroeconomic Theory of Incidence of Federal and State Taxes

Following on from the PKK dynamic tax incidence model of the previous section, but allowing for taxes on wages, the shares of profits and wages of industry value added are given as

$$\pi/Y = [(k - 1)(1 + j) - O/W]/[(k - 1)(1 + j) + 1] \quad (9)$$
$$W/Y = (1 - t_w)/[(k - 1)(1 + j) + 1] \quad (10)$$

where π = aggregate industry profits; Y = value added; k = average industry markup; j = ratio of material costs to industry wage bill; O— industry overhead costs; W — industry wage bill; and t_w = the tax rate on the wage bill. As reflected in Equations (9) and (10), assuming profits taxes are not part of prime costs, the distribution of income is affected directly through changes in the tax rate on the wage bill and indirectly through the impact of taxation on industry mark-ups, k (see Mair & Laramie, 1992; Laramie & Mair, 1993).

The macroeconomic implications of Kalecki's theory of income distribution are as follows. The post-tax wage and salary share of gross private sector income is defined as

$$V/Y = \beta/Y + \alpha \quad (11)$$

where V = wage and salary income; β = after-tax salaries (a part of overhead costs); α = wages' share of value-added. Assuming that k and j represent economy-wide aggregates, the right-hand side of (11) is set equal to a. This term is used to derive the basic Kaleckian income multiplier $1/(1 - \alpha)$, where the level of national income is given as[2]

$$y = (\beta + \Pi)/(1 - \alpha) \quad (12)$$

where $\Pi = \pi + T$.

National income is expressed as a function of expenditures by finding an expression for after-tax profits. If we define aggregate profits simply as corporate profits, like Levy & Levy (1983),[3] then

$$\pi = I + X + (G - T_n) + D - S_p - Z \quad (13)$$

where π = post-tax gross corporate profits; I = gross private domestic investment less the inventory valuation adjustment; X = net foreign investment; T_n = net (of transfer payments) government receipts; G = government purchases; D = the sum of corporate net interest and dividends; S_p = personal savings; and Z = the sum of non-corporate consumption of fixed capital, wage accruals less disbursements, capital grants received and the statistical discrepancy. Then, the sum of corporate profits and tax receipts can be written as

$$\pi = I + X + G + D - S_p - Z \qquad (14)$$

Substituting (14) into (12) yields

$$Y = [\beta + I + X + G + D - S_p - Z]/(1 - a) \qquad (15)$$

If we assume that dividends and interest payments are fixed in the short period, i.e.

$$D = D_0 \qquad (16)$$

and that personal savings are a linear function of the national income; i.e.

$$S_p = S_{p0} + s(Y) \qquad (17)$$

then the expression for national income is given as

$$Y = [\beta + I + X + G + D_0 - S_po - Z]/(1 - \alpha + s) \qquad (15')$$

From (15') it can be seen that taxation plays no explicit role in affecting the level of national income but that the structure of taxation can affect the distribution factors, a and β (since β is after-tax salaries, where pre-tax salaries are assumed to be fixed).

Thus, it can be seen from our PKK model that the equations critical for an examination of the macroeconomic incidence and effects of state and local taxation in a federal context are (14), (15) and (15'). We present below results we have obtained for the US as illustrative of the macroeconomic effects of state and local taxation.

7. The Macroeconomic Incidence of State Taxation

The macroeconomic incidence of taxation of profits is determined by two sets of effects (Laramie, 1994): (i) a public sector effect, which depends upon the government's budget stance; and (ii) a private sector effect which, in turn, depends upon: (a) the reaction of personal savings to the tax/budget stance; (b) the reaction of investment to the tax in the long period; (c) the change in corporate mark-ups with respect to the tax; and (d) a foreign sector effect. As implied, a dollar increase in the taxes, holding other things constant, results in a dollar reduction in post-tax corporate profits, but this effect is mitigated depending upon the public and the private sector effects. If the government spends the tax receipts on final goods and services, the incidence of the profits tax on corporations is reduced depending upon the reaction of personal savings to the resultant change in aggregate income.

Moreover, if corporations respond to a tax by altering mark-ups, then the economic incidence of the tax may further vary from the legal incidence. These various effects impact on future investment through their impact on profits, which may lead to cumulative incidence effects.

In determining the economic incidence of any tax, the relative strengths of these various effects must be considered. In the US, the Federal Government's budget stance is a policy decision and typically little can be said about it a priori. However, it is possible to indulge in some speculation about the relative strengths of the private sector effects. These are expected to be relatively weak. First, consider the behaviour of savings. If the marginal propensity to save is small, then a change in income, given a change in any tax, is likely to have a small impact on post-tax corporate profits. Secondly, the extent to which taxes impact on aggregate post-tax profits, via the degree to which taxes are shifted through changes in corporate mark-ups, is diluted by a number of factors.

For example, in considering the incidence of the US corporate profits tax, Pechman (1987) stressed that businesses only know their tax liability *ex post* and, therefore, the immediate shifting of the profits tax through mark-up changes is unlikely; also, inter-firm rivalry may inhibit the degree to which the tax is shifted forwards or backwards. These sentiments were also expressed by Sylos-Labini (1979) when he argued that non-direct costs may not be passed along due to interfirm differences. However, Coutts et al. (1978), in analysing the relationship between profit margins and corporate taxes with UK data, have suggested that little shifting occurs in the short period (a year or less), but that there is some full, or more than full shifting, in the medium and long runs respectively.

Even if full or more than full shifting is the outcome, then the extent to which such shifting impacts on the level of aggregate post-tax corporate profits depends upon: (i) the change in aggregate income with respect to the change in profit margins; and (ii) the extent to which personal savings changes with respect to the change in aggregate income. Again, if the marginal propensity to save is relatively small, the change in corporate profits with respect to a change in corporate mark-ups is also expected to be relatively small. With the private sector effects relatively insignificant, the incidence of the corporation income tax depends largely upon the government budget stance. The economic incidence of the profits tax is determined politically or institutionally by the way in which these are reflected in the government's budget stance.

To consider the incidence of US state taxes on corporate profits, we reexamine (14) and consider the institutional/political factors that have determined the budget stances of state governments. Moreover, we reconsider some effects that develop in response to state government budget stances. The budget deficits of state governments are separated in (14'); i.e.

$$\Pi = I + X + (G - T)_F + (G - T)_S + D - S_p + Z \qquad (14')$$

where the subscripts F and S represent respectively the Federal and State Governments.

The following factors, as mitigated by private sector reactions, will have an impact on the incidence of state taxes: (i) the structure of the tax receipts of state governments; (ii) the expenditure functions of state governments; (iii) the budget stances of states as determined by their permitted deficits and debt limitations; and (iv) intergovernmental relations between the federal and state governments. We examine each of these briefly in turn.

7.1 The Structure of State Government Receipts

To begin, we examine the impact of the structure of government receipts by assuming that tax receipts are simply held, not used, by the state governments. By doing so, we consider how the private sector responses to the structure of taxation alone impacts on corporate profits. Holding other things constant (on the right-hand side of (14')), the change in state tax receipts is inversely related to corporate profits (dollar for dollar). The impact of taxation on corporate profits is mitigated by the extent to which personal savings changes, given a change in state tax receipts. To consider the impact of state taxes on personal savings, we consider the incidence of these state taxes on household incomes.

State taxes can affect personal savings by altering the distribution of income to households that are affected in two ways: (i) through an income effect; and (ii) through a mark-up shifting effect. The income effect arises when the state tax reduces the income flows to households. For example, corporate businesses may reduce their dividends or owners of non-corporate businesses may have less personal disposable income following an increase in the state property tax. The mark-up shifting effect occurs when businesses alter their mark-ups in an attempt to shift the tax. A change in mark-up, see (10), alters the distribution of income and the flow of income to wage earners. Given wage earners' marginal propensities to save, the level of personal savings falls and the level of profits increases, *ceteris paribus.*

7.2 The Expenditure Functions of State Governments

As indicated above, one of the factors that influences the incidence of state taxes on corporate profits is the reaction of the private sector to the government budget stance. The private sector reaction depends on what state governments do with their receipts. If state government receipts are saved and paid for via declines in consumption expenditures, corporate profits decline by the full amount of tax receipts, regardless of the source of tax receipts. If receipts are used to finance expenditures, then the impact of taxation depends on how these expenditures flow into the corporate sector. Government purchases of goods from the corporate sector, for example, flow directly back into the corporate sector and, therefore, offset the negative impact of taxes on corporate profits. Government purchases from the non-corporate sector, ignoring the foreign sector, compensation to employees, government transfer payments and government interest payments are payments to households, and the flow of these expenditures back to the corporate sector depends upon households' marginal propensities to save.

The functions of state governments are summarized in state government budgets, the bulk of which are devoted to government purchases. US data suggest that much of the incidence of state taxes on corporate profits depends on the relative impacts of taxes and expenditures on personal savings. The imposition of taxes reduces personal savings whereas the spending of tax receipts increases personal savings. To determine the relative impacts of these, the state government budget stance and the relative marginal propensities to save (with respect to changes in various state tax receipts and expenditures) must be ascertained. We now consider the state budget stance and the impact of intergovernmental relations.

7.3 The State Budget Stance

As is well known, most states in the US have some form of legal restrictions, constitutional or statutory, that limit budget deficits. The existence of these restrictions has accounted historically for the surpluses in state budgets. State budgets have typically maintained a budget surplus over the 1980s from about 6% to 12% of gross receipts. In the 1990s, much of this surplus was eliminated. In 1992, the states' budget surplus was only about 0.8% of gross receipts and can be attributed to the surplus in the state and local social insurance fund.

This government budget stance implies that the distribution of gross receipts to various uses (as reflected in expenditures) follows a pattern similar to the distribution of expenditures and that the impact of state taxes on corporate profits depends upon the redistributive effects of state budgets and the resultant impact on personal savings.

7.4 Intergovernmental Relations

Governmental relations between the federal and state governments encompass many activities, ranging from federal government mandates, to the deductibility of state taxes, to exclusion from federal taxes of state and municipal bonds, to grants-in-aid. During the 1980s, two of the major changes in fiscal intergovernmental relations that occurred were: (i) the elimination of the deduction for sales taxes; and (ii) consolidation and reduction in grants-in-aid to state governments.

The elimination of the deduction for sales taxes appears to have had little impact. In contrast, the reduction in federal grants-in-aid has induced state governments to reduce their budget surpluses and to increase their reliance on income and property taxes in order to balance rising expenditures. Thus, in determining the incidence of state taxes, we are particularly concerned with the impact of federal grants-in-aid to state governments.

Federal grants-in-aid impact on the incidence of state taxes on corporate profits by altering the government and budget stance. If the federal government has a marginal propensity to spend greater than that of the state governments, then the transfer of tax revenues from the federal to the state governments reduces the aggregate propensity to spend out of tax receipts and, thus, alters the impact of taxes on aggregate profits. Moreover, if state governments substitute federal grants-in-aid for other revenue sources, like personal and property tax receipts, the incidence of state taxes on corporate profits and other forms of income may be altered.

We have looked above at ways in which US state taxation interacts with federal taxation. We now wish to consider some possible macroeconomic effects. As shown in (15'), state taxation impacts on national income through three variables: (i) the post-tax salary bill, β; (ii) the wage share, a; and (iii) government purchases, G, *ceteris paribus.*

By differentiating (15') with respect to β, G and a, we conclude that increases in tax rates that reduce the post-tax salary bill or the wage share have a negative impact on national income. In contrast, an increase in the profits tax, assuming the profits tax has no impact on the wage share, will increase national income if the profits tax is used to fund an increase in government purchases.

This US result raises interesting questions for the future role of corporate profits taxation in the post-Maastricht EU. In the US, state governments make only minimal use of the corporate profits tax and it is their weakest revenue source. Due to capital mobility and the pressures of local business and threats of exit, individual states are constrained in their ability to use the profits tax to fund projects even though such taxes are likely to stimulate growth and have no aggregate incidence impact on corporate profits. Instead, state governments choose clearly inferior policies, which play income classes off against each other. For example, an increase in indirect business taxes, household property or sales taxes reduces household consumption on the one hand but is then redistributed back to households or to government purchases. The net effect is that some households, like middle or lower income households who do not receive transfer payments or have major stakes in corporations, are made worse off while corporate profits are unaffected. Corporate profits and household incomes, in aggregate, could be unaffected if the corporate profits tax was used to fund state government purchases. To the extent that the same pressures from the business sector will constrain the use of corporate taxation in a post-Maastricht EU, considerations similar to those that have arisen for the US may arise.

The reluctance of state governments to use the corporate profits tax suggests an added rationale for federal grants-in-aid. The federal government has much greater latitude and does not face the same constraints, even in a global economy, as state governments in levying corporate profit taxes. The federal government could rectify the deficiency in public investment by increasing the corporate profits tax and by applying these funds to federal grants-in-aid. The results would be more balanced economic growth.

8. Conclusion

The purpose of this paper has been to show that implementation of the Treaty of Maastricht raises important issues for fiscal policy. There are two levels at which we think the debate should proceed. The first is the theoretical and we have shown in this paper how a PKK model can be constructed to examine the macroeconomic incidence and effects of national fiscal policy in a federal Europe. It seems to us that this is an important theoretical issue. The widespread mainstream practice of grafting pre-Keynesian microeconomic assumptions—perfect competition, full market clearing, perfect factor mobility, etc.—onto a Keynesian macro-economic model seems to us to render mainstream theory incapable of analysing in any meaningful sense the macroeconomic effects of taxation. We argue for a PICK approach in which both micro and macro elements are combined in the way we have demonstrated.

Our analysis suggests that stabilisation need no longer depend on the application of orthodox Keynesian policies of running budget deficits during recessions and surpluses during periods of recovery. Stabilisation objectives can be achieved within given volumes of public revenue and spending by altering the structure of taxation. Recognition of this possibility means that compliance by a member state to the 3% budget deficit constraint of the Maastricht Treaty need not act as a constraint on its ability to use fiscal policy as an instrument of stabilisation. Appropriate and suitably timed switches between taxation of wages and profits, for example, could have desired macroeconomic effects for member states.

A corollary of this PKK conclusion is that there would then be a tendency towards greater heterogeneity in the structure of taxation of member states. This, of course, would be at variance with the long-standing desire for fiscal harmonisation within the EU. However, this could provide an opportunity to address one of the major issues likely to delay successful completion of Stage Three, namely, the reluctance of certain member states, notably the United Kingdom, to surrender autonomy for economic and monetary policy to the EU. It would still be possible for member states to exercise discretion over national macroeconomic priorities while still complying with the fiscal criteria of Stages Two and Three. The *quid pro quo* for the Council would be to forego the quest for fiscal harmonisation.

If PKK theory is suggesting greater fiscal heterogeneity within a post-Maastricht EU as a means of reconciling member states' stabilisation objectives and the Council's convergence criteria, then it is important to recognise that the macroeconomic incidence and effects of EU taxation and spending may be quite different from the macroeconomic incidence and effects of the taxation and spending of the member states. As we have shown in this paper, due to institutional and political factors in the US, the macroeconomic effects and incidence of state and local taxes are different from the incidence of similar federal taxes. Due to statutory or constitutional requirements, State governments have deficit and debt limitations. The US federal government appears to have an *ad hoc* budget process with little apparent connection between the revenue and expenditure sides of the budget. These state fiscal constraints, coupled with federal grants-in-aid, cause the state governments' propensity to consume out of tax receipts to exceed one and, therefore, have a negligible, though positive, impact on corporate profits.

The fiscal policy implications for the EU of adopting the sort of PKK approach outlined in this paper can only be identified after a detailed examination of the macroeconomic issues identified in this paper. We have specified the sort of PKK model that can be estimated for the US (see Laramie & Mair, 1995). A corresponding EU model would require us to take into account: (i) a macroeconomic theory of the incidence of taxation; (ii) the structure of the tax receipts of the governments of member states; (iii) the expenditure functions of the governments of member states; (iv) the budget stances of the member states; and (v) the intergovernmental relations between the EU and its member states.

Notes

1. The Treaty contains provision for some relaxation of these conditions, but these are not important for the purposes of this paper.
2. We are ignoring post-tax proprietors' income, rental income and non-corporate net interest.
3. Levy & Levy (1983) showed that manipulation of the savings and investments identity in the US National Income and Product Accounts yields the following expression for corporate profits:

Post-tax corporate profits (with inventory valuation and capital adjustments) = gross investment + government budget deficit + dividends – personal savings — consumption of fixed capital — wage accruals (less disbursements) — capital grants received by US (net) — statistical discrepancy.

By recognising that the consumption of fixed capital can be broken down into corporate and non-corporate elements; and by adding the corporate component to both sides; and by subtracting the capital consumption and inventory valuation adjustments from both sides; and by adding corporate net interest to both sides, gross post-tax corporate profits can be written as:

Gross post-tax corporate profits (= undistributed corporate profits + dividends + corporate net interest + corporate consumption of fixed capital) = gross investment – corporate capital consumption adjustment + government budget deficit + dividends + corporate net interest – personal savings – non-corporate capital consumption allowance (with inventory valuation and capital consumption adjustments) – wage accruals (less disbursements) – capital grants received by US (net) – statistical discrepancy.

For more detail, see the appendix in Laramie (1994) for the complete derivation.

References

Asimakopulos, A. & Burbidge, J. B. (1974) The short-period incidence of taxation, *Economic Journal,* 84, pp. 267–288.

Atkinson, A. B. & Stiglitz, J. E. (1980) *Lectures on Public Economics* (Maidenhead, McGraw-Hill).

Bayoumi, T. & Eichengreen, B. (1994) The political economy of fiscal restrictions: implications for Europe from the United States, *European Economic Review,* forthcoming.

Bryant, R., Henderson, D. W., Holtham, G., Hooper, P. & Symansky, S. A. (Eds) (1990) *Empirical Macroeconomics for Interdependent Economies* (Washington, DC, Brookings Institution).

Buiter, W., Corsetti, G. & Roubini, N. (1993) Excessive deficits: sense and nonsense in the Treaty of Maastricht, *Economic Policy,* 16, pp. 57–100.

Canzoneri, M. & Diba, B. (1991) Fiscal deficits, financial integration and a central bank for Europe, *Journal of the Japanese and International Economies,* 5, pp. 481–503.

Coutts, K., Godley, W. & Nordhaus, W. (1978) *Industrial Pricing in the United Kingdom* (Cambridge, Cambridge University Press).

Damania, D. & Mair, D. (1992) The short period incidence of taxation revisited, *Cambridge Journal of Economics,* 16, pp. 195–206.

Eichengreen, B. (1990) One money for Europe? Lessons from the US currency and customs union, *Economic Policy,* 10, pp. 117–187.

Eichengreen, B. (1992a) Is Europe an optimum currency area?, in: S. Bomer & H. Grubel (Eds) *European Integration: the view from outside,* pp. 138–161 (London, Macmillan).

Eichengreen, B. (1992b) Should the Maastricht treaty be saved?, *Princeton Studies in International Finance,* 74, December.

Eichengreen, B. (1993) European monetary unification, *Journal of Economic Literature,* 31, pp. 1321–1357.

Eichengreen, B. (1994) Fiscal policy and EMU, in: B. Eichengreen & *J.* Frieden (Eds) *The Political Economy of European Monetary Unification,* pp. 167–190 (Boulder, Westview Press).

Harberger, A. C. (1962) The incidence of the corporation income tax, *Journal of Political Economy,* 70, pp. 215–240.

Kalecki, M. ([1968] 1971) *Theory of Economic Dynamics* (New York, Monthly Review Press).

Kalecki, M. ([1937] 1971) A theory of commodity, income and capital taxation, *Economic Journal,* 47, pp. 444–450. Reprinted in: *Selected Essays on the Dynamics of a Capitalist Economy, 1933–1970* (Cambridge, Cambridge University Press).

Kenen, P. B. (1969) The optimum currency area: an eclectic view, in: R. Mundell & A. Swoboda (Eds) *Monetary Problems of the International Economy,* pp. 41–60 (Chicago, University of Chicago Press).

Kriesler, P. (1989) Methodological implications of Kalecki's microfoundations, in: M. Sebastiani (Ed) *Kalecki's Relevance Today,* pp. 121–141 (London, Macmillan).

Kotlikoff, L. & Summers, L. (1987) Tax incidence, in: A. J. Auerbach & M. J. Feldstein (Eds) *Handbook on Public Economics,* Vol. 2, pp. 1043–1092 (Amsterdam, North Holland).

Laramie, A. J. (1991) Taxation and Kalecki's distribution factors, *Journal of Post-Keynesian Economics,* 4, pp. 583–594.

Laramie, A. J. (1994) *The Incidence of the Corporate Profits Tax Revisited: a Post Keynesian approach* (Jerome Levy Economics Institute) Working Paper No. 109.

Laramie, A. J. & Mair, D. (1993) The incidence of business rates: a post-Keynesian approach, *Reviezo of Political Economy*, 5, pp. 55–72.

Laramie, A. J. & Mair, D. (1995) The short-period macroeconomic incidence and effects of state and local taxes, in: G. France & R. Viaggi (Eds) *New Issues in Local Government Finance: theory and policy* (forthcoming).

Laramie, A. J. & Mair, D. (1996) Taxation and Kalecki's theory of the business cycle, *Cambridge Journal of Economics* (forthcoming).

Laramie, A. J. Mair, D., Miller, A. G. & Reynolds, P. J. (1994) Kalecki's degree of monopoly theory of income distribution: some new results, Department of Economics, Heriot-Watt University, mimeo.

Levy, S. J. & Levy, D. A. (1983) *Profits and the Future of American Society* (New York, Harper and Row).

Mair, D. & Laramie, A. J. (1992) The incidence of business rates on manufacturing industry, *Scottish Journal of Political Economy*, 39, pp. 76–94.

Mieszkowski, P. M. (1972) The property tax: an excise tax or a profits tax? *Journal of Public Economics*, 1, pp. 73–96.

Oudiz, G. & Sachs, J. (1983) Macroeconomic policy coordination among the industrial economies, *Brookings Papers on Economic Activity*, 1, pp. 1–64.

Pechman, J. A. (1987) *Federal Tax Policy*, 5th ed (Washington, DC, The Brookings Institution).

Reynolds, P. J. (1984) An empirical analysis of the degree of monopoly theory of income distribution, *Bulletin of Economic Research*, 36, pp. 59–84.

Roberti, P. & Visaggio, M. (1994) Fiscal adjustments between fiscal harmonization and the Maastricht convergence criteria, in: M. Baldassarri & M. Roberti (Eds) *Fiscal Problems in the Single-Market Europe*, pp. 261–293 (Basingstoke, Macmillan, St. Martin's Press).

Sala-i-Martin, X. & Sachs, J. (1992) Federal fiscal policy and optimum currency areas, in M. Canzoneri, V. Grilli & P. Masson (Eds) *Establishing a Central Bank: Issues in Europe and Lessons from the US*, pp. 195–220 (Cambridge, Cambridge University Press).

Sylos-Labini, P. (1979) Industrial pricing in the United Kingdom, *Cambridge Journal of Economics*, 3, pp. 153–163. Reprinted in: M. C. Sawyer (Ed.) *Post Keynesian Economics* (Aldershot, Edward Elgar).

Douglas Mair, Heriot-Watt University, Edinburgh, UK

Chapter 3: Kalecki's *A Theory of Commodity, Income and Capital Taxation* Revisited

Abstract: Given the timing of its publication in 1937 immediately after Keynes's *General Theory*, it might have been expected that Kalecki's *A Theory of Commodity, Income and Capital Taxation (ATOCICT)* would have been recognized as the *locus classicus* of macroeconomic public finance theory. Instead it has been largely ignored. In his intellectual biography of Kalecki, Toporowski (2013) argues that a proper understanding of Kalecki can only come from a knowledge of his journalistic writings in the 1920s and 1930s. This highlights the important distinction Kalecki draws between investment *decisions* and *actual* investment expenditures, subsequently developed by Courvisanos (1996) into the idea of the investment susceptibility cycle. Mair et al. (2014) demonstrate that the Kalecki-Courvisanos susceptibility cycle can be estimated econometrically to provide an explanation of recent investment volatility in the US thereby resulting in a fuller understanding of *ACOCICT.* This has important implications for the role of fiscal policy in stimulating investment and growth.

1. Introduction

Kalecki is a notoriously difficult economist to understand and not just because of his unfortunate tendency of writing in the wrong language, in the wrong place, and at the wrong time. He was an autodidactic maverick who owed no allegiance to any particular school of thought. As a result, economists of more conventional persuasions have never quite known what to make of him. Nowhere is this bemusement more acute than in the reaction to *A Theory of Commodity, Income and Capital Taxation (ATOCICT)* (Kalecki, 1937). Published within a year of Keynes's *General Theory,* it might have been expected that Kalecki's introduction of effective demand analysis into the study of the macroeconomic effects and incidence of taxation would occupy thereafter a central role in the literature on public finance. Not so. The micro/macro dichotomy that has prevailed in neoclassical economic theory, particularly in the incidence of taxation, has resulted in *ATOCICT* being widely ignored, as, for example, Atkinson and Stiglitz (1980: 222):

> The general equilibrium analysis of tax incidence has to date been undertaken largely independently of the literature on macroeconomics. Thus, competitive equilibrium models, with all markets clearing, have been used to investigate the incidence of different

> taxes, whereas a quite separate literature, using aggregate demand/monetary models, has examined the implications of taxes for the level of employment and the rate of inflation. In other areas of economics, this gap has been narrowed, a notable example being the integration of relative price effects and income-expenditure determination in international economics; *but in public finance this separation has lasted much longer.* (emphasis added)

Without further elaboration, they add in a footnote:

> However, note should be made of work in the Keynesian tradition. An early example is Kalecki (1937).

Even sympathetic post-Keynesians have found it difficult to know what to make of *ATOCICT.* Feiwel (1975: 187–8), for example, devotes only one paragraph to Kalecki's views on taxation and does not mention *ATOCICT* explicitly. Sawyer's (1985: 130, 221–2)) discussion of Kalecki on taxation focuses on *Three Ways to Full Employment* and his later writings on less-developed economies, with no reference to *ATOCICT.* There is a chapter by Paladini in Sebastiani (1989: 220–30) entitled *Kalecki and Fiscal Policy* in which he does little more than summarise *ATOCICT* before confessing to finding a 'baffling situation' over which a 'veil of silence' has been drawn. Osiatyński (1990: 319–25, 357–76 and 557–63) faithfully reproduces *ATOCICT* and *Three Ways to Full Employment* as well as the pre-publication correspondence on *ATOCICT* between Kalecki and Keynes in his capacity as editor of the *Economic Journal* but with little elaboration. The first serious attempt to build on *ATOCICT* was Asimakopulos and Burbidge (1974), although they were subsequently criticised by Damania and Mair (1992) for their overly simplified presentation of the forces determining prices in non-competitive markets. More recently, De Vecchi (2008) has argued that while Keynes may have approved of Kalecki's conclusions in *ATOCICT,* he was not particularly happy with the method by which Kalecki arrived at them.

In part, Kalecki himself may be at fault for the failure of *ATOCT* to make a bigger impact. In the opening sentences of the original 1937 *Economic Journal* version, though not in the later 1972 version, he writes:

> Mr Keynes' theory [the *General Theory*] gives us a new basis for the enquiry into the problems of taxation. The analysis of the influence of various types of taxes on effective demand leads, as we shall see, to quite unexpected results which may be of practical importance (Kalecki, 1937: 444).

The intrepid pre-war reader of the *EJ*, perhaps struggling to get his/her head round the *General Theory,* might have been tempted by Kalecki's enticing 'come on' signal to read *ATOCICT* in the hope of finding therein clues to the exciting new vistas of 'unexpected' and 'practically important' fiscal policy options that

Kalecki claimed were waiting to be discovered in the *General Theory*. He/she would have been sadly disappointed. There is nothing in the *General Theory* that could have inspired *ATOCICT*. Indeed, in the pre-publication correspondence between Keynes and Kalecki, Keynes had the good grace to admit that on the issue of the macroeconomic effects of taxation, Kalecki was ahead of him:

> I have been conscious for some time of the relevance of the theory you refer to the choice between income tax and a capital tax, but I had not myself worked out the conclusions as rigorously as you have done. (Osiatyński, 1990: 558).

Had our intrepid reader been fluent in Polish, French or German (which Keynes, on his own admission, was not) he/she might have consulted some of Kalecki's earlier works in search of inspiration. But even there, I suspect he/she would have been disappointed. Finally, to compound matters, Kalecki rather sold himself short in the last paragraph of *ATOCICT*:

> It follows from the above that capital taxation is perhaps the best way to stimulate business and reduce unemployment. It has all the merits of financing the state expenditure by borrowing, but is distinguished from borrowing by the advantage of the state not becoming indebted. *It is difficult to believe, however, that capital taxation will ever be applied for this purpose on a large scale*; for it may seem to undermine the principle of private property, and therefore in this case, as in general, 'any government which had both the power and the will to remedy the faults of the capitalist system would have the will and the power to abolish it altogether' (Joan Robinson, review of R. F. Harrod, The Trade Cycle, in the Economic Journal, Dec. 1936) (Osiatynski, 1990: 325) (emphasis added).

For the intrepid reader to satisfy him/herself that the implementation of Kalecki's theory of taxation would have the 'unexpected' and 'important' results that he claimed it would, he/she would have had to wait patiently for the demise of capitalism. In the meantime, '*faux*-Keynesian' macroeconomic tax theory went skipping merrily down the yellow brick road to the land of the Grand Neoclassical Synthesis.

2. Kalecki's early career

It might have been hoped that Toporowski's (2013) biography of Kalecki's pre-war career would shed some light on the 'baffling situation' that has surrounded *ATOCICT*. A first reading is not encouraging. Like previous Kaleckian biographers, Toporowski (2013: 94–6) simply provides a brief summary of *ATOCICT*, with no discussion of how it fits into the wider schema of Kalecki's thought. However, this is too facile a criticism. On closer reading, there are valuable insights in Toporowski which help to explain why *ATOCICT* has been generally ignored by later generations of economists. In correspondence with the author, Toporowski has confirmed that in his searches of Kalecki's personal papers and archives, he found no early drafts of *ATOCICT* or other papers that might provide clues to Kalecki's thinking on taxation. In the absence of original archive material, it is necessary, therefore, to infer from the context of Kalecki's career and writing in the late 1920s and early 1930s clues as to how he came to write *ATOCICT*.

Toporowski's biography is important to understand the evolution of Kalecki's thinking. Despite his childhood ambition to be a zoo-keeper, economic circumstances in Poland in the 1920s determined otherwise. Following the collapse of his father's textile firm and military service in the Polish army in the war with Soviet Russia, Kalecki was obliged to find employment wherever he could in the depressed economic conditions in Poland in the 1920s. Although he had not completed his own studies at Gdańsk Polytechnic, he worked initially as a tutor for high school pupils preparing for their matriculation examinations. Drawing on the business experience he had picked up from his father, he persuaded a local businessman in Łodź to finance a short-lived business periodical to which Kalecki was the principal contributor. This led to employment with another local businessman who ran an agency investigating the credit-worthiness of firms mainly in the local textile industry. This, as Toporowski observes, was to be an important phase in Kalecki's intellectual development:

> From this very practical experience arose Kalecki's later preoccupation with firms' internal finance in his later theories of the firm and investment (Toporowski, 2013: 18).

He then moved to Warsaw in 1927 where he obtained casual employment for two years designing concrete structures for civil construction projects.

During the gaps in his civil engineering employment in the late 1920s, Kalecki began writing seriously in the dual capacities of journalist and economic theorist. In his assessments of Kalecki's intellectual development, Toporowski (2013:19) notes that academic commentators have focused mainly on his writings as an economic theorist, regarding his journalism as being of secondary importance. This dichotomy, Toporowski argues, is of critical importance in understanding Kalecki's intellectual development:

> ... this is not how Kalecki's ideas developed. With Kalecki, his journalism came first, and his theoretical writings grew out of it. This chronological order has to be respected, if only because in his theoretical writings Kalecki, throughout his publishing life, tended to repeat his theories, with important modifications, rather than change the subject matter of his analysis with each new work he undertook. The result is that no single work is definitive, nor, because of the successive modifications that differentiate each work, can his collected writings be regarded as definitive, since each one contains an important revision of an

> earlier view. *If Kalecki's views are to be understood in their entirety, the starting point has to be his journalism, which was informed not only by his own work experience and business researches but by his interest in politics, which was broadening out into reading in economic theory* (Toporowski, 2013:19, emphasis added)

It would appear, therefore, that a principal problem academics have had in understanding Kalecki has stemmed from their unfortunate practice of putting the Kaleckian academic cart before the Kaleckian journalistic horse!

So, what were the issues on which Kalecki the journalist was writing in the late 1920s and early 1930s? Not reading Polish myself I am obliged to rely on Toporowski. Kalecki's first published article *'American-Russian Economic Rapprochement and Poland'* came out in 1927 in the business fortnightly *Przeglad Gospodarczy*, published by the Polish Association of Industry, Mining, Trade, Industry and Finance. This was followed in the first 1928 issue of the same periodical by an article entitled *'The Economic Consequences of the British-Soviet Dispute'*. In a later article in 1932 in the more political journal *Przeglad Socjalistyczny*, writing under the pseudonym of Henryk Braum, Kalecki commented with relish on the fall of Deterding 'the financier of intervention and master of corruption'.

Toporowski (2013: 23–4) observes that Kalecki's early articles showed him to be familiar with the business literature of London, Berlin, Paris and Moscow. The bulk of his economic journalism in 1928 was concerned with conditions in particular markets and the progress of various international raw materials cartels, including metals, rubber, linoleum, matches, coal, cotton and oil. He found additional outlets for his journalism in *Przeglad Polityczny* (*Political Review*) and *Przemysł i Handel* (*Industry and Trade*), a Polish government journal designed to promote Polish industry and commerce. Here, he was concerned with French petroleum policy and the international steel cartel.

Toporowski (2013:23) notes two important articles in *Przemysł i Handel* that indicate the extent to which Kalecki's understanding of economic relations had gone beyond the intrigues of businessmen to control markets. In *'Control over German Industry by Foreign Capital'* (1928) Toporowski (2013:24) concludes that Kalecki's ideas had matured from mere reportage by pointing out that Germany's steel industry was heavily cartelised, thereby allowing German steel companies to finance themselves to a greater extent by debt. In *'On Activating the Balance of Trade'* (1929), Toporowski (2013:24) reckons that Kalecki had shown an unusual ability to illuminate how individual decisions and government policy affect the evolution of the economy as a whole, not by the mere aggregation of economic units, but through their impact on the circular flow of income. Thus, Toporowski (2013:25) concludes:

> Kalecki's economic journalism up to the eve of the 1929 Crash had given him a systematic understanding of the key decisions that drove business activity, financial balances in the economy and its unstable progress. The Crash and its catastrophic consequences, as well as his professional engagement as an economist, inspired him to present that understanding in a coherent form.

Kalecki's growing reputation as a journalist was to provide the platform for the next phase of his career. In 1926, a chemical engineer, Eugeniusz Kwiatkowski, was appointed Minister of Trade and Industry by the Polish Prime Minister, Marshal Piłsudski. In 1928, Kwiatkowski set up the Institute for the Study of Business Cycles and Prices in Warsaw with the academic economist Edward Lipiński as its first director. Shortly after the founding of the institute, Lipiński offered Kalecki his first serious employment as an economist working as a consultant on cartels. At the same time as progressing his career as a journalist, Kalecki embarked on the serious study of economics, reading Tugan-Baranovsky, Lenin, Rosa Luxembourg and Hobson but not, apparently, Mill, Walras or Marshall! He also engineered an entrée into the Polish academic circles through an acquaintanceship with the economist and university professor Henryk Tennenbaum, a prolific writer on economic stabilisation policy and left-wing political activist.

This brief account of Kalecki's early career as business journalist and civil engineer, maturing into economic analyst, policy adviser and economic theoretician from the late 1920s into the early 1930s presents a picture of a man who through his journalistic experience had acquired a detailed understanding of the operation of business and commerce across a wide range of industries in Poland, Europe and the US. His growing understanding of economic theory allowed him to take both a bottom-up and top-down perspective of global economic conditions in the periods immediately before and after the Great Crash of 1929. As economic theorising became progressively more important in his career development from the early 1930s, he was uniquely well equipped to provide insights beyond the ken of other academic economists of the period.

3. Evaluation of *ATOCICT*

From this perspective, it is possible to evaluate *ATOCICT*. First, Kalecki presents his analysis of the macroeconomic effects of taxes within a national income accounting framework. At the Institute for the Study of Business Cycles and Prices, he was involved in a number of pioneering studies aimed at quantifying the magnitudes of the various sectors of the Polish economy, including investment. He collaborated in the publication in the early 1930s of the first estimate of social income in Poland for 1929. Thus, it was logical for him to adopt a national income accounting framework in *ATOCICT*, an approach in which he had a clear comparative advantage.

Second, he differentiates between taxes on commodities, incomes and capital by reference to whether or not they are costs of production. He begins by considering the effects of state expenditure financed by wage goods (commodities) taxation:

> It is obvious that this type of tax constitutes a new kind of prime cost (Osiatyński, 1990:320)

Thus, if wage goods taxation is increased by 2% to finance doles for the unemployed who consume all of their increased doles, the total demand for wage goods also rises by 2% as do their marginal costs and prices. But there is no stimulus in this situation for any change in capitalist consumption or investment, apart from an increase in the rate of interest which he assumes to be very small.

Next, he introduces a tax on capitalist incomes:

> It is obvious that these taxes are not prime costs but form part of gross profits (Osiatyński, 1990:322)

The immediate effect of an increase in income tax is a rise in gross profits which he considers to be 'not at all surprising' since new state expenditure has taken place and no other spending has been curtailed. However, there may be a disincentive to investment as the consequence of the increase in income tax will be a compensating rise in the rate of interest. By means of a simple back of the envelope calculation, he demonstrates that there is 'nothing surprising' in this result since the lenders' reward is not diminished by an increase in the income tax and, therefore, the whole burden falls on the entrepreneur planning investment.

Finally, he introduces a capital tax levied at a uniform rate on every type of owned capital:

> Of course, as with income taxation, it does not constitute a prime cost (Osiatyński, 1990: 324).

Unlike increases in wage-good or income taxation, whose impact on investment is via changes in the rate of interest, an increase in the rate of capital taxation does not tend to lower the profitability of investment or raise the rate of interest. But, because expectations of gross profits increase under a capital taxation regime, the inducement to invest is enhanced by the increase in capital taxation, resulting in a new rise in gross profits and employment. Thus, Kalecki concludes that increasing capital taxation results in a win-win outcome:

> Curiously enough, capital taxation not only makes the gross profit rise by the total amount of this taxation, but also the income $C_c + I$ [capitalist consumption plus investment],

> which remains to capitalists after they have paid the taxes, increases significantly. (In the case of income taxation, C_c + I remains unaltered and the gross profit is increased by the amount of the taxation.) The increase via the real wage bill is higher than in the case of income taxation, due to the stronger rise of employment. *It follows from the above that capital taxation is perhaps the best way to stimulate business and reduce unemployment* (Osiatyński, 1990: 324–5) (emphasis added).

This brief summary of *ATOCICT* suggests that its origins do indeed derive from Kalecki's early career. His use of a national income framework follows from his early experience in national income accounting at the Institute for the Study of Business Cycles and Prices in Warsaw. This methodology is consistent with the continental circular flow of income approach he had acquired from his study of Marxist economics, an approach which did not sit comfortably with the views of economists trained in the Marshallian tradition. His classification of taxes into prime or fixed costs shows familiarity with the nature of business costs and pricing, which will have come from his early experience as a credit investigator. His use of a simple arithmetic example to illustrate the relationship between an increase in commodity or income taxation and the rate of interest involves no economic jargon and would have been readily understood by businessmen and their accountants. This leads to the conclusion that the appearance of *ATOCICT* in 1937 as a solution to the problem of identifying the macroeconomic effects of taxation would have come as a surprise to the majority of academic economists.

4. Actual investment and investment decisions

Kalecki develops *ATOCICT* on the basis of a number of assumptions which serve to simplify his analysis without seriously restricting its relevance, for example:

> I assume, above all, that workers do not save, and that capitalists' standard of living (their real consumption) does not depend on their income. Both of these assumptions sharply emphasize tendencies *which are unquestionably real* (emphasis added) (Osiatyński, 1990:493).

These assumptions, although perhaps 'unquestionably real' are not original to Kalecki. A century earlier, John Rae (1965:326) had argued that workers have zero propensity to save:

> The labourer seeks pre-eminence in displaying his abilities to spend, and employs any spare funds he may possess in the purchase of fineries, in treating his companions at the alehouse, and in similar extravagancies.

On the question of the relationship between capitalists' standard of living and their incomes, once again Kalecki held views which, though not shared by most of his neoclassical contemporaries, were not exclusively his own. Again, we find a strong link between Kalecki and Rae. Rae held strong moral and religious views on the evils of conspicuous consumption and is recognised by Mason (1998: 107) as having made a significant early contribution to work on luxury expenditure and status-seeking consumption. It was Rae's fate to have seen his work overshadowed by Veblen's *Theory of the Leisure Class* and its attack on the evils of American finance capitalism. As Kalecki generally never acknowledged his sources, there is no means of knowing whether he had read Rae. Certainly, Veblen was widely read in socialist circles in the early 20th century, but there is nothing in Kalecki to suggest he was influenced by Rae's moralistic or Veblen's censorious views of conspicuous consumption, motivated by vanity or wider social considerations. But a central tenet of the neoclassical tradition that dominated economic thinking in the 1930s was the assumption of independent consumer preferences, so that economists could adopt the assumption of 'additivity', which allowed them to calculate demand from the summation of individual demand schedules. To accept that the concept of additivity was flawed would have resulted in calling into question the legitimacy of the neoclassical approach to the measurement of aggregate demand.

Kalecki's two most critical assumptions are those relating to investment I and capitalists' propensity to consume C_c:

> (i) the rate of investment I does not change *immediately*, because it is the result of previous investment decisions requiring a certain not very short time for completion;
> (ii) the capitalists' propensity to consume is insensitive to the expectation of changes in income, and it is only the actual rise (or fall) in income which can induce them to raise (or lower) their standard of living
>
> It follows from these assumptions that the gross profit $P = C_c + I$ can be altered by the change of basic conditions with only a certain time-lag, and one which is not very short. For in the meantime the rate of investment I remains unaltered, while the capitalists' propensity to consume is not affected by the expectations of the change in their income (Osiatyński, 1990:320) (emphasis in original).

Consider first his assumption that the rate of investment does not change *immediately*, because it is the result of previous investment decisions requiring a not very short time for completion. The importance Kalecki attaches to this assumption is underlined by the fact that he emphasises it in italics in the original. Toporowski (2013:95) sees this assumption as central to Kalecki's schema:

> An essential distinction, one that differentiates his analysis from that of Keynes and the neoclassical analysis of investment, is between *actual* investment, the investment

expenditure in any given time period and investment *decisions*. Investment *decisions* take time to implement.

Between 1927 and 1929 Kalecki had experience of working as a civil engineer designing concrete structures for civil construction projects. According to Toporowski (2013: 19) he obtained some of his work from the largest Polish construction firm of the time, *Polski Towarzystwo Budowlane,* for whom he designed a large aircraft hangar and collaborated in the designs for the roof of the Army Museum in Warsaw. Thus, Kalecki had personal industrial experience in the design and manufacture of large civil engineering projects with their attendant design problems, changes in specification and choice of materials, procurement delays, cost over-runs, industrial disputes, weather and other delays.

Kalecki maintained the distinction between *actual* investment and investment *decisions* throughout his entire career. Thus, Kalecki (1971/1968: 173) expresses fixed investment decisions D as:

$$(1)\quad D = E + r_0[I(\pi) - I] + B(t),$$

where E = entrepreneurial savings, I = the *actual* rate of investment, $I(\pi)$ the rate of investment that generates the normal or expected rate of profit, r_0 the intensity of reaction of entrepreneurs and $B(t)$ a semi-autonomous function depending on 'past economic, social and political developments' that he assumed would change slowly over time. Equation (1) represents the quintessential essence of Kalecki's economics and marks the great divide between Kaleckian and Keynesian economics.

> The determination of investment decisions by, broadly speaking, the level and rate of change of economic activity … remains the central pièce de résistance of economics (Kalecki, 1968: 263).

In his review of *General Theory* Kalecki saw Keynes's approach as falling into two fundamental parts, (i) the determination of short-period equilibrium with a given production apparatus; and (ii) the determination of the volume of investment. Kalecki agreed that Keynes had solved the first problem but:

> The matter is quite different so far as the second fundamental problem is concerned, namely, the analysis of the factors determining the level of investment. It is not only the exposition, but the construction itself, that reveals serious deficiencies … it is difficult to consider Keynes's solution of the investment problem to be satisfactory. The reason for this failure lies in an approach which is basically static to a matter which is by its nature dynamic (Osiatyński, (1990: 223, 231).

However, he considered Keynes's solution to the investment problem to be unsatisfactory—a static solution to a dynamic problem. The critical issue, as he saw it, was the effect investment will have on expectations.

> It is here that one can glimpse the road one must follow in order to build a realistic theory of investment, its starting point should be the solution of the problem of investment decisions, of *ex ante* investment. (Osiatyński, 1990: 231).

From a certain state of expectations of future incomes, given prices of investment goods and a given rate of interest, Kalecki asks how much investment will entrepreneurs intend to undertake in a given period of time? Prophetically, he concluded that this would be impossible without introducing some special assumptions on the psychology of entrepreneurs.

5. Susceptibility cycle

It took sixty years for Kalecki's prophecy to be fulfilled before Courvisanos (1996) refined and extended Kalecki's theory of investment by synthesizing Kalecki's 'objective' and Keynes's 'subjective' determinants of investment into what he termed the 'susceptibility cycle' which seeks to explain the fragility of fixed investment decisions. Fragility is the result of tensions that investment decisions create concerning firms' future profitability and viability. These tensions are a function of exposure to risk and uncertainty over time and lead to the emergence of a cycle. It is this susceptibility cycle of investment orders that drives the investment cycle and plays a significant role in the shape and intensity of the business cycle.

By identifying these tensions, or behavioural elements, Courvisanos provides a link between Kalecki's (1971/1968) rather mechanical theory of the business cycle and Keynes's views on the role of conventions or rules of thumb (event-regularities) in the investment decision process. Courvisanos argued that the tangible (quantifiable) behavioural elements of this Kalecki-Courvisanos (K-C) susceptibility cycle would be reflected in profits, the gearing (debt to equity) ratio and in the level of capacity utilization. Recognition of the latent behaviourist foundations of Kalecki's investment theory is a major step in confirming his contemporary relevance in a global economy that has changed significantly since he wrote about it between the 1930s and the 1960s (Courvisanos, 2004).

Mair et al. (2014) (see Chapter 10) have applied the K-C theory of the susceptibility cycle to understanding the determinants of new orders of investment goods in the US and their relationship to shipments (expenditures on investment goods). The K-C theory of the susceptibility cycle argues that new orders of investment goods depend on profits (cash flows), capacity utilization, sales, and financial conditions. Mair et al. provide a statistical illustration for the US by examining data from 1992 to 2013. To satisfy the stationarity conditions required for time series analysis they check for co-integration, and find, when testing for the susceptibility cycle, that the levels of some of the variables are stationary, and conclude, therefore, that co-integration analysis is not applicable in understanding the susceptibility cycle. Given that some of the variables are stationary in levels, and other variables are non-stationary in levels, and all the variables are stationary when first differenced, Mair et al. first difference all the variables to test for the susceptibility cycle.

Using auto-correlated corrected regressions, they show that new orders of non-defence capital goods are positively related to profits, the net increase in financial liabilities (a complement to new orders), the capacity utilization rate, and manufacturing sales, are inversely related to the net acquisition of financial assets (a substitute for new orders), the interest rate spread, and the share of GDP of national defence spending. They find no statistical relationship between the gearing (debt-to-equity) ratio or the wage share and new orders of capital goods.

Second, they consider how new orders of capital goods are related to expenditures or shipments of capital goods. They show that shipments of capital goods follow very closely new orders, and that relationship during the post 9/11 era has been 'looser'. To illustrate the relationship between shipments and orders, they considered a number of variants of the model using both quarterly and monthly data and using different econometric techniques (auto-correlated regressions and vector error correction models). When auto-correlated corrected regressions were used, they found that both the intercept dummy (to account for post 9/11 changes) and the slope dummy (to account for shifts in the relationship between shipments and orders during the Great Recession) were negative and statistically different from zero. In addition, they found that changes in the debt-to-equity ratio negatively affect the relationship between shipments and orders. They also consider the possibility that a co-integrated relationship might exist between shipments, new orders and the debt-to-equity ratio. Co-integration tests show that two co-integrated relationships exist, and the vector error correction model finds a co-integrated relationship between shipments and new orders and new orders and the debt-to-equity ratio. Shocks to the error terms in these co-integrated equations explain variations in shipments.

The results reported by Mair et al. lead to the conclusion that the K-C investment susceptibility cycle theory provides a relevant 21st century explanation of investment volatility. The Mair et al. study recognises the importance of studying investment behaviour *ex ante*, incorporating the behavioural and institutional influences that impact on business investment decision-making.

6. Implications for fiscal policy

As observed by Toporowski (2013:95), the foundation of Kalecki's analysis of taxation was his profits equation on the basis of which, under certain simplifying assumptions, results in the profits realised by capitalists being equal to the sum of their total expenditure on consumption and investment. The critical distinction, as noted above, between Kalecki on the one hand and Keynes and the neoclassicals on the other, in their analyses of investment is between *actual* investment, i.e. investment expenditure in any given time period and investment *decisions*, which take time to implement.

> **These investment *decisions* will therefore be affected by prices, excess capacity and debt considerations *but not by taxes* because investment (being the outcome of decisions taken in the past) cannot be reduced immediately in response to a capital tax (Toporowski, 2013: 95) (emphasis added).**

But whereas Keynes and the neoclassicals were concerned with establishing the conditions under which an equilibrium might be determined, this was not Kalecki's perception of the central problem of the capitalist economy.

Laramie and Mair (2003) use a Kaleckian growth model to consider the macroeconomic effects of balanced budget changes in the structure of taxation

The principal features of the Kaleckian model are:

(i) capacity utilisation is variable
(ii) the expenditure side of the government budget is fixed
(iii) analysis of the macroeconomic consequences of varying the revenue side of the government budget
(iv) attachment of first order importance to the effects of taxation on the functional distribution of income
(v) recognition that tax-induced changes in the functional distribution of income can, under certain circumstances, result in higher investment and faster growth
(vi) recognition that tax shifting can result in significantly different macroeconomic outcomes
(vii) attachment of second order importance to the resource-allocating effects of taxation

By contrast with the neoclassical approach, the crux of the Kaleckian approach is that the effects on aggregate demand of tax-induced changes in the functional distribution of income are explicitly considered when assessing the macroeconomic effects and incidence of taxation. The micro- and macro-economic foundations of the Kaleckian model stand side by side and are present in the analysis of taxation. At the macroeconomic level, aggregate spending flows determine the level of profits. At the microeconomic level, the degree of monopoly determines the distribution of income. Tax policy can affect the aggregate flow of spending and profits, but business pricing decisions determine the distribution of income. Ultimately, the confluence of these factors determines the short-period incidence of taxes and this incidence, insofar as it has an influence on business investment decisions, generates a long-period effect (Laramie and Mair, 1997: 175–8).

Laramie and Mair (2003) use a Kaleckian investment function to consider the impact of the tax system on the trend level of investment, the trend capital stock and the trend rate of capacity utilisation. The channels through which the tax system impacts on trend levels of investment, capital stock and capacity utilisation are (Laramie and Mair, 2003):

(i) the rate of depreciation (δ)
(ii) the level of profits (P)
(iii) the rate of capacity utilisation (c)[1]

The impact of taxation on δ operates by affecting the real tax bill associated with old equipment. Technical progress, through new investment, results in increases in the productivity of new equipment which, *ceteris paribus*, results in lower prices. This increases the real costs and lowers the real profits associated with existing equipment, accelerating its obsolescence. Thus, an increase in corporation tax (CT) will increase the rate of depreciation and, hence, the level of profits and *vice versa*. A change in income tax (IT) will have no impact on the rate of depreciation (Laramie and Mair, 2003: 333–4). The impact of taxation on the level of profits, P, occurs directly through an effect brought about by changes in the rates of CT and IT and indirectly through changes in the share of wages in national income (Laramie and Mair, 2003: 335–6).

1 Introduction of the rate of capacity utilisation as a variable in the model is important as this is the critical distinguishing feature between the Cambridge (UK) and Kaleckian models of growth and income distribution. Without a variable rate of capacity utilisation, the Kaleckian model would be constrained to analysing growth under conditions of full employment and in that respect no different from the neoclassical approach.

The impact of taxation on the rate of capacity utilisation, *c*, depends on the impact of taxation on national income, which in turn depends on the effects of taxation on pre-tax profits and the wage share. For example, under certain assumptions concerning the government budget, *G*, and the propensities to consume out of profits and wages, a balanced budget increase in *G* will push up pre-tax profits, national income and the rate of capacity utilisation (Laramie and Mair, 2003: 336–7).

In the Kaleckian growth model, the macroeconomic impact of taxation depends on:

(i) the relative marginal propensities to consume out of employment incomes and out of profits
(ii) the compensating changes made in the government budget
(iii) the extent to which a tax change is shifted through changes in business markups

In Table 1 below, I show the effects on δ, *P* and *c* of maintaining *G* unchanged but altering the structure of taxation by making equal yield substitutions between IT and CT. The only tax substitution that will have a positive impact on δ is a reduction in IT and an increase in CT, provided the increase in CT is not shifted. For all other tax substitutions, the impact is negative or neutral. The only tax substitution that will result in an increase in *P* is an increase in IT and a reduction in CT, although tax shifting will modify this effect. The effects on *c* are either negative or ambiguous.

Table 1: Effect of tax substitution on δ, P and c

	Effect of ΔIT > 0			Effect of ΔCT < 0	
	No tax shifting	Tax shifting		No tax shifting	Tax shifting
Effect on δ	0	0		-	n.a.
Effect on *P*	+	+/0		+	n.a.
Effect on *c*	+	-		-	n.a
	Effect of ΔIT < 0			Effect of ΔCT > 0	
	No tax shifting	Tax shifting		No tax shifting	Tax shifting
Effect on δ	0	n.a.		+	-
Effect on *P*	-	n.a.		-	0
Effect on *c*	-	n.a.		+	-

Source: Laramie and Mair (2003)

Table 1 illustrates a fiscal scenario within which the Kaleckian approach identifies the possibilities of influencing growth by targeting the principal determinants of growth by altering the structure but not the level of taxation. Whether the net effect on growth is positive or negative depends on the relative impacts on investment of changes in the rate of depreciation and in the level of profits. Changes in IT have no impact on the rate of depreciation, so if a government were to use its tax varying powers to influence the rate of depreciation and stimulate technological change, it could only do so by increasing CT. This, of course, runs counter to the received neoclassical wisdom that the only way to stimulate investment and technological change is to cut CT. But as Table 1 illustrates, the neoclassical approach only considers the positive impact on P of a cut in CT and does not take into account the negative impacts on δ and c. Also, the neoclassical approach does not take into account the incidence of a reduction in CT and the possible distributional effects.

7. Conclusion

In *ATOCICT,* Kalecki made a contribution to the development of the macroeconomic effects of fiscal policy far in excess of what his contemporaries (including Keynes) ever appreciated. Perhaps he even exceeded his own expectations. For reasons that have never been fully understood, Kalecki never returned to the theme of fiscal policy in his later writings. Perhaps he recognised it was conditional on developing a satisfactory theory of investment, something that he recognised towards the end of his life that he had never adequately achieved: perhaps he recognised that his vision of optimal taxation would never be achieved in a capitalistic world.

Toporowski argues that part of the reason for the apparent failure of *ATOCICT* is Kalecki's refusal to fit price theory into Marshallian methodology. This resulted in mutual incomprehension between Kalecki and his pre-war contemporaries at Cambridge (and, by extension, the rest of the British academic profession):

> Keynes, who already in 1937 had sought to disentangle some more familiar presuppositions from Kalecki's theory of taxation, remained uncomprehending of Kalecki's 'assumptions'. But the incomprehension arose because Kalecki was not a Marshallian. The arguments over method were to concentrate Kalecki's thinking even more on the circular flow of income, out of which was to come yet more arguments with Keynes and the centre-piece of Kalecki's economics, his theory of profits. (Toporowski, 2013:149).

As De Vecchi (2008;179) concludes:

> The discussion between Keynes and Kalecki on the 1937 text can be reduced to an aphorism: Kalecki formulated a theory of taxation that was only partly 'in the light of the Keynesian theory'. If we consider it from the point of view of method, it was formulated 'in the light of the Kaleckian theory'.

That method was based on detailed journalistic examination of economic events and their causes allied to an outstanding ability to put these into their wider macroeconomic context.

References

Asimakopulos, A. and Burbidge, J., 1974, The Short-period Incidence of Taxation, *Economic Journal,* 84, 2.

Atkinson, A. and Stiglitz, J., 1980, Lectures on Public Economics, London, McGraw-Hill.

Courvisanos, J., 1996, Investment Cycles in Capitalist Economies, Cheltenham, Edward Elgar.

Courvisanos, J., 2004, Michal Kalecki as a Behavioural Economist: Implications for Modern Evolutionary Economic Analysis, in Sadowski, Z. L. and Szeworski, A. (eds) Kalecki's Economics Today, London, Routledge, 27–41.

Damania, D. and Mair, D, 1992, The Short-period Incidence of Taxation Revisited, *Cambridge Journal of Economics*, 16, 2, 195–206.

De Vecchi, N., 2008, Keynes on Kalecki's Theory of Taxation: Contents Approved, Method Questioned, *History of Political Economy*, 40, 1, 163–182.

Feiwel, G. R., 1975, The Intellectual Capital of Michał Kalecki, Knoxville, University of Tennessee Press.

Kalecki, M., 1937, A Theory of Commodity, Income and Capital Taxation, in Osiatyński (op. cit.) 318–325.

Kalecki, M., 1944, Three Ways to Full Employment, in Osiatyński (op. cit.) 357–376.

Kalecki, M. 1971/1968, Selected Essays on the Dynamics of the Capitalist Economy, Cambridge, Cambridge University Press.

Mair, D., Evangelos, C., Kazemi, H. and Laramie, A. J., 2014, The Determinants of New Orders of Non-Defence Capital Goods and Its Relationship to Business Fixed Investment Expenditures: 1992 to 2010, *European Research Studies*, XVI, 3, 71–92.

Osiatyński, J., 1990, Collected Works of Michał Kalecki, Volume 1, Capitalism, Business Cycles and Full Employment, Oxford, Clarendon Press.

Paladini, R., 1989, Kalecki and Fiscal Policy, in Sebastiani, M. (ed) Kalecki's Relevance Today, Basingstoke, Macmillan.

Sawyer, M., 1985, The Economics of Michał Kalecki, Basingstoke, Macmillan.

Toporowski, J., 2013, Michał Kalecki: An Intellectual Biography, Volume 1: Rendezvous in Cambridge, Basingstoke, Palgrave Macmillan.

Anthony J. Laramie, Merrimack College, MA, USA
Douglas Mair, Heriot-Watt University, Edinburgh, UK

Chapter 4: Regional Tax Differentials: A Kaleckian Approach*

Abstract: The paper presents a Kaleckian approach to the analysis of the incidence and macroeconomic effects of national and local taxes. The approach offers a number of advantages over the neoclassical approach. The micro- and macroeconomic foundations of the model are developed. These are then used to identify the effects on the UK, Scottish and rest of UK economies if the Scottish Parliament were to exercise its income tax-varying powers under the Scotland Act. The paper concludes that because Scotland is a small open economy, the Scottish Parliament would be advised not to increase government spending in Scotland funded by an increase in the standard rate of income tax in Scotland.

1. Introduction

In earlier work (Laramie and Mair, 2000), we have set out the arguments for a Kaleckian approach to the study of the macroeconomic effects and incidence of taxation. We have shown how, in a Kaleckian framework, the introduction of taxation can have an impact on the dynamic performance of the economy by affecting the amplitude of the business cycle and the long-run rate of growth (Laramie and Mair, 1996, 2002a). Most of our previous work has been undertaken at the national level and in this paper we show how a Kaleckian approach can be modified to take account of regional tax differentials. In particular, we demonstrate the economic consequences that we expect to follow if the Scottish Parliament were to exercise its income tax-varying powers, the so-called Tartan Tax.

Before we proceed to develop the Kaleckian model that forms the basis of this paper, we should justify why we have taken this approach. Kalecki is remembered primarily for his contributions to business cycle theory and to development economics. Paradoxically, he is not remembered as a public finance economist despite having had the early insight (Kalecki, 1937) that the publication of Keynes's *General Theory* required a whole new approach to the study of taxation. This he never developed himself and it is only comparatively recently that Asimakopulos (1978)

* Laramie, Anthony and Mair, Douglas, "Regional Tax Differentials: A Kaleckian Approach," Regional Studies, Volume 39, Number 3, May 2005. Reprinted by permission of the publisher Taylor and Francis, Ltd, http://www.tanfonline.com

and Laramie and Mair (2001) have demonstrated that Kalecki and not Keynes is the more appropriate starting point for the Post-Keynesian approach to taxation.

There are two principal reasons for adopting a Kaleckian approach. The first relates to the compatibility of the micro- and macroeconomic elements of his schema. As has been emphasised by Kriesler (1996), the micro and macro lie side by side, neither dominating the other but each a necessary part of the whole. This contrasts with the concerns expressed by a number of leading public finance economists, for example, Atkinson and Stiglitz (1980), Kotlikoff and Summers (1987) and Musgrave (1997), at the continuing dichotomy between the micro and macro elements of mainstream public finance theory.

The other reason for preferring a Kaleckian approach is its greater realism. Sawyer (1985) argues that Kalecki provides a more realistic starting-point for the development of an alternative (i.e. non-monetarist/Keynesian) approach to macroeconomics. This is because Kalecki's macroeconomics fits in well with many widely accepted features of developed capitalist economies, for example, mark-up pricing and investment dependent on demand and profits. Lee (2002) argues that the philosophical foundations of Post Keynesian (including Kaleckian) economics include realism and critical realism, thus differing from the positivist, empirical realist and deductivist foundations of neoclassical (including public finance) economics. From a Post-Keynesian (Kaleckian) perspective, economic phenomena are perceived to be real phenomena and Post-Keynesian (Kaleckian) explanations or theories refer to real things, represent real entities and are judged to be good or bad, true or false, by virtue of the way the economy is. As Lee explains, Post Keynesians (Kaleckian) have embraced a particular form of realism, critical realism, which starts with an account of what the economic world must be like before economic analysis is possible. Thus, for Post-Keynesian (Kaleckian) economists their scientific purpose is to identify structures and causal mechanisms and describe their way of influencing or acting on specific events in an open economic world.

2. Basic Elements of Kaleckian Theory

There are seven principal theoretical building blocks in a dynamic Kaleckian theory of taxation—a theory of the state, a theory of taxation, a theory of income determination, a theory of income distribution, a theory of investment, a theory of the business cycle and a theory of economic growth. They fit together in a structurally coherent manner. The introduction of taxation into this integrated theoretical framework allows us to identify the dynamic macroeconomic effects and incidence of taxation (Laramie and Mair, 2000).

Kalecki's tax analysis is worked out in an economic environment characterised by persistent under-utilisation of capacity and large oligopolistic enterprises. At the macro level, aggregate spending flows determine the level of profits. At the micro level, Kalecki's degree of monopoly theory of income distribution, based on the pricing decisions of firms, determines the distribution of income. Tax policy can affect the aggregate flows of spending and profits, but pricing decisions, as reflected in firms' markups of price over prime cost, determine the intra- and inter-industry and class distributions of income. Ultimately, the confluence of these factors determines the short-period incidence of taxation and this incidence, insofar as it has an influence on firms' investment, generates long-period effects.

Laramie (1991) was the first to bring Kalecki's theories of taxation and income determination together. He showed that the critical elements to be considered are: (1) the impact of taxation on the level of profits; and (2) the impact of taxation on the distribution of income. Assuming that the introduction of taxation is accompanied by a balanced change in government spending, Laramie concluded that taxes have no impact on the level of profits. However, the surplus—the sum of profits plus corporation taxes—expands by the amount of the change in government taxes and, therefore, national income expands by a multiple amount. Thus, an increase in taxation, insofar as it leads to an increase in government purchases, causes the level of national income to expand, holding unchanged the factors that determine the distribution of income.

To make Kalecki's tax theory dynamic, it is necessary to integrate it with his theories of income determination and investment (Laramie and Mair, 1996, 2002c). Kalecki's theory of investment is particularly important because it underlies his theories of the business cycle and the long-run trend. The standard neoclassical approach to investment theory posits profit maximising behaviour by firms and has two principal formulations, the user cost of capital approach and the *q* approach. As observed by Courvisanos (1996), neither has been able to generate satisfactory econometric estimates of investment behaviour. This is because neither has been able to link macroeconomic cyclical behaviour with microeconomic firm behaviour without resort to the expedient of incorporating *ad hoc* exogenous explanations. Courvisanos develops the idea of a 'susceptibility cycle' of investment behaviour in which firms' investment decisions are influenced by the impact of risk and uncertainty on the psychological tensions experienced at various stages of the business cycle. This 'susceptibility' cycle can be made operational in Kaleckian terms by examination of what happens to firms' investment decisions as a result of changes in the level of firms' profits and the rate of change therein to their financial gearing ratios and to their rates of capacity utilisation. Laramie, Mair and Miller

(2003) have successfully estimated a Kaleckian 'susceptibility cycle' investment decisions function for the United Kingdom.

In Kalecki's theory of investment, the tax system has an impact on investment through two channels: (1) the rate of depreciation; and (2) the level of profits. The impact of depreciation on investment is by affecting the real tax bill associated with old equipment. By means of new investment, technical progress results in increases in productivity, which result in lower prices. This increases the relative costs and lowers the profits associated with existing capital equipment. The decline in real profits to existing equipment accelerates its obsolescence.

Taxation affects profits through three effects: (1) the effect of the tax change on government expenditures; (2) the effect of the tax change on consumption of out wages and profits, and (3) the effect of the tax change on business markups and the distribution of income. We consider these effects in the following sections.

Kalecki's tax and investment theories are made dynamic by integrating them with his business cycle theory (Laramie and Mair, 1996). In order to identify the effect of taxation on the business cycle, it is necessary to know four things: (1) the stage of the business cycle at which the economy happens to be; (2) the long-run trend of investment, whether rising, falling or stationary; (3) the direction of tax policy; and (4) the process and degree of tax shifting. Depending on the assumptions made about the extent of tax shifting and the direction of the long-run trend in investment, balanced changes in the structure of taxation will either dampen or attenuate the amplitude of the business cycle.

The long-run effects of taxation on stability, growth and unemployment can be derived by incorporating Kalecki's theory of taxation into his theory of growth. The results are complex to derive mathematically and, again, are conditional on the assumptions made about the extent of tax shifting and the long-run trend of investment. A full account is given in Laramie and Mair (2002a).

The critical aspect of a dynamic Kaleckian theory of taxation is the sensitivity of the outcomes to the assumptions made about tax shifting. In a Kaleckian model, tax shifting occurs when firms adjust their markups of price over unit prime cost in response to a change in the taxation of employment incomes or profits. Their ability to do so is determined by the degree of monopoly they enjoy. Thus, Kalecki's degree of monopoly theory of income distribution occupies a pivotal role in his theory of taxation. It stems from his realisation of the interdependence between the determination of the level of national income and its distribution.

Kalecki's approach to income distribution is set out in his *Theory of Economic Dynamics* (Kalecki, 1954). This is an integrated treatment of the theory of income determination and the theory of income distribution in which both micro- and macroeconomic forces work together. Employment income's share of national income is determined by the process of firms marking up unit prime costs to obtain prices. The level of profits is determined by past investment decisions and:

> National output will be pushed up to the point where the profits carved out of it are in accordance with the 'distribution factors' (Kalecki, 1954, p. 47).

Kalecki's theory of income distribution is consistent with an approach to economics in which the levels of national income and employment are determined by effective demand and in which persistent unemployment is possible.

Kalecki argued that prices, at the industry level, are set by a markup, k, over unit prime costs of production, u (wages plus material costs), i.e. price = ku. From this price equation, Kalecki derived his degree of monopoly theory of income distribution in which the share of employment income in national income is inversely related to the markup, k. The markup, k, will be influenced by a set of institutional and environmental conditions under which firms are operating. The 'degree of monopoly' factors may vary both between economies and over time.

3. Kaleckian Approach to National and Regional Taxation

Having set out the basic principles of a Kaleckian approach to the incidence and macroeconomic effects of taxation, we now demonstrate how a Kaleckian model can be used to examine the national and regional effects of taxation and of a change in income tax in particular. We illustrate the model by considering the implications of the introduction of a regional variation in income tax by the Scottish Parliament. We define these implications according to: (1) those that appear in the short-period (where current investment expenditures are fixed by past investment decisions), such as compensating changes in the budgets of national and regional governments, or changes in business markups; and (2) those that appear in the long period, such as changes in the level and patterns of business investment.

In this section of the paper we show: (1) the national and regional dimensions of national tax policy; and (2) how regional taxation affects both the national and the regional economies. We identify the various channels through which the national tax policy works itself out in regional government jurisdictions, and we highlight the various channels through which regional tax policies generate inter-regional effects.

To begin with, we present the simplest version of the model that is based on the following assumptions:

- two regional jurisdictions with separate fiscal authorities.
- a single national government with independent fiscal authority.
- one integrated sector operating over the two jurisdictions.
- the unit costs of production (prime costs), markups and prices are identical across the two regional jurisdictions.
- trade between the two regional jurisdictions is free while foreign trade is nonexistent.
- trade between the two regional jurisdictions is assumed to be initially in balance, i.e. exports from each jurisdiction equal imports into each jurisdiction.
- to avoid complications, we assume that tax shifting, when allowed, is reflected in changes in business markups without affecting the market price of output. Increases in wage taxes when shifted result in a lower markup.
- we assume the supply of labour is perfectly elastic, and, that movements in labour between jurisdictions, in response to real wage differentials, do not take place in the short period.

We begin with the microeconomic foundations. Value added for jurisdiction *j* is defined as:

$$Y_j = (k_j - 1)(W_j + M_j) + O_j + W_j \tag{1}$$

where Y = value added, k = the price/cost mark up, W = the employment income bill, M = the materials bill and O = overhead costs

Business profits plus overheads for jurisdiction *j* are defined as:

$$P_j + O_j = (k_j - 1)(W_j + M_j) \tag{2}$$

where P = profits.

The distribution of value added is found by defining the employment income share. From equation (1) the employment income share is given as:

$$W_j/Y_j = 1/[1 + (k_j - 1) + (1 + j_j)] \tag{3}$$

where $j_j = M_j/W_j$. The share of profits plus overhead costs of value added is simply $(1 - W_j/Y_j)$.

The question now arises as to what determines the level of employment income and material costs in specific sectors. Kalecki considered an economy operating below full employment, with ample unused production possibilities. Similarly, we hypothesise that the rate of innovations and technical progress are such that aggregate demand has difficulty keeping pace with the growth in production possibilities. As is standard with Kalecki, we consider a model where the levels of employment income and material costs are constrained by aggregate demand. To consider this further, we must examine the macroeconomic foundations of the model.

The macroeconomic foundations are as follows. Value added for the economy as a whole is defined as:

$$Y = \Sigma Y_j = Y_1 + Y_2 \tag{4}$$

We derive the aggregate markup from equation (4) and define aggregate value added in terms of the aggregate markup. For example, by substituting equation (1) into equation (4), we derive aggregate value added as:

$$Y = (k_1 - 1)(W_1 + M_1) + W_1 + O_1 + (k_2 - 1)(W_2 + M_2) + W_1 + O_2 \tag{5}$$

Since aggregate value added can also be written as:

$$Y = (k - 1)(W + M) + W + O \tag{5'}$$

where the unsubscripted variables represent aggregates, the aggregate prime cost markup can be written as the weighted average of the industry markups; i.e.:

$$(k - 1) = (k_1 - 1)(W_1 + M_1)/(W + M) + (k_2 - 1)(W_2 + M_2)/(W + M) \tag{6}$$

Given equation (5), the aggregate employment income share can be written as:

$$W/Y = \alpha \tag{7}$$

where 〈 = the employment income share. Given equation (3), the aggregate employment income share can be written as:

$$\alpha = 1/[1 + (k - 1) + (1 + j)] \tag{8}$$

From equation (7), we derive an expression for national income by defining $\Pi = Y - W$, where a is pre-tax profits, i.e.:

$$Y = (\Pi)/(1 - \alpha) \tag{9}$$

Kalecki (1968) stated that equation (9) shows how the distribution factors, in this case, a, push up the level of income so that profits out of income are realised, where realised profits are determined by aggregate spending flows. Kalecki used national income accounts to derive a definition for aggregate profits. He defined aggregate profits (net of taxes), assuming that government transfer payments were completely consumed, as:

$$P = I + Ge - T + Ex - Im + C_c - W_s \tag{10}$$

where I = gross private domestic investment, Ge = government expenditures, T = total tax receipts, Ex = exports, Im = imports, C_c = consumption out of non-employment income (profits, rentier incomes and transfer incomes) and W_s = workers' savings (defined as pre-tax wages and salaries less wage and salary taxes less consumption out of employment income).

Before going further, we consider the effects of profit and wage taxation on aggregate profits. To simplify, we assume that T = Tp + Tw, Ex – Im = 0 and C_c = cc(P) and W_s = sw(W–Tw), Tw = tw(W), and Tp = tp(P+Tp). In addition, we assume a balanced budget constraint (Ge = T) and we recall that W = αY.[1] To further simplify, we initially assume a zero marginal propensity to consume out of profits, a zero marginal propensity to save out of wages and that business markups are unaffected by the changes in wages and profit taxes. With these simplifying assumptions, a balanced budget increase in profit taxes increases pre-tax profits, leaves unaffected post-tax profits and increases both national income and the pre-tax wage and salary bill. If the marginal propensity to consume out of profits is between zero and one, then the tax increase reduces spending out of profits dampening the effects of the increase in government expenditures on pre-tax profits and, therefore, reducing after-tax profits.

If an increase in government expenditure is financed by an increase in wage taxes, then government spending replaces worker spending, leaving after-tax profits, national income and pre-tax wages unchanged. If the marginal propensity to consume out of wages is between zero and one, then the balanced budget change in the wage tax reduces worker savings and increases aggregate spending relative to the wage bill. The effect of the increase in aggregate spending relative to the wage bill is to increase pre-tax and post-tax business profits and to increase national income. The increase in national income increases pre-tax wages and dampens the fall in after-tax wages.

Finally, if a tax change affects business markups, the distribution of income and the composition of spending change. The change in the composition of spending affects the level of pre-tax and post-tax profits and national income. For example, if the increase in the wage tax is shifted, then business markups decrease. The decrease in business markups increases workers' share of aggregate income. If workers have a positive marginal propensity to save, the redistribution of income increases worker savings and reduces worker consumption relative to the wage bill. The relative reduction in worker consumption reduces pre-tax and post-tax profits and decreases

---

1 In this case, the aggregate level of profits is given as:
$P = [I(1\text{-}tp)(1\text{-}tw)]/[(1\text{-}tp)(1\text{-}\alpha)(1\text{-}cc) + sw(\alpha)(1\text{-}tw)]$.

national income. If the increase in the profit tax is shifted, then business markups increase. The increase in business markups decreases workers' share of aggregate income. If workers have a positive marginal propensity to save, then the redistribution of income increases worker consumption relative to the wage bill (reduces worker savings), and pre-tax and post-tax profits increase and national income increases. The change in the business markups with respect to a change in taxes has no effect on aggregate profits if the marginal propensity to consume out of wage is zero.

Given the above circumstances, the effects of profit and wage taxes on business profits is an empirical question. Any theoretical discussion is contingent upon the government's budget constraint, the marginal propensities to consume out of profits and wages, and the extent to which business markups shift with respect to changes in the wage and profits taxes. Keeping these points in mind we now proceed to consider the effects of national and local taxes on the national and local economies.

For the present, we continue to ignore the inter-regional trade balance and we assume capitalists' consumption, savings out of employment income and government transfer payments to be zero. Thus, we rewrite equation (10) simply as:

$$P + Tp = \Pi = I + G - Tw \tag{10'}$$

where P = post-tax profits, Tp = profits taxes, G = government purchases, and Tw = income tax.

From equations (10) or (10'), we can see that the level of realised profits is determined by the interaction of the right-hand-side variables. Given the aggregate distribution factors, the level of national income is pushed up so that profits are realised according to equations (10) or (10'). The aggregate level of income is distributed to sectors/jurisdictions in accordance with sectoral/jurisdictional distribution factors. At this point, ignoring the re-distributional role of national and regional governments, these sectoral/jurisdictional distribution factors are reflected in the jurisdictional price/cost markups and in the jurisdictional ratios of the material bills to the wage income bills.

4. Example of Tax Model

The regional and aggregate effects of national and regional taxation can be best illustrated by a simple example. From this example, we go on to consider extensions and further implications. In order to minimise the amount of algebra in the paper, we present our results in tabular form. We identify three tax jurisdictions; Scotland, Rest of United Kingdom (RUK) and United Kingdom (UK). For each jurisdiction, we identify three parameters, the markup, k, the ratio of the materials bill to the wage bill, j, and the wage share, α. We subscript them for Scotland,

RUK and UK and identify the initial (pre-tax change) value of the parameters by '*'. Similarly, we designate the four policy variables, profits tax, T_p, profits tax rate, t_p, income tax, T_w, and income tax rate, t_w, for each jurisdiction and identify its initial value by '*'. We repeat the above process for the five variables in the model, the wage bill, W, the materials bill, M, value added, Y, post-tax profits, P, and the rate of profit, r.

For the two tax changes discussed below, we indicate the change in the parameter or variable (>0, <0) that we would expect to occur in response to: (i) an increase in income tax levied by the UK government, ($\Delta t_{wuk} > 0$, $\Delta t_{ws} = 0$) (see Table 1); and (ii) to an increase in income tax levied by the Scottish parliament ($\Delta t_{wuk} = 0$, $\Delta t_{ws} > 0$) (see Table 2). For these two tax changes, we show the change in post-tax profits (ΔP), in pre-tax wages (ΔW), and in post-tax wages (Δ(W–Tw)) for each of the three jurisdictions.

Finally, we calculate two measures of tax burden for each jurisdiction. The first, the tax burden ratio, measures the additional tax burden on wage income and profits relative to the additional tax revenues raised. This is interpreted as the decline in private sector income as a result of a £ increase in taxation. The second, the excess tax burden ratio, is the additional tax burden on wages and profits minus the additional tax receipts, which is then divided by the additional tax receipts. The excess tax burden ratio is interpreted as the decline in private sector income in excess of the tax receipts as a result of a £ increase in taxation. Again, we calculate these tax burdens for Scotland, RUK and UK as deviations >0 or <0 from their initial positions prior to the tax change. We initially assume no change in expenditure by either the UK government or the Scottish parliament. We also assume no tax shifting and that workers spend all their income.

To start, suppose the UK wage (income) tax rate increases. The increase in the UK rate of income tax, t_{wuk}, will reduce the consumption of wage and salary earners relative to the employment income bill, W, and also reduce business profits, P. In other words, a national income tax, T_{wuk}, bears a double incidence. The tax reduces the disposable incomes of both employment income earners and capitalists simultaneously. Given our assumptions, post-tax profits, P, fall by the amount of the tax, T_w, while national income, Y, falls as a result of the operation of the income multiplier. Post-tax income from employment, W – Tw, falls as a result of both the decline in national income, Y, and the increase in income tax, T_w. These two effects together cause post-tax employment incomes, W – Tw, to decline more than the tax increase, T_w, and together create an excess tax burden i.e. the loss in private sector income is greater than the additional tax receipts. These results are summarised in Table 1. Given the assumptions above, but assuming no balanced budget constraint (see footnote 4), national income can be written as:

$$Y = (I + Ge)/[(1 - cc(1\text{-}tp))(1\text{-}\alpha) + tw \langle(1\text{-}sw) + \alpha sw)] \tag{11}$$

Assuming no short period response to the tax change, T_w, that is, where investment is fixed by past investment decisions and assuming the capital stock remains constant, the increase in income tax, T_w, has an equi-proportional effect on both Scotland and RUK. The rate of profit, r, falls in each jurisdiction but remains constant across both. If worker saving is nonzero, the qualitative conclusions remain the same. The effect of the nonzero savings is to dampen the negative effect as some of the tax increase is paid for via a reduction in savings.

Table 1. Example of regional tax model if UK government increases rate of income tax (Δt_{wuk} >0) with (i) no change in government spending and (ii) no tax shifting

Jurisdiction: **Scotland:** *RUK:* UK	Symbol	Initial Value	Δ(Initial Value) if $\Delta t_{wuk} > 0$
Parameters			
Markup	k_s: k_{ruk}: k_{uk}	k^*_s: k^*_{ruk}: k^*_{uk}	**0:** *0:*0
Materials Bill/Wage Bill	j_s: j_{ruk}: j_{uk}	j^*_s: j^*_{ruk}: j^*_{uk}	**0:** *0:* 0
Wage Share	α_s: α_{ruk}: α_{uk}	α^*_s: α^*_{ruk}: α_{uk}	**0:** *0:* 0
Policy Variables			
Profits Tax	T_{ps}: T_{pruk}: T_{puk}	T^*_{ps}: T^*_{pruk}: T^*_{uk}	**0:** *0:* 0
Profits Tax Rate	t_{ps}: t_{pruk}: t_{puk}	t_{puk}: t_{puk}: t_{puk}	**0:** *0:* 0
Income Tax	T_{ws}: T_{wruk}: T_{wuk}	T^*_{ws}: T^*_{wruk}:T^*_{wuk}	**0:** *0:* >0
Income Tax Rate	t_{ws}: t_{wruk}: t_{wuk}	t_{wuk}: t_{wuk}: t_{wuk}	**0:** *0:* >0
Variables			
Wage Bill	W_s: W_{ruk}: W_{uk}	W^*_s: W^*_{ruk}: W^*_{uk}	**<0:** *<0:* <0
Materials Bill	M_s: M_{ruk}: M_{uk}	M^*_s: M^*_{ruk}: M^*_{uk}	**<0:** *<0:* <0
Value Added	Y_s: Y_{ruk}: Y_{uk}	Y^*_s: Y^*_{ruk}: Y^*_{uk}	**<0:** *<0:* <0
Post-Tax Profits	P_s: P_{ruk}: P_{uk}	P^{*s}: P^*_{ruk}: P^*_{uk}	**<0:** *<0:* <0
Rate of Profit	r_s: r_{ruk}: r_{uk}	r^*_s: r^*_{ruk}: r^*_{uk}	**<0:** *<0:* <0
Tax Burden Assessment			
ΔPost-Tax Profits	ΔP_s: ΔP_{ruk}:ΔP_{uk}		**<0:** *<0:* <0
ΔPre-Tax Wages	ΔW_s: ΔW_{ruk}: W_{uk}		**<0:** *<0:* <0
ΔPost-Tax Wages	$\Delta(W\text{–}Tw)_s$: $\Delta(W\text{–}Tw)_{ruk}$: $\Delta(W\text{–}Tw)_{uk}$		**<0:** *<0:* <0
Tax Burden Ratio			**>0:** *>0:* >0
Excess Tax Burden Ratio			**>0:** *>0:* >0

5. An Increase in Income Tax Levied by the Scottish Parliament

Now, we consider what happens if the Scottish Parliament raises the standard rate of income tax, t_{ws}. We assume for the moment that there is no corresponding increase in spending by the Scottish Executive, and no change in trade flows between Scotland and RUK. We further assume that business markups, k, are constant and that the increase in income tax, t_{ws}, is not shifted through lower business markups (an increase in the unit costs of labour relative to the price of output). The effect of the increase in income tax in Scotland, t_{ws}, is to reduce wage and salary earners' consumption for the UK as a whole relative to the wage and salary bill. The result, like in the previous case, is a reduction in the aggregate level of profits, P, national income, Y, the wage and salary bill, W, and the materials bill, M. The declines in national income, Y, and in the wage and salary bill, W, and the materials bill, M, are distributed over Scotland and RUK based on the distribution or composition of industry in each jurisdiction. As a result, the jurisdiction that has not increased income tax, RUK, has to bear some of the burden, in terms of declining profits and wages, of the Scottish Parliament's decision to increase the rate of income tax, t_{ws}. The increase in income tax in Scotland, t_{ws}, reduces the value of the income multiplier, which reduces UK national income, Y_{uk}.

As in the case of a national income tax, t_{uk}, profits, P_{uk}, fall by the full amount of the increase in the income tax levied by the Scottish Parliament, T_{ws}. The decline in profits is distributed to Scotland and RUK according to each sector's share of aggregate prime costs. Again, as in the case of an increase in the UK rate of income tax, pre-tax wages and salaries, W_{uk}, fall as a result of the decline in national income, Y_{uk}, associated with the increase in the income tax rate, t_{ws}. The decline in pre-tax wages and salaries, W_{uk}, is distributed to Scotland and RUK according to the distribution of aggregate prime costs. It is the decline in national income, Y_{uk}, that is distributed to RUK that causes RUK's labour, W_{ruk}, to bear some of the burden of Scotland's tax decision. For this reason, labour in RUK, W_{ruk}, should oppose an increase in income tax in Scotland (assuming Scottish government spending remains constant!). In addition, labour in Scotland, W_s, has to bear an additional burden of paying the higher Scottish income tax rate, t_{ws}, on its now lower pre-tax income, W_s. The income tax burden in Scotland, and on labour in general, is greater than the income tax revenues raised. The excess tax burden ratio for Scotland and for RUK is >1. These results are shown in Table 2. Again, these negative results are dampened if the some of the Scottish income tax increase is paid for by a reduction in savings.

Table 2: Short period changes if Scottish Parliament raises the standard rate of income tax with (i) no change in government spending; (ii) no inter-regional trade flows; and (iii) no tax shifting

Jurisdiction: **Scotland:** *RUK:* UK	Symbol	Initial Value	Δ(Initial Value) if $\Delta t_{ws} > 0$
Parameters			
Markup	$\mathbf{k_s}$: k_{ruk}: k_{uk}	$\mathbf{k^*s}$: k^*_{ruk}: k^*_{uk}	**0**: *0*:0
Materials Bill/Wage Bill	$\mathbf{j_s}$ j_{ruk}: j_{uk}	$\mathbf{j^*s}$: j^*_{ruk}: j^*_{uk}	**0**: *0*: 0
Wage Share	$\boldsymbol{\alpha_s}$: α_{ruk}: α_{uk}	$\boldsymbol{\alpha^*s}$: α^*_{ruk}: α_{uk}	**0**: *0*: 0
Policy Variables			
Profits Tax	$\mathbf{T_{ps}}$: T_{pruk}: T_{puk}	$\mathbf{T^*_{ps}}$: T^*_{pruk}: T^*_{uk}	**0**: *0*: 0
Profits Tax Rate	$\mathbf{t_{ps}}$: t_{pruk}: t_{puk}	$\mathbf{t_{puk}}$: t_{puk}: t_{puk}	**0**: *0*: 0
Income Tax	$\mathbf{T_{ws}}$: T_{wruk}: T_{wuk}	$\mathbf{T^*_{ws}}$: T^*_{wruk}:T^*_{wuk}	**>0**: *0*: 0
Income Tax Rate	$\mathbf{t_{ws}}$: t_{wruk}: t_{wuk}	$\mathbf{t_{wuk}}$: t_{wuk}: t_{wuk}	**>0**: *0*: 0
Variables			
Wage Bill	$\mathbf{W_s}$: W_{ruk}: W_{uk}	$\mathbf{W^*_s}$: W^*_{ruk}: W^*_{uk}	**<0**: *<0*: <0
Materials Bill	$\mathbf{M_s}$: M_{ruk}: M_{uk}	$\mathbf{M^*_s}$: M^*_{ruk}: M^*_{uk}	**<0**: *<0*: <0
Value Added	$\mathbf{Y_s}$: Y_{ruk}: Y_{uk}	$\mathbf{Y^*_s}$: Y^*_{ruk}: Y^*_{uk}	**<0**: *<0*: <0
Post-Tax Profits	$\mathbf{P_s}$: P_{ruk}: P_{uk}	$\mathbf{P^{*s}}$: P^*_{ruk}: P^*_{uk}	**<0**: *<0*: <0
Rate of Profit	$\mathbf{r_s}$: r_{ruk}: r_{uk}	$\mathbf{r^*_s}$: r^*_{ruk}: r^*_{uk}	**<0**: *<0*: <0
Tax Burden Assessment			
ΔPost-Tax Profits	$\mathbf{\Delta P_s}$: ΔP_{ruk}:$\Delta \mathrm{P}_{uk}$		**<0**: *<0*: <0
ΔPre-Tax Wages	$\mathbf{\Delta W_s}$: ΔW_{ruk}: W_{uk}		**<0**: *<0*: <0
ΔPost-Tax Wages	$\mathbf{\Delta(W-Tw)_s}$: $\Delta(W-Tw)_{ruk}$: $\Delta(\mathrm{W-Tw})_{uk}$		**<0**: *<0*: <0
Tax Burden Ratio			**>0**: *>0*: >0
Excess Tax Burden Ratio			**>0**: *>0*: >0

6. Further Implications

As in any model, the assumptions play a pivotal role in determining the outcomes. We now begin to consider the results of relaxing some of our assumptions. In particular, we consider implications arising in the short period, implications arising in the long period, and other implications. The short-period implications arise as a result of compensating changes in the government budget. Other implications arise as a result of two forces: (1) changes in business markups in response to the tax change; and (2) changes in investment in response to changes in the rate of profit.

So far, we have assumed that the UK and Scottish governments raise tax revenues for the sake of doing so. Now we consider the incidence and effects of taxation when both governments spend their increased tax revenue, i.e. when the governments either use the tax receipts to purchase goods and services, transfer the tax receipts to earners of employment incomes, or transfer the tax receipts to capitalists. We assume that both governments operate with a balanced budget constraint.

7. Short Period Implcations Associated with a National Income Tax

If we assume that workers do not save and profit earners do not spend, and if the UK government levies a tax on employment income, T_{wuk}, to finance government purchases of goods and services, equation (10') reduces to:

$$P + Tp = \Pi = I \tag{12}$$

and national income is rewritten as:

$$Y = I/(1 - \alpha) \tag{13}$$

The result is that an income tax, T_{wuk}, has no impact on the pre- or post-tax levels of profits, the pre-tax wage and salary bill and level of national income. The UK government in this case simply takes disposable income from wage and salary earners, which reduces their consumption relative to the wage and salary bill, and substitutes its spending for that of wage and salary earners, leaving the level of profits unaffected. In this case, capitalists in the wages-good industry lose profits to the gain of capitalists in the government-goods-and-service industry, but the overall rates of profits in Scotland and RUK are unaffected. The tax burden ratio is one and the excess tax burden ratio is zero. If the marginal propensity to consume out of employment income were less than one, employment income earners would pay for some of the tax by reducing their savings and the tax would stimulate national income, pre-tax and post-tax profits and the pre-tax wage bill. Thus, the tax burden ratio would be less than one and the excess tax burden ratio would be negative.

If the increased income tax receipts are used to transfer income to employment income earners, the results are similar to those above, assuming that the marginal propensity to spend out of employment income is one. The increase in income tax, T_{wuk}, on the one hand, reduces income earners' consumption relative to the wage bill, W_{uk}, which reduces profits, P_{uk}, but, on the other hand, the tax transfer to income earners restores consumption back to its original level. This story may be further complicated if the tax distribution is other than a transfer distribution or if the marginal propensity to spend is less than one.

If the higher income tax receipts are used to transfer income to profit earners, and profit earners' marginal propensity to consume is zero, then the result is the same as presented in Table 1. Consumption out of income from employment falls relative to the wage and salary bill, with no offset, and profits fall by the amount of the tax. The tax burden ratio is equal to one and the excess tax burden ratio is greater than one. In contrast, however, if profit earners' marginal propensity to consume is nonzero, then the falls in profits, the rate of profits, national income and the wage and salary bill are offset to some degree, and the tax burden and excess tax burden ratios decline.

8. Short-Period Implications Associated with a National Income Tax

Now we suppose that the Scottish Parliament increases its purchases/expenditures in response to an increase in its income tax, T_{ws}. To begin, we assume that the marginal prospensity to save out of wages is zero. In this case, the results in Scotland and RUK depend upon how the Scottish Parliament's purchases/expenditures affect the balance of trade between Scotland and RUK and on the marginal propensity to save wages (income). If, for example, the increase in the Scottish income tax, T_{ws}, results in an increase in the Scottish Executive's purchases from local contractors in Scotland, without affecting the balance of trade between Scotland and RUK, then the Scottish income tax, T_{ws}, has no impact on national income, Y_{uk}, value added in Scotland, Y_s, and RUK, Y_{ruk}, aggregate or jurisdictional pre-tax or post-tax profits, P_{uk}, P_s, P_{ruk}, and the pre-tax wage and salary bill in each jurisdiction. However, in Scotland, the post-tax wage and salary bill, W_s, will fall by the full amount of the income tax, T_{ws}, as Scottish Executive purchases displace local consumption by employment income earners in Scotland.

The story gets more complicated if we allow for purchases by the Scottish Executive to spill out of Scotland, or, more generally, if the additional Scottish Executive purchases upset the balance of trade between Scotland and RUK. If the Scottish Executive purchases goods and services from non-local RUK contractors, exports increase in RUK, pushing up its value added, Y_{ruk}, its wage and salary bill, W_{ruk}, its level of profits, P_{ruk}, and its rate of profits, r_{ruk}. At the same time, imports increase into Scotland reducing its value added, Y_s, wage and salary bill, W_s, its level of profits, P_s, and its rate of profits, r_s.

We consider in more detail the effects with inter-jurisdictional trade flows. At the aggregate level, little will change. The aggregate levels of pre- and post-tax profits, P_{uk}, income, Y_{uk}, wage and salary bill, W_{uk}, materials bill, M_{uk}, and rate of profits, r_{uk}, are all unchanged. Since there are no changes to profit tax, t_{puk}, the difference between pre-tax and post-tax profits remains unchanged. However, at the jurisdictional level, a redistribution of income from Scotland to RUK has taken place. The Scottish Executive purchases have increased by the amount of the income tax increase, T_{ws}. The net result is that pre- and post-tax profits, P_s, in Scotland decline. Through the income multiplier, this reduction in profits pushes down value added in Scotland, Y_s. The wage and salary bill, W_s, and materials bill, M_s, in Scotland adjust accordingly. Likewise, RUK's profits, P_{ruk}, increase by the amount of the Scottish Executive's purchases from RUK contractors. Value-added in RUK, Y_{ruk}, increases. As a consequence, the rate of profit in Scotland, **rs**, declines while that in RUK, r_{ruk}, increases. The loss in income in Scotland relative to the increased income tax receipts is <0, causing the excess tax burden ratio to be >1 (see Table 3). Thus, the example shows that a jurisdiction like Scotland, which has fiscal discretion, has an incentive not to raise income tax, if other jurisdictions do not do the same, while at the same time, it is in the interest of non-tax increasing and spending jurisdictions, i.e. RUK, to encourage others, like Scotland, to spend and to tax.

Table 3. Example of the local tax model if the Scottish Parliament increases the standard rate of income tax (tws) with (i) a compensating change in Scottish Executive purchases and (ii) trade flows between Scotland and RUK.

Jurisdiction: Scotland: *RUK*: UK	Symbol	Initial Value	Δ(Initial Value) if $\Delta t_{ws} > 0$
Parameters			
Markup	$\mathbf{k_s}$: k_{ruk}: k_{uk}	$\mathbf{k^*_s}$: k^*_{ruk}: k^*_{uk}	**0:** *0*:0
Materials Bill/Wage Bill	$\mathbf{j_s}$: j_{ruk}: j_{uk}	$\mathbf{j^*_s}$: j^*_{ruk}: j^*_{uk}	**0:** *0*: 0
Wage Share	$\boldsymbol{\alpha_s}$: α_{ruk}: α_{uk}	$\boldsymbol{\alpha^*_s}$: α^*_{ruk}: α^*_{uk}	**0:** *0*: 0
Policy Variables			
Profits Tax	$\mathbf{T_{ps}}$: T_{pruk}: T_{puk}	$\mathbf{T^*_{ps}}$: T^*_{pruk}: T^*_{uk}	**0:** *0*: 0
Profits Tax Rate	$\mathbf{t_{ps}}$: t_{pruk}: t_{puk}	$\mathbf{t_{puk}}$: t_{puk}: t_{puk}	**0:** *0*: 0
Income Tax	$\mathbf{T_{ws}}$: T_{wruk}: T_{wuk}	$\mathbf{T^*_{ws}}$: T^*_{wruk}:T^*_{wuk}	**>0:** *0*: 0
Income Tax Rate	$\mathbf{t_{ws}}$: t_{wruk}: t_{wuk}	$\mathbf{t_{wuk}}$: t_{wuk}: t_{wuk}	**>0:** *0*: 0

Jurisdiction: Scotland: *RUK:* UK	Symbol	Initial Value	Δ(Initial Value) if $\Delta t_{ws} > 0$
Variables			
Wage Bill	$\mathbf{W_s}$: W_{ruk}: W_{uk}	$\mathbf{W^*_s}$: W^*_{ruk}: W^*_{uk}	**<0:** *>0:* 0
Materials Bill	$\mathbf{M_s}$: M_{ruk}: M_{uk}	$\mathbf{M^*_s}$: M^*_{ruk}: M^*_{uk}	**<0:** *>0:* 0
Value Added	$\mathbf{Y_s}$: Y_{ruk}: Y_{uk}	$\mathbf{Y^*_s}$: Y^*_{ruk}: Y^*_{uk}	**<0:** *>0:* 0
Post-Tax Profits	$\mathbf{P_s}$: P_{ruk}: P_{uk}	$\mathbf{P^*_s}$: P^*_{ruk}: P^*_{uk}	**<0:** *>0:* 0
Rate of Profit	$\mathbf{r_s}$: r_{ruk}: r_{uk}	$\mathbf{r^*_s}$: r^*_{ruk}: r^*_{uk}	**<0:** *>0:* 0
Tax Burden Assessment			
ΔPost-Tax Profits	$\Delta\mathbf{P_s}$: ΔP_{ruk}:ΔP_{uk}		**<0:** *>0:* 0
ΔPre-Tax Wages	$\Delta\mathbf{W_s}$: ΔW_{ruk}: W_{uk}		**<0:** *>0:* 0
ΔPost-Tax Wages	$\Delta\mathbf{V_s}$: ΔV_{ruk}: ΔV_{uk}		**<0:** *>0:* 0
Tax Burden Ratio			**>0:** *<0:* 0
Excess Tax Burden Ratio			**>0:** *<0:* 0

If the Scottish Executive transfers the increase in income tax back to Scottish wage and salary earners, and if Scottish wage and salary earners spend all the tax transfers locally in Scotland, the results are the same as if the Scottish Parliament had not increased income tax at all. If income earners in Scotland pay for some of the tax by reducing their savings, then UK and RUK national income increases, and in Scotland value-added increases, profits increase and the pre-tax wage bill increases relative to what is described in Table 3. The effect of the Scottish income tax increase becomes an empirical question where two offsetting effects have to be considered. The spillover of spending into the RUK reduces Scottish profits and Scottish income (value added), but the decrease in Scottish savings increases Scottish profits and Scottish income (value added). Whether the effects of the Scottish income tax increases are positive or negative on Scottish profits and Scottish national income depends upon the relative sizes of local taxpayers and local governments' marginal propensities to spend locally and on the marginal propensity to save.[2] In any case, the RUK has the incentive to encourage the Scottish Executive

2 Consider the following example. Recall that pre-tax profits can be written as:

$\Pi = I + Ge - Tw + Ex - Im + Cc - Ws$.

Suppose $\Delta Tw = \Delta Ge = 10$, then the ΔPi = zero, ceteris paribus.

Now suppose $\Delta Tw = \Delta Ge = 10$ and $\Delta Ws = -2$, $\Delta\Pi = 2$, ceteris paribus, and the economy is stimulated.

to increase its income tax and increase its spending. However, locally, the Scottish Executive will face political pressure to behave as fiscal conservatives.

If the Scottish Executive transfers the income tax increase to capitalists, and capitalists do not consume, then the result is the same as described in Table 2. But if capitalists do have a nonzero marginal propensity to consume out of transfer income, then the declines in the various incomes are offset according to the degree to which capitalists spend the transfer income. The decline in incomes in Scotland is offset according to the degree to which capitalists spend their income locally in Scotland.

In each of the previous scenarios, we have assumed that the UK government evenly spends or distributes the tax receipts back to each of the jurisdictions according to the initial set of dis-aggregation weights. Also, we have assumed that each jurisdiction's spending is distributed over the national economy according to the relative size of each jurisdiction's economy. In an actual economy, of course, this might not be the case. The UK government may play favourites, as is alleged with respect to the Barnett formula (McLean and McMillan, 2002) or the Scottish Executive may attempt to direct its purchases to local Scottish contractors, as the recipients of jurisdictions' transfers are generally likely to be local. Under this sort of scenario, the playing at favourites by the UK or Scottish governments could result in a change in the balance of economic power between jurisdictions. This scenario is more of a long-period story that we discuss further below.

Now suppose, $\Delta Tw = \Delta Ge = 10$, $\Delta Ws = -2$, and local government and workers have the same marginal propensity to spend locally (say equal to 25%). So worker consumption of imported goods falls by .75 of 8 = 6 and government imports rise by .75 of 10 or 7.5

As such the $\Delta P = \Delta Ge - \Delta Tw - \Delta IM - \Delta Ws$

Or $\Delta \Pi = 10 - 10 - (-6) - (7.5) - (-2) = +.5$ (a mild stimulis)

Now suppose that the government has a smaller marginal propensity to spend locally than workers do. Suppose the government spends 20% locally and workers spend 25% locally,

In this case, the $\Delta \Pi = 10 - 10 - (-6) - (8.0) - (-2) = 0$ (then no stimulus).

A reduction in marginal propensity to save, an increase in local workers' marginal propensity to spend locally and a decrease in the local government's marginal propensity to spend locally reduce the economic stimulus associated with the balanced budget increase in local taxes. If local taxes are highly regressive and if the economy of the local jurisdiction is relatively small, then a balanced budget increase in local income (wage) taxes is likely to have a contractionary effect.

There are two further implications that may have a significant influence on a regional economy: (1) changes in investment with respect to changes in taxation; and (2) changes in the business price/cost markup, k, with respect to a change in taxation.

9. Taxation and Investment

So far we have presented only a short-period version of a Kaleckian tax model. In the short period, the level of investment expenditure is unchanged having been determined by investment decisions taken in some previous time period. The length of the time lag between an investment decision and the subsequent expenditure depends on the rate at which new physical capacity can be planned and installed. With the passage of time businessmen's expectations and confidence will change in response to changing economic and political conditions. One of the factors influencing business susceptibility and, hence, future investment decisions is tax policy.

To move from a Kaleckian short-period situation to the long period means that it is now necessary to consider factors that influence investment decisions in the longer term, for example, the rate of capacity utilisation. We have shown elsewhere (Laramie and Mair, 1996) the conditions under which balanced changes in the structure of taxation can influence the amplitude of the business cycle for an economy in which the trend rate of investment is zero. However, balanced changes in the structure of taxation may also influence the trend rate of investment. When these changes in tax structure are disaggregated to the regional level they may have an impact on aggregate and jurisdictional levels and rates of profits, r_{uk}, r_s, r_{ruk}. These changes may then have an impact on the aggregate and jurisdictional levels of investment, which, in turn, affect the aggregate growth rate and relative jurisdictional rates of growth. For example, in Tables 2 and 3 we have shown that that there are circumstances under which increases in regional income tax, T_{ws}, can reduce the aggregate level of profits, P_{uk}, and the rate of profits, r_{uk}.

Kalecki (1971/1968) and Gomulka et al. (1990) have explained business fixed investment decisions and aggregate investment decisions in a Kaleckian model as a lagged function of business savings, derived from profits, and the rate of profits. Laramie and Mair (1996, 1998) have connected these investment decisions to the structure of taxation via the level and rate of profits. Not surprisingly, Laramie and Mair have shown that taxation that depresses the level of profits and the rate of profits also depresses economic growth, and, thus, the long-period incidence effects of taxation need to be considered.

In Kaleckian theory, the determinants of current investment expenditures are: (1) the lagged level of profits; (2) the change in the level of past profits; (3) a past level of investment expenditure and an innovations factor, given a number of parameters relating to changes in business confidence, the savings behaviour of capitalists, the rate of capacity utilisation, the payback period of investment, the rate of obsolescence and the profits generated by new investment. Laramie and Mair (2002a) show how the introduction of taxation into a Kaleckian growth model impacts on the trend level of investment, the trend capital stock and the trend rate of capacity utilisation.

The impact of the tax system in a Kaleckian model is either via the rate of depreciation or the level of profits. If no income tax shifting occurs, an increase in income tax has no effect on the rate of depreciation and, therefore, no impact on the level of investment. If, however, an increase in income tax is shifted, then this will result in a fall in business markups which, given the level of profits, will increase the wage and salary bill and the level of income and, therefore, the rate of depreciation, leading to an increase in investment. If no shifting of income tax occurs, a rise in income tax will result in a fall in the savings of wage and salary earners and an increase in the level of post-tax profits. If the increase in income tax is shifted then this positive impact on profits will be reduced by the extent to which shifting increases the income share of employment income, the wage and salary bill and savings out of employment incomes. It will also increase the rate of capacity utilisation. The effects of an increase in income tax on the trend level of investment, whether shifted or not, are indeterminate because of the presence of offsetting effects. An increase in income tax that is not shifted will increase the long-run rate of capacity utilisation via an increased income multiplier effect. However, if the increase in the tax is shifted, the long-run effects on the rate of capacity utilisation again become indeterminate because of offsetting effects. These results show that fiscal policy, even with a balanced budget, affects the long-run performance of the economy. The incidence and effects of taxation depend critically on whether or not taxes are shifted.

10. Tax Shifting via Changes in the Business Price/Cost Markup

As we have shown elsewhere (Laramie, 1991, Laramie and Mair, 1996), further complications arise when we allow for changes in the markup with respect to a change in taxation. Basically, we introduce a tax shift parameter into the markup function. Employment income earners, for example, may attempt to shift an increase in income tax by squeezing or reducing the price/cost markup. This sort of shifting may go on even when the aggregate levels of post-tax profits or post-tax employment incomes are unaffected by taxation because of changes in the intra-industry distributions of profits and employment incomes. The most that can be said at this point is that the precise nature of the dynamic process of tax shifting is unknown, but tax shifting may take place both over the short and long periods.

If the increase in income tax in Scotland, T_{ws}, is shifted, then business markups in Scotland, k_s, will be reduced, and the pre-tax employment income share, $\square_s$, will increase. This, in turn will increase national income, Y_s, and the pre-tax and post-tax wage and salary bills, W_s and $(W-Tw)_s$, and, holding Scottish Executive purchases constant, will reduce the level of business profits in Scotland, P_s. Again, this story is further complicated by the savings behaviour of wage and salary earners. For example, if wage and salary earners are savers and have a nonzero propensity to save, then the shifting of the increase in Scottish income tax, T_{ws}, may further reduce business profits, P_s, while increasing national income, Y_s.

We also have to consider changes in business markups at the jurisdictional level. In Table 2, we showed that the Scottish Parliament's increase in income tax, T_{ws}, reduced not only the post-tax wage bill in Scotland, $(W-Tw)_s$, but also in RUK, $(W-Tw)_{ruk}$. Employee groups in both jurisdictions may attempt to shift the increase in income tax, T_{ws}, but with the pressure to do so being greater in Scotland than in RUK, where the tax shifting in Scotland may be constrained by the efforts of employees in RUK.

It is at this stage that the importance Kalecki attached to income distribution becomes significant. As we have argued in this paper, fiscal policy, even with a balanced budget, can affect the long-run development of a capitalist economy depending on whether or not taxes are shifted. This reflects the blending of both macroeconomics and microeconomics in Kalecki's theory of growth. Kalecki's theory of profits is macroeconomic while his theory of income distribution is microeconomic, dependent on the degree of monopoly. The macroeconomics and the microeconomics have different implications for tax shifting. As we have shown above, quite different macroeconomic effects can occur if the Scottish Parliament increases income tax, depending on whether or not the tax increase is shifted.

Crucial, therefore, to assessing the macroeconomic effects of a regional increase in income tax is an understanding of how the distribution of income is determined in Kaleckian theory. In Kaleckian economics, the distribution of income is determined by firms in the process of setting prices. The factors determining price setting are, therefore, responsible for determining income distribution. Kalecki (1954) identified the factors determining the markup as the growth of concentration among giant corporations, the development of sales promotion through advertising, selling agents etc., the influence of changes in the level of overhead costs in relation to prime costs, and the power of trade unions. Laramie, Mair and Reynolds (2003) have estimated the determinants of the degree of monopoly for a sample of UK manufacturing industries incorporating the factors identified by Kalecki as well as others suggested by the literature on industry price/cost markups.

For two different samples of the UK manufacturing industry, the first in the late 1980s and the second in the mid 1990s, regression analysis confirms the importance of the factors Kalecki thought would be determinants of industry markups. Both equations have R-bar squared values of around 0.6. In particular, the advertising-to-sales ratio and the degree of market openness, as measured by import and export penetration, are statistically significant determinants as well as entry barriers such as scale economies and minimum capital requirements. These estimates have been generated by data at the UK level. No work has yet been done to replicate them at regional level. It is, however, particularly important to note that at the UK level, an industry's degree of exposure to foreign competition is a significant determinant of its price setting ability and, hence, of the distribution of income. At the regional level, firms are, of course, subjected not only to competition from overseas but also from other regions in the UK, which will act as a further constraint on their ability to set prices. At the UK national level, Laramie and Mair (2002b) have observed a sustained increase since the mid 1970s in the share of profits in national income at the expense of income from employment. These considerations suggest that shifting any increase in income tax levied by the Scottish Parliament may be unlikely.

11. Conclusion

The exercise of the income tax-varying powers of the Scottish Parliament is, like matrimony, something that should not be entered into lightly. As we have tried to demonstrate in this paper, it is likely to be neither a universally bad thing nor a universally good thing. The likely outcomes are heavily dependent on certain conditions being fulfilled. In particular, the outcomes depend upon the government's budget constraint (balanced or not), the marginal propensity to save out of (wage) income, the extent to which the income tax is shifted through changes in business price/cost markups, and the relative sizes of local income earners and local governments' marginal propensity to spend locally. Should it ever contemplate exercising its tax varying powers, it is important that the Scottish Parliament be clear as to the social or economic objectives it wishes to achieve. If the objective is to fund an increase in social expenditure in Scotland, as, for example, the recent introduction in Scotland but not in the rest of the UK of free personal care for the elderly, then a significant part of the benefit of this increased expenditure is likely to accrue to income earners in RUK. The extent to which Scotland benefits from the tax change depends on income earners' marginal propensity to save and marginal propensity to spend locally, the Scottish government's marginal propensity to spend locally to make the program operational, and the extent to which the tax is shifted through a change in business price/cost markups. This is an inevitable consequence of Scotland being a small open economy with substantial trade flows with RUK.

If the objective of the Scottish Parliament is economic, for example, to use its tax-varying powers to mitigate the impact of the business cycle on the Scottish economy, then perverse consequences ***may*** arise. Assuming that a balanced budget constraint is maintained, an increase in income tax, $\mathbf{T}_{ws}$, that is not shifted, and we think, is the most likely outcome, then, as we show in our analysis of the impact of taxation on the business cycle (Laramie and Mair, 2000), the probable effect will be to attenuate rather than dampen the cycle. Again, this conclusion is based on the assumption that workers have a nonzero marginal propensity to save and that the trade balance between Scotland and the RUK is unaffected by the tax. Insofar as the tax causes a spillover in demand for products from the RUK, a leakage of spending flows from Scotland to the RUK, the attenuation of the Scottish business cycle is dampened and the RUK business cycle is attenuated. When such spillover effects are significant (see footnote 2), local government authorities have the incentive to be fiscally conservative. When local government authorities are fiscally conservative, the likelihood of national stagnation rises, and the national government must play a greater policy role, be fiscally liberal, to offset the behaviour of local governments.

In this paper, we have attempted to provide a new approach to the theory of the incidence and effects of taxation. In particular, we have attempted to consider how national taxation affects the performance of the economies of regional jurisdictions, and how regional/jurisdictional taxation affects the regional economy, other regional economies and the national economy. Essentially, we have considered these effects when taxation changes independently of government expenditures and when governments are constrained to maintain balanced government budget stances. Our results show that national taxes, even with a balanced budget constraint, are preferable to regional taxes, because regional tax policies tend to drive a wedge between jurisdictional rates of profits. The exception to this rule is if regional government spending of its tax receipts does not create an imbalance of trade between the jurisdictions.

These results have many policy implications. However, we must recognise that our model poses a paradox for policy makers. On the one hand, policy makers tend to want to extend the principle of subsidiarity and bring the government closer to the people. Granting regional jurisdictions more autonomy to raise taxes and giving these authorities more responsibilities to provide public expenditure may result in regressive tax policies and 'beggar thy neighbour' policies that will undercut national economic objectives of full employment, high incomes and high growth rates.

Notes

This paper was presented at the 32nd Annual Conference of the Regional Science Association International (British and Irish Section), Brighton, UK 21–23 August 2002.

References

Courvisanos, J. 1996 *Investment Cycles in Capitalist Economies: A Kaleckian Behavioural Contribution*, Cheltenham, Edward Elgar.

Gomulka, S., Ostaszewski, A. and Davies, R. O. 1990 The innovation rate and Kalecki's theory of the trend, unemployment and the business cycle, *Economica,* **57**, 525–40.

Kalecki, M. 1937 A theory of commodity, income and capital taxation, *Economic Journal,* **47**, 444–50.

Kalecki, M. 1954, *Theory of Economic Dynamics,* London, Unwin University Books.

Kalecki, M. 1971/1968 *Selected Essays on the Dynamics of the Capitalist Economy,* Cambridge, Cambridge University Press.

Laramie, A. J. 1991 Taxation and Kalecki's distribution factors, *Journal of Post Keynesian Economics,* **13**, 583–94.

Laramie, A. J. and Mair, D. 1996 Taxation and Kalecki's theory of the business cycle, *Cambridge Journal of Economics*, **20**(4), 451–64.

Laramie, A. J. and Mair, D. 2000 *A Dynamic Theory of Taxation: Integrating Kalecki into Modern Public Finance,* Cheltenham, Edward Elgar.

Laramie, A. J. and Mair, D. 2001 Tax incidence in Holt, R. and Pressman, S. (eds), *A New Guide to Post Keynesian Economics,* pp. 42–51, London, Routledge.

Laramie, A. J. and Mair, D. 2002a The effects of taxation in a Kaleckian growth model, *Metroeconomica,* forthcoming.

Laramie, A. J. and Mair, D. 2002b Full employment: gift horse or Trojan horse?, *Review of Social Economy,* **LX**, 567–594.

Laramie, A. J., Mair, D. and Miller, A. 2003 Kalecki's investment theory reconsidered in *Proceedings of International Conference to mark the Centenary of Kalecki's Birth, T. Kowalik and* S. Zydowski (ed). London, Routledge, forthcoming.

Laramie, A. J., Mair, D. and Reynolds, P. J. 2003 Kalecki's theory of income distribution: the answer to a maiden's prayer?', *Contemporary Post Keynesian Analysis: A Compendium of Contributions to the Seventh International Post Keynesian Conference,* L. R. Wray and M. Forstater (eds) Cheltenham, Edward Elgar, forthcoming.

Lee, F. S. 2002 Theory creation and the methodological foundations of Post Keynesian economics, *Cambridge Journal of Economics,* **26**, 789–804.

McLean, I. and McMillan, A. 2002 The fiscal crisis of the United Kingdom', Nuffield College Working Papers in Politics, 2002, W10.

Douglas Mair, Heriot- Watt University, Edinburgh, UK
Anthony J. Laramie, Merrimack College, MA, USA

Chapter 5: The Effects of Taxation in a Kaleckian Growth Model*

Abstract: The paper analyses the effects of balanced budget changes in the tax rates on wages and profits on the trend component of fixed investment, on the trend rate of growth of capital stock and on the trend rates of capacity utilisation. A modified version of Kalecki's growth model is used to analyse the long-term effects of taxation on the growth performance of the economy.

1. Introduction

The issue we explore in this paper is the feasibility of influencing the growth path of the economy by changing tax rates within a balanced budget framework. We consider this issues from within the Kaleckian paradigm. Our principal reason for doing so is that a critical feature of Kalecki's approach is the assumption of unused capacity of plant and labour. At first sight, adopting a Kaleckian approach to analyse the role of taxation on the long-term growth performance of the economy may appear unusual for two reasons: 1) In his writings on business cycles and growth Kalecki tended to assume away or minimise the role of the government budget; and 2) Kalecki did not explicitly incorporate the effects of taxation into the corpus of his work on long-term economic growth. Kalecki (1971/1937) had pointed out that an important implication of the publication of Keynes' *General Theory* was that a whole new approach to the study of the effects of taxation on effective demand was required, but, Kalecki never developed his tax analysis beyond a simple short period model. We can only speculate to the reasons as to why this was the case. We believe that Kalecki was concerned with developing the core, investment driven, theory of growth.

We consider the effects of taxation on the trend component of fixed investment, on the trend rate of growth in the capital stock, and on the trend rate of capacity utilization. Kalecki attempted to explain the behaviour of these variables

---

* Laramie, Anthony and Mair, Douglas, "The Effects of Taxation in Kaleckian Growth Model," *Metroeconomica*, Volume 54, No.s 2 & 3, May/September 2003, pp. 326–345. Reprinted by Permission John Wiley and Sons, copyright 2003.ß

using two different approaches. Kalecki (1962) essentially relied on version II of his theory of fixed investment. In this version, fixed investment decisions depend on the entrepreneurial capital of the firm, the change in the rate of profits and technological change. However, as was pointed out by Gomulka, et al. (1990) there was a serious flaw in this version of Kalecki's theory which they corrected (see Laramie and Mair 2000). They then used this corrected version to analyze further the dynamic properties of Kalecki's model to show that, depending on the parameters in the model, his approach can be used to explain 'cautious' capitalism, i. e. capitalism with a dampening cycle, and 'rash' capitalism, i.e. capitalism with an explosive cycle. Gomulka et al. conclude that, when corected, Kalecki's theory of growth was evolving closer towards Schumpeter and further away from Marx. In order to move Kalecki towards Schumpeter, the rate of innovations and the investment-inducing power of innovations have to be sufficiently high to absorb a growing labor force. Kalecki (1971/1968) was not satisfied with his 1962 Version II theory of investment and modified it to what is popularly known as Version III. In Version III, new investment is governed by the increment in profits captured by new investment, as opposed to being simply dependent on changes in the past rate of profits. In addition, Kalecki reformulated the theory of the trend stating:

> … the rate of growth at a given time is a phenomenon rooted in past economic, social and technological developments rather than determined fully by the coefficients of our equations as is the case with the business cycle [and] mechanistic theories (based… on such fallacious a priori assumptions as a constant degree of long-run utilization of equipment).

Kalecki concluded Version III by stating:

> … future inquiry into the problems of growth should be directed not towards doing without semi-autonomous magnitudes . . but rather towards treating the coefficients of equations … as slowly changing variables rooted in past development of the system.

In this paper, we attempt to follow Kalecki's suggestion. In particular, we attempt to consider how the trend growth rate is affected by the tax structure when the capacity utilization rate and the balance sheet matter in affecting business fixed investment decisions. We consider this topic particularly important at a time when fiscal policy has been, at best, relegated to the back seat of macroeconomic policy making, when monetary policy seems to have reached its limits and when the word 'deficit' is considered vulgar.

The paper is structured as follows. First, we develop Kalecki's theory of fixed investment modifying it to account for the effects of the capacity utilization rate, the balance sheet, and the structure of taxation. Second, we re-develop Kalecki's theory of the trend level of investment, the trend capital stock, and the trend rate of capacity utilization accounting for the same factors. Third, we consider the implications for growth and public policy.

2. Kalecki's Theory of Investment

Kalecki (1971/1968, p. 171) considered three determinants of new investment decisions: 1) entrepreneurial savings; 2) the prerequisites for their reinvestment; and 3) an innovation factor. Entrepreneurial savings, E, influence investment decisions because of capital market limits and increasing risk (Kalecki, 1971/1968, p. 172). Whether entrepreneurial savings are reinvested depends upon the relationship between the actual level of gross investment, I, and the investment that generates the standard ('normal') rate of profits, $I(\pi)$, where π is the standard rate of profit and it is the reciprocal of the pay-off period. Assuming that as investment increases, the rate of profits is reduced, investment decisions will be in excess of, equal to, or less than entrepreneurial savings, if actual investment expenditures are respectively less than, equal to, or greater than the level of investment that yields the standard rate of profits. The extent to which the difference between investment that generates the standard rate of profits and actual investment impact on investment decisions depends upon the "intensity of the reaction of entrepreneurs," r_o (Kalecki, 1971/1968, p. 172). To these determinants, Kalecki (1971/1968, p. 173) adds innovation-induced investment decisions, B(t). This factor is represented as a semi-autonomous function, depending upon "past economic, social and technological developments" (Kalecki, 1971/1968, p. 173), that is assumed to change slowly over time. Accordingly, Kalecki expressed that fixed investment decisions, D, can be written as (1):

(1) $D = E + r_o(I(\pi) - I) + B(t).$

We now modify the expression for investment decisions by including a gearing ratio and the capacity utilization rate as determinants. The reason for including the gearing ratio, defined as total liabilities to net worth, is to capture the effects of increasing risk associated with investment. An increase in the gearing ratio puts more of the firm's capital at risk in case of failure (see Kalecki, 1968, pp. 92 -94). Thus, an increase in the gearing ratio is likely to diminish entrepreneurs' reactions to the stimulus provided by the situation where investment that yields the standard rate of profits, $I(\pi)$, is greater than actual investment, I. Likewise, an increase in the gearing ratio will accelerate the contraction of investment decisions when $I(\pi)$ is less than I.

The capacity utilization rate will also modify entrepreneurs' reactions to the difference between $I(\pi)$ and I. Businesses are assumed to desire a certain capacity utilization rate. See Courvisanos (1996, pp. 20–24). If the actual capacity utilization rate rises above the desired capacity utilization rate, the increase will heighten businesses' reactions to the positive difference between I(π) and I. If the actual capacity utilization rate decreases below the desired capacity utilization rate, the decrease will dampen businesses' reaction to the positive difference between I(π) and I. When the difference between I(π) and I is negative and businesses have the incentive to contract investment decisions, an increase in the capacity utilization above the desired level will dampen such a contraction, and a decrease in the capacity utilization rate below the desired level will accelerate the contraction of investment decisions.

Given these considerations, we now write investment decisions as:

(2) $$D = E + r_0 (I(\pi) - I) + r_1 (gr) + r_2(u - u_d) + B(t);$$

where gr = the gearing ratio, u = actual capacity utilization rate, u_d = desired capacity utilization rate, and where $r_1 < 0, r_2 > 0$.

We now proceed to modify equation (2) to consider the role of profits and taxation in affecting investment decisions. Kalecki finds expressions for entrepreneurial savings, E, and investment that generates the standard rate of profits, I(π). We do likewise, but make some modifications. We will also reconsider the determinants of gearing ratio and the capacity utilization rate.

Kalecki (1971/1968, p. 172) assumes that entrepreneurial savings are a fraction of gross savings (worker savings assumed to be zero). Since we have assumed non-zero workers' savings, we write entrepreneurial savings as a fraction of total post-tax profits; thus:

(3) $$E = \lambda P;$$

where P = aggregate post-tax profits.

In order to find an expression for investment that generates the standard rate of profits, Kalecki (1971/1968, p. 170) assumes "ample unused productive capacities" and that new investment that generates the standard rate of profits will capture only a portion, n, of the new 'real' profits generated, ΔP.[1] This amount is augmented by the extent to which new investment results in productivity increases. The productivity increases associated with new investment increase real costs to existing

1 Since some businesses operate with unused productive capacity so as to as to capture profits from unexpected increases in demand (and, for example, as a barrier to entry), then the desired capacity utilization rate is below the full capacity utilization rate. As such, the unused capacity will cause firms to capture only a portion of the profits generated by their new investment expenditures.

equipment, cause some shift in production from existing to new investment, reduce the real profits to existing equipment and increase profits to new equipment. The loss in profits to existing equipment (the gain to new equipment) is assumed to be proportional to real costs, the difference between national income, Y, and aggregate profits, P, i.e.: $\omega(Y- P)$. The greater the rate of technical progress, the greater the value of □, and the greater the gain in profits to new equipment. As a consequence, the profits generated by new investment is $\pi[I(\pi)] = n\Delta P + \omega(Y- P)$, and, thus investment that yields the standard rate of profit is written as:

(4) $I(\pi) = [n\Delta P + \omega(Y - P)]/\pi.$

In turn, (4) can be rewritten by finding an expression for national income as a function of profits. Following Kalecki (1968), businesses set markups over prime costs to cover overheads and attain profits. On the aggregate, profits are largely determined by capitalist spending decisions independently of business pricing decisions. Pricing decisions, as reflected in business markups, inter alia, determine the wage bill's share of national income. To simplify, we write the wage share as:

(5) $W/Y = \alpha,$

where W = the wage bill, Y = national income, and α = the wage share. From the definition of the wage share, an expression for national income is derived. Assuming $W = Y - \Pi$, where Π is pre-tax profits, and $\Pi = P + Tp$, and assuming that $Tp = tp(\Pi)$, national income, Y, is written as:

(6) $Y = P/(1 - tp)(1 - \alpha)$; tp = the tax rate on profits; and α= the wage share.

Equation (6) is important because it shows that the tax system influences the relationship between aggregate profits (P) and national income (Y) directly through the profits tax and indirectly through profits and wage taxes' impact on the level of profits (P) and the wage share (α). We will discuss these points further below. By substituting (6) into (4), the level of investment fetching the standard rate of profit, $I(\pi)$, can be rewritten as:

(4') $I(\pi) = [n\Delta P + \delta P]/\pi;$

where:

(7) $\delta = \omega[\alpha + t_p (1 - a)]/(1 - t_p)(1 - \alpha);$

and where δ = the rate of depreciation (Kalecki 1971/1968, p. 171, fn) in the sense that it represents the rate at which profits are lost to existing capital as the result of technical progress.

Combining equations (3), (4') and (2) yields the investment decision equation:

(8) $D = \lambda(P) + r_o ([n\Delta P + \delta P]/\pi - I) + r_1 (gr) + r_2 (u - u_d) + B(t)$ or:
(8') $D = [\lambda + (r_o \delta/\pi)]P + [n r_o /\pi] \Delta P - (r_o)I + (r_1)gr + (r_2)(u - u_d) + B(t)$

Now we reconsider the determinants of the gearing ratio (gr) and the capacity utilization rate (u). We define the gearing ratio as the ratio of the firm's total liabilities to net worth. We suppose that the gearing ratio increases in response to the anticipation of higher future profits. The effect of expected higher income on future investment is reflected in Kalecki's investment equation in the difference between I(π) and I. Thus, an increase in expected future profits has a set of contradictory effects. On the one hand, it encourages investment, on the other hand, it pushes up the gearing ratio which, in turn, depresses or dampens future investment. By assuming that changes in expected future income are reflected in the difference between investment that yields the standard rate of profits and actual investment, we express the gearing ratio as:

(9) $gr = \gamma_o + \gamma_1(I(\pi) - I)$;

where g_o and g_1 are greater than zero and change with respect to changes in the 'state of credit' and changes in the state of confidence, where the 'state of credit' depends on the financial system's willingness to extend credit, and the state of confidence depends on firms' willingness to seek credit. An increase in the state of credit increases the gearing ratio allowed by lenders. An increase in the state of confidence increases the gearing ratio desired by firms. By introducing (9) into equation (8'), investment decisions are written as:

(10) $D = r_1(\gamma_0) + [\lambda + (\delta/\pi)[r_o + r_1(\gamma_1)]]P + [n/\pi][r_o + r_1 (\gamma_1)]\Delta P - (r_o + r_1(\gamma_1)])$
$I + (r_2)(u - u_d) + B(t)$.

The capacity utilization rate is measured as the ratio of actual output to potential output. Actual output is described in equation (6). That is:

(11) $u = Y/ Y^P = P/[Y^P (1 - tp)(1 - \alpha)]$

where Y^P= is potential output. For this paper, we assume that Y^P is constant. By plugging (11) into (10), the investment decisions equation is rewritten as:

(12) $D = r_1(\gamma_0) - r_2 u_d + [\lambda + (\delta/\pi)[r_o + r_1(\gamma_1)] + r_2/((1 - tp)(1 - \alpha) Y^P)]P + [n/\pi]$
$[r_o + r_1 (\gamma_1)]\Delta P - (r_o + r_1(\gamma_1)])I + B(t)$

Following Kalecki, investment decisions taken in the time period t are translated into investment expenditures in t+τ so that $I_{t+\tau} = D_t$, and, therefore, the fixed investment equation is given as:

(12') $I_{t+\tau} = r_1(\gamma_0) - r_2\, u_d + [\lambda + (\delta/\pi)[r_o + r_1(\gamma_1)] + r_2/((1 - tp)(1 - \alpha)Y^P)]$
$P + [n/\pi][r_o + r_1\,(\gamma_1)]\Delta P - (\,r_o + r_1(\gamma_1)])I + B(t).$

From equation (12') we can summarize the determinants of investment expenditures. Current investment expenditures depend on the lagged level and the change in the level of past profits, a past level of investment expenditures and an innovations factor (given the parameters: λ, r_o, r_1, r_2, γ_0, γ_1, u_d, n, δ and π). An increase in profits results in a rise in entrepreneurial savings and an increase in the profitability of new investment relative to actual investment. The rise in entrepreneurial savings reduces the risk associated with new investment and provides greater access to capital markets. The rise in profits and the increase in the change in profits causes new investment to become more profitable (makes more investment possible at the standard rate of profits), since the volume of profits captured by new investment increases, given n and d. The rise in investment that yields the standard rate of profits relative to actual investment induces entrepreneurs to undertake investment expenditures in excess of entrepreneurial savings, given the intensity of entrepreneurs' reactions, r_0. These effects on investment decisions are dampened by the impact of the increased profitability on the gearing ratio. If the increased profitability induces businesses to expand their debt relative to equity, the higher debt slows down businesses' reactions in response to the increased profitability of investment. Also, these effects are heightened by the increase in the capacity utilization rate's effects on investment. The increased profitability pushes up the actual capacity utilization rate relative to the desired capacity utilization rate. This increase speeds up businesses' reactions to the increased profitability.

We now proceed to use the investment function as specified in equation (12') to consider the impact of the tax system on trend level of investment, the trend capital stock, and the trend capacity utilization rate. The tax system impacts on these variables through the rate of depreciation, the level of profits, and the capacity utilization rate. An analysis of the effects of the tax system on these variables provides us with the underlying causal mechanisms in the model.

2.1 The impact of taxation on the rate of depreciation

The impact of the tax system on investment operates via the rate of depreciation and the level of profits. The impact of taxation on depreciation is by affecting the real tax bill associated with old equipment. Technical progress, through new investment, results in increases in the productivity of new equipment which, *ceteris paribus*, result in lower prices. This increases the real costs and lowers the real profits associated with existing equipment. The decline in real profits from existing equipment accelerates its obsolescence. Thus, an increase in the tax on profits will increase the rate of depreciation, given the rate of technical progress.

To consider how a change in the tax rates on wages or profits has an impact on the rate of depreciation, we recognize that a change in any of the parameters that increases national income relative to profits, given the rate of technical progress, increases the rate of depreciation. We consider here and in the next two sections how changes in the tax rates on wages and profits have an impact on depreciation for two cases: 1) no tax shifting; and 2) tax shifting.

In the no tax shifting case, the markup, k, is constant with respect to a change in the tax rates, t_w and t_p. In the tax shifting case, we assume an inverse relationship between the markup and the wage tax rate, t_w, and a positive relationship between the markup and the profits tax rate, t_p.[2]

By differentiating the rate of depreciation, equation (7), with respect to a change in either tax rate, we consider the impact of taxation on the rate of depreciation, i. e.:

(13) $$d\delta/dt_i = \partial\delta/\partial t_i + (\partial\delta/\partial\alpha)(\partial\alpha/\partial k)(\partial k/\partial t_i);$$[3]

where i = w and p.

With no tax shifting, an increase in the tax rate on wages, t_w, has no impact on the rate of depreciation (see Laramie and Mair, 2000). When the wage tax shifting effect is considered, the fall in business markups, given profits, increases the wage bill and national income and, therefore, increases the rate of depreciation (see Laramie and Mair, 2000).

With no tax shifting, an increase in the tax rate on profits, t_p, given post-tax profits, causes pre-tax profits to increase thereby increasing national income, Y, relative to aggregate profits, P, and increases the rate of depreciation. With profits tax shifting, the increase in business markups reduces the wage bill, dampens the

2 The inverse relationship between the wage tax rate and the markup is assumed because the higher wage tax, if shifted, increases unit labor costs. Businesses, depending upon the degree of monopoly, might not be able to shift the increase in unit labor costs forward or backward, and, therefore, the markup is squeezed. Likewise, an increase in the profits tax could cause firms to shift the tax by increasing price and/or reducing unit labor costs, thus causing the markup to increase.

3 As shown in equation (13), the shifting effect is through a change in the impact of the markup on the wage share. Kalecki (1971/1968) argued that the markup and the ratio of materials costs to wage costs move counter-cyclically causing the wage share to be relatively constant. Whether such a counter-cyclical movement exists with respect to a change in the tax rates is an empirical question and beyond the scope of this paper.

increases in both national income and in the rate of depreciation (see Laramie and Mair, 2000). The significance of these results is discussed more fully below. Given that a change in the rate of depreciation affects the level of new investment, taxation will have an impact on the level of investment and the structure of the business cycle.

2.2 Taxation and the level of profits

Kalecki (1968) showed that aggregate profits, as measured by the difference between aggregate sales and prime costs (materials and wages), can be represented as the sum of gross private investment, the government budget deficit, the trade surplus and the difference between capitalists' consumption and workers' savings. Thus, assuming that the trade balance is zero, the level of profits is expressed as:

(14) $P = I + G - T + Cc - Ws$

where G = government purchases, T = tax receipts, Cc = capitalists' consumption and Ws = workers' savings.

Assuming a balanced budget constraint, $G = T$, and that $Cc = A(t) + c_c(P)$, (where A(t) is a semi-autonomous component of capitalist consumption) and $Ws = (1 - t_w)s_w(W)$, where c_c = the propensity to consume out of profits, and s_w = the propensity to save out of wages, the profit function can be written as:

(15) $P = [I + A(t)](1 - \alpha)(1 - t_p)/[(1 - t_p)(1 - \alpha)(1 - c_c) + s_w(1 - t_w)\alpha]$.

As reflected in equation (15), aggregate profits are equal to investment, when workers do not save and capitalists do not consume, and the government budget is in balance. The impact of taxation on the level of profits can be formally represented by a differentiating equation (15) with respect to a change in the rates of tax on wages and profits, i.e.:

(16) $dP/dt_i = (\partial P/\partial a)(\partial a/\partial k)(\partial k/\partial t_i) + (\partial P/\partial t_i)$ where i = w and p.

As evidenced in equation (16), assuming a balanced budget constraint, the direct effect of taxation on the level of profits in the short period is directly through a change in the tax rates and the indirect effect is through a change the wage share. In the no tax shifting case, a balanced budget increase in the wage tax causes a reduction in workers' savings which increases the level of post-tax profits. If the wage tax is shifted, then this positive impact on profits is reduced by the extent to which shifting increases the wage share, α and the wage bill and workers' savings. If workers' savings are zero, then the balanced budget tax change has no impact on post-tax profits (see Laramie and Mair, 2000).

By contrast, an unshifted balanced budget increase in the profits tax reduces after tax profits, because the rise in pre-tax profits increases national income, the wage bill and workers' savings. However, if the profits tax is shifted, the effect is dampened as the increase in workers' savings is reduced. If workers do not save, the balanced budget increase in the profits tax has no effect on post-tax profits.

2.3 Taxation and the capacity utilization rate

Given Y^p, the capacity utilization rate moves in the same direction and constant proportion to national income, Y. The impact of taxation on national income depends upon the effects of taxation on pre-tax profits and the wage share. The effect of taxation on pre-tax profits depends upon the government budget and the propensities to consume out of profits and wages. For example, equation (6), can be rewritten as:

(17) $Y = \Pi/(1 - \alpha)$;

where Π = pre-tax profits, and where

(18) $\Pi = I + G - Tw + Cc - Ws$.

From equation (18), we can see that a balanced budget increase in the profit tax rate increases G. The increase in G pushes up pre-tax profits, national income, and the capacity utilization rate. The increase in national income is dampened by a decrease in capitalist consumption and/or an increase in worker savings. The dampening effect depends upon the marginal propensities to consume out of profits and wages. In contrast, a balanced budget increase in the wage tax rate has no effect on pre-tax profits, assuming no changes in capitalist consumption or worker savings. However, if the wage tax results in a reduction in worker savings, then both pre-tax and post-tax profits increase. The increase in pre-tax profits pushes up national income and the capacity utilization rate.

The effects of the tax rates on capacity utilization are modified if the taxes are shifted. A shifted profit tax increases business markups (decreases the wage share) and further dampens the balanced budget effect. In contrast, a shifted wage tax reduces business markups (increases the wage share) and increases the balanced budget effect.

We have now shown that taxation has an impact on investment through three channels: 1) the rate of depreciation, 2) the level of profits, and 3) the capacity utilization rate. To summarize, an increase in the profit tax increases the rate of depreciation (assuming no tax shifting), and reduces post-tax profits and increases the capacity utilization rate, assuming a balanced budget constraint and no tax shifting. An increase in the wage tax has no effect on the rate of depreciation (assuming no tax shifting), increases post-tax profits and the capacity utilization rate. The shifting of the wage tax reduces post-tax profits but increases the capacity utilization rate.

3. The Trend Level of Investment, the Trend Capital Stock and Trend Capacity Utilization Rate.

3.1 The trend level of investment

We now derive an expression for the trend, we simply rewrite equation (12') as:

(19) $I_{t+\tau} = b_o + b_1 (P) + b_2 (\Delta P) - b_3 (I) + B(t)$; where:
$b_o = r_o + r_1(\gamma_1)] - r_2 u_d >=< 0$;
$b_1 = [\lambda + (\delta/\pi)[r_o + r_1(\gamma_1)] + r_2/((1 - tp)(1 - \alpha)Y^p)] > 0$ if $r_o > r_1 (\gamma_1)$ (sufficient but not necessary condition);
$b_2 = [n/\pi][r_o + r_1 (\gamma_1)] > 0$, if $r_o > r_1 (\gamma_1)$;
$b_3 = (r_o + r_1(\gamma_1) < 0$, if $r_o > r_1 (\gamma_1)$.

To derive an expression for the trend, we need to covert (19) into a difference equation. The difference equation is derived by plugging (15) into (19); i.e.:

(20) $I_{t+\tau} = b'_1 (I_t) + b'_2 (\Delta I_t) + F(t)$;
where:
$b'_1 = [b_1 (1 - \alpha)(1 - t_p)/[(1 - t_p)(1 - \alpha)(1 - c_c) + s_w(1 - t_w)\alpha]] - b_3$;
$b'_2 = b_2 (1 - \alpha)(1 - t_p)/[(1 - t_p)(1 - \alpha)(1 - c_c) + s_w(1 - t_w)\alpha]$;
$F(t) = B(t) + b'_1 A(t) + b'_2 \Delta(A(t)) + b_o$.

From equation (20), the trend level of investment, y, is given as:

(21) $y_{t+\tau} = b'_1 (y_t) + b'_2 (\Delta y_t) + F(t)$;

Following Kalecki, this expression can be used to find the determinants of trend investment in time t. From (21), it follows that

(22) $F(t) = y_{t+\tau} - b'_1 (y_t) - b'_2 (\Delta y_t)$.

By adding and subtracting y_t on the right-hand-side, and by noting that $y_t = F(t)/F(t)/y_t$, and therefore $y_t = F(t)/[(1 - b'_1)y_t + y_{t+\tau} - y_t - b'_2\Delta y_t]/(yt) = F(t)/[(1 - b'_1) + [y_{t+\tau} - y_t - b'_2\Delta y_t]]/(y_t)$. By letting $v = [y_{t+\tau} - y_t - b'_2\Delta y_t]/(y_t) <=> 0$, then $y_t = F(t)/[(1 - b'_1) + v]$, or by defining $d_t = 1/[1+v/(1+ b'_1)]$, then the trend level of investment is given as:

(23) $y_t = [d_t /(1 - b'_1)] F(t)$.

Kalecki concluded that the major factor determining the trend is F(t). Assuming dt is roughly stable, then parameter shifts, such as changes in tax rates, affect the trend rate of growth through changes in b'1 and F(t). Any parameter shift that increases b'1 and F(t) increases the trend level of investment. We will return to this discussion later, but first we consider the determinants of the trend capital stock and the long-run capacity utilization rate.

3.2 The trend capital stock

Following Kalecki (1971/1968), the trend value of the capital stock, Kt, is the sum of gross fixed investment less depreciation over n years; i.e.:

(24) $K_t = y_t + y_{t-1}(1 - \delta) + y_{t-2}(1 - \delta)^2 + \dots$

By substituting (23) into (24), and by assuming that the rate of growth in F(t) is ζ, so that $F(t) = F(t - 1)(1+\zeta)$, the trend capital stock can be written as:

(24') $K_t = F(t)(1+\zeta)/(1 - b'_1 + v)(\zeta + \delta)$.

The change in the capital stock and the rate of growth in the capital stock is given as:

(25) $\Delta K_t = y_t - \delta K_t$;

and;

(26) $\Delta K_t/K_t = (y_t/K_t) - \delta$.

By combining (23) and (24'), (y_t/K_t), is given as:

(27) $(y_t/K_t) = (\zeta + \delta)/(1 + \zeta)$.

By substituting (27) into (26), the trend rate of growth in the capital stock can be written as:

(26') $\Delta K_t/K_t = \zeta(1 - \delta)/(1 + \zeta)$.

Equation (26') shows how the tax system affects the trend rate of growth in the capital stock. Taxation affects the rate of growth in F(t) and, thus, affects ζ. In addition, as described above, taxation affects the rate of depreciation.

3.3 The trend capacity utilization rate

Following Kalecki (1971/1968), the long-run capacity utilization rate is defined as the ratio of trend national income to the practical productive capacity. The practical productive, or economically useful, capacity is defined as some portion, h, of the trend capital stock; i. e.:

(28) $u_{trend} = Y_{trend}/hK$.

The trend level of national income is found by combining (6) and (16) and noting that the trend value of I_t is y_t; i.e.:

(29) $Y_{trend} = [y_t + A(t)]/[(1 - t_p)(1 - \alpha)(1 - c_c) + s_w(1 - t_w)\alpha]$;

or:

(29') $Y_{trend} = [y_t]\ [1+ A(t)/\ y_t]/[(1 - t_p)(1 - \alpha)(1 - c_c) + s_w(1 - t_w)\alpha]$.

Combining (27), (28) and (29) yields:

(28') $u_{trend} = [1/h[(1 - t_p)(1 - \alpha)(1 - c_c) + s_w(1 - t_w)\alpha]]\ [1 + A(t)/y_t]\{(\zeta + \delta)/(1 + \zeta)\}$.

Not surprisingly, the income multiplier, the semi-autonomous portion of capitalist consumption relative to the trend level of investment, and the ratio of trend gross investment to the capital stock determine the long-run capacity utilization rate. These factors, of course, are in turn influenced by the tax system. We now return to these issues.

3.4 Taxation and the trend, the rate of growth in capital stock and the long-run capacity utilization rate.

The effects of taxation on the trend level of investment, the trend rate of growth in the capital stock and the long-run capacity utilization rate are reflected in (23), (26') and (28').

Taxation and the trend. The effects of taxation on the trend level of investment depend on two terms, b'_1, the investment coefficient, and F(t), the semi-autonomous component of fixed investment, given dt. F(t), given B(t), A(t) and b_o, depends upon b'_1 and b'_2. Any factor that increases b'_1 and F(t) increases the trend level of investment. To put it more formally, the change in the trend level of investment with respect to a change in the tax rate, ti, i = p, w, is:

(30) $dy/dti = [\partial y/\partial F(t)][\partial F(t)/\partial ti] + [\partial y/\partial b'_1][\partial b'_1/\partial ti]$;

where:

(31) $\partial F(t)/\partial ti = [\partial F(t)/\partial b'_1][\partial b'_1/\partial ti] + [\partial F(t)/\partial b'_2][\partial b'_2/\partial ti]$;

(32) $\partial b'_1/\partial ti = [\partial b'_1/\partial d][\partial d/\partial ti] + [\partial b'_1/\partial m_o][\Delta m_o/\Delta ti]$;
(33) $\Delta m_o/\Delta ti = [\partial m_o/\partial a][\partial a/\partial ti] + [\partial m_o/\partial ti]$;
(34) $\partial b'_2/\partial ti = [\partial b'_2/\partial m_o][\partial m_o/\partial ti]$;

and where m_o is the profit multiplier in equation (15), i.e.:

(35) $m_o = (1 - \alpha)(1 - t_p)/[(1 - t_p)(1 - \alpha)(1 - c_c) + s_w(1 - t_w)\alpha]$.[4]

To simplify the analysis, we assume that r1, the gearing ratio reaction coefficient, and r2, the capacity utilization reaction coefficient equal zero. Tax shifting is reflected in the term, $\partial\alpha/\partial ti$, where alpha, the wage share, equals 1/k, and k = the price/cost markup. An increase in the profits tax rate, if shifted, increases k, and reduces the wage share. An increase in the wage tax rate, if shifted, decreases k, and increases the wage share. Finally, we assume that A(t) and ΔA(t) are both positive, and we continue with the assumption that the government maintains a balanced budget. With these simplifications, we now consider the effects of a change in the profits tax rate and the wage tax rate on the trend level of investment.

Allowing for tax shifting and nonzero worker savings, the effects of changes in the profits tax rate and the wage tax rate are indeterminate. Thus, perhaps the best way to consider the effects of a profits tax rate on the trend level of investment is to consider the conditions sufficient for the relationship to be positive. A sufficient condition for the profits tax rate to have a positive effect on the trend level of investment is if the profits tax is unshifted and workers do not save. An increase in the profit tax rate that is not shifted increases national income and worker savings and reduces profits and the profits multiplier. However, if workers don't save, then: $\Delta m_o/\Delta tp = 0$. As shown above, an unshifted increase in the profit tax rate increases the rate of depreciation; and an increase in the rate of depreciation raises the investment coefficient, b'_1. These positive effects are dampened if workers do save and if the profit tax is shifted. These effects are further dampened if the gearing ratio reaction coefficient, r1, is nonzero negative, and these effects are further heightened if the capacity utilization rate coefficient, r2, is nonzero positive.

A sufficient condition for a change in the wage tax rate to have no effect on the trend level of investment is if the wage tax is not shifted and workers do not save. With no tax shifting, a change in the wage tax has no effect on the profit multiplier, the rate of depreciation, and the trend level of investment. If the wage tax is shifted and workers save, then the profit multiplier decreases. The increase in the rate of depreciation increases trend level of investment, but the decrease

---

4 Formal proofs of the effects of taxes are available upon request.

in the profit multiplier reduces the trend level of investment, and the result is indeterminate.

3.5 Taxation and the rate of growth in capital stock

From equation (26'), we can see that the trend rate of growth in the capital stock depends on rate of growth in F(t), ζ, and the rate of depreciation, δ. The rate of growth in the capital stock is positively related to rate of growth in F(t), and inversely related to the rate of depreciation. The effects of a change in tax rates, ti, where i = p, w, on trend rate of growth in the capital stock is formally given as:

(36) $d(\Delta K_t/K_t)/dti = [\partial(\Delta K_t/K_t)/\partial\zeta][\partial\zeta/\partial ti] + [\partial(\Delta K_t/K_t)/\partial d][\partial d/\partial ti]$.

The rate of growth in F(t) with respect to a change in the tax rate ti, $[\partial\zeta/\partial ti]$, is a positive function of $\partial F(t)/\partial ti$, which is given in (31). The change in F(t) with respect to a change in the profits tax is positive if the tax is not shifted and if workers do not save. Again, if the tax is shifted and workers do save, the effect of the profits tax is dampened. The effect of the profit tax on F(t) is offset by the degree to which the profit tax increases the rate of depreciation, δ.

The change in the trend capital stock with respect to a change in the wage tax rate is zero if the tax is not shifted. If the wage tax is shifted and workers' savings are nonzero, then the profit multiplier decreases, which reduces F(t) and the trend rate of growth of the capital stock. In addition, under these same conditions, an increase in the wage tax increases the rate of depreciation and also reduces the trend rate of growth in the capital stock.

3.6 Taxation and the long-run rate of capacity utilization

As shown in equation (28'), the long-run rate of capacity utilization is positively related to both the rate of growth in F(t), the rate of depreciation, δ, and the income multiplier ($= 1/[(1 - t_p)(1 - \alpha)(1 - c_c) + s_w(1 - t_w)\alpha]$). Again, an increase in the profit tax rate increases both F(t) and the rate of depreciation, and it also increases the income multiplier, assuming workers do not save and the profits tax is not shifted. In contrast, an unshifted wage tax has no effect on F(t), the rate of depreciation, but increases the income multiplier if workers save, and, therefore, increases the long-run rate of capacity utilization. If the wage tax is shifted, the positive effect on the income multiplier increases, the rate of depreciation increases which raises F(t), but the profit multiplier decreases, which reduces F(t), and, therefore, the effect on the long-run capacity utilization rate is indeterminate.

4. Conclusion

Fiscal policy, even with a balanced budget, affects the long-run development of a capitalist economy. The incidence and effects of taxation influence the course of capitalist development, given a balanced budget, depending on whether or not workers save or taxes are shifted. Both of these factors reflect the blending of both macroeconomics and microeconomics in Kalecki's theory of growth. Kalecki's theory of profits is macroeconomic, while his theory of distribution is microeconomic—dependent on the degree of monopoly. The macroeconomics and the mircroeconomics have different implications for tax shifting. For example, following an increase in the profits tax, if the government maintains a balanced budget and workers don't save, then after-tax profits are unaffected by the tax. However, the imposition of the tax can alter the microeconomic distribution of profits, depending upon the nature of the profits tax, and thus can alter industry markups, the aggregate markup, wage share and national income. Given that tax policies can be designed to leave unaffected the aggregate level of profits, we nonetheless conclude that some profit tax shifting will occur unless tax policies can be designed to leave unaltered the industrial (microeconomic) distribution of profits.

Absent from the analysis of the effects and incidence of taxation is a discussion of the standard tax incentive approaches to investment. In neoclassical theory, investment is stimulated by reducing the marginal costs (user costs) associated with new investment. In these approaches, accelerated depreciation schedules or investment tax incentives reduce the user costs associated with new investment and stimulate investment. The approach presented here emphasizes the effects of the average profits and wage tax rates. These factors affect the level of profits generated by new investment, where new investment only captures a portion of those new profits.

Clearly, Kalecki's approach can potentially capture these effects. In the paper, we have introduced Kalecki's assumption that new investment, ignoring technical progress, only captures a portion, n, of the new profits generated by the new investment. Tax incentives, such as accelerated depreciation and the investment tax credit, are likely to increase n. Neoclassical theorists have had difficulty in capturing the effects of these incentives on investment. However, our model suggests that perhaps they are approaching the analysis in the wrong way.

An alternative approach might be to consider the effects of these incentives in a more fully specified Kaleckian or Post-Keynesian model. The effects of such tax incentives without simultaneously accounting for cash flow and depreciation effects are bound to get lost in the analysis. In addition, another avenue along which tax policy affects investment is through the tax deductibility of interest expenses. This factor favors debt financing over equity financing as a way to stimulate investment. In our model, one way to capture this effect, and changes in the deductibility of interest expenses, is through the gearing ratio reaction coefficient we have added to the model. The deductibility of the interest expense related to investment diminishes the negative effect that higher gearing ratios have on future investment.

Two final extensions to the model might be considered. First, the effects of the functional distribution of income on tax policy might also be considered. Growing income inequality, due, for example, to increases in business markups, might lead to re-distributive tax policies. Second, in the model above, we assumed that the desired capacity utilization rate was independent of the tax rate on profits. Re-distributive tax policies that result in changes in aggregate demand might cause businesses to alter their desired capacity utilization rates[5] (see Courvisanos (1996, p. 64, notes 7 and 10).

References

Commendatore, P., D'Acunto, S., Panico, C. and Pinto, A., (2001), 'Keynesian theories of growth', Dipartmento di Teoria Economica e Applicazioni, Università 'Federico II', Via Rodinò 22, 80138, Napoli, Italy.

Courvisanos, J. (1996), *Investment Cycles in Capitalist Economies*, Edward Elgar, Cheltenham.

Fazzari, S., Hubbard, G. and Petersen, B., (1988b), 'Investment, financing decisions and tax policy', *American Economic Review*, 78, 2, 200–205.

Gomulka, S., Ostaszewski, A. and Davies, R. O., (1990), 'The innovation rate and Kalecki's theory of the trend, unemployment and the business cycle', *Economica*, 57, 525–540.

Harrod, R. F. (1939), '*Value and Capital* of John Hicks', *Economic Journal*, 49.

Harrod, R. F. (1973), *Economic Dynamics*, Macmillan, London.

Kaldor, N. (1957), 'A model of economic growth', *Economic Journal*, 67, 591–624.

Kalecki, M., (1971/1937), 'A theory of commodity, income and capital taxation,' *Economic Journal*, 47, 444–450, reprinted in *Selected Essays on the Dynamics of the Capitalist Economy*, Cambridge University Press, Cambridge.

Kalecki, M., (1971/1968), 'Trend and the Business Cycle Reconsidered', *Economic Journal*, 78, reprinted in *Selected Essays on the Dynamics of the Capitalist Economy*, Cambridge University Press, Cambridge.

5 We are grateful to an anonymous referee for making these last two points.

Kalecki, M., (1962) 'Observations on the theory of growth', *Economic Journal,* 72, 134–153.

Keynes, J. M., (1936), *The General Theory of Employment, Interest and Money,* New York, Harcourt Brace.

Laramie, A. J. and Mair, D. (1996), 'Taxation and Kalecki's theory of the business cycle', *Cambridge Journal of Economics,* 20 (4), 451–464.

Laramie, A. J., and Mair, D. (2000), *A Dynamic Theory of Taxation*, Edward Elgar, Cheltenham.

Laramie, A. J. Mair, D., Miller, A.G. and Stratopoulos, T., (1996), 'The impact of taxation on gross private nonresidential fixed investment in a Kaleckian model: some empirical evidence', *Journal of Post Keynesian Economics*, 19, 2, 243–256.

Pasinetti, L. L. (1962), 'Rate of profit and income distribution in relation to the rate of economic growth', *Review of Economic Studies,* 29 (4), 103–120.

Robinson, J. (1956), *The Accumulation of Capital,* London, Macmillan.

Robinson, J. (1962), *Essays in the Theory of Economic Growth,* London, Macmillan.

Sawyer, M. C., (1985), *The Economics of Michal Kalecki*, London, Macmillan.

Jerry Courvisanos, University of Ballarat, Victoria AU
Anthony J. Laramie, Merrimack College, MA, USA
Douglas Mair, Heriot-Watt University, Edinburgh, UK

Chapter 6: Tax Policy and Innovation: A Search for Common Ground[*1]

Abstract: The paper is motivated by a desire to find common ground between mainstream and Post-Keynesian approaches to fiscal policy. A Post-Keynesian approach with origins in Kalecki offers a promising line of enquiry which is developed here. The paper identifies the principal differences between the Keynesian and Kaleckian approaches. The possibilities are explored of finding accommodation between the mainstream and Kaleckian approaches to the taxation of greenhouse gases. The macroeconomic implications of taxing greenhouse gases are identified. However, these may be thwarted by the emergence of 'political aspects of innovation', akin to Kalecki's 'political aspects of full employment'. A Kaleckian balanced budget approach allied to fiscal incentives to innovate offers some prospect of common ground with the mainstream.

1. Introduction

The themes of the 2008 Research Network Macroeconomics and Macroeconomic Policies conference are to examine the changes that are taking place in mainstream economics; to establish what, if any, is the new orthodoxy; and to identify the implications for Post-Keynesian economics. In particular, the conference organisers have asked contributors to examine the role of fiscal policy in both mainstream and Post-Keynesian[2] macroeconomics with a view to establishing whether there is any possible common ground between them. This is the task we have set ourselves in this paper.

---

* Courvisanos, Jerry, Laramie, Anthony and Mair Douglas, "Tax policy and innovation: A search for common ground," *Intervention* (now known as: *The European Journal of Economics and Economic Policies: Intervention)* , Volume 6, Number 2, pp. 271–287. Reprinted with permission from the lead editor, Torsten Niechoj and Edward Elgar (https://www.elgaronline.com)

1 We wish to thank Eckhard Hein and an anonymous refer for helpful comments on an earlier draft.

2 We distinguish two categoris of Post-Keynesian economics. The category that has its origins in Keynes we designate as Post Keynesian (JMK). The category that has its origins on Kalecki we designate as Post keynedian.

In a sense, our task is 'mission impossible' because the principal emphasis of mainstream macroeconomics is on monetary policy, denying any substantive role for fiscal policy, except possibly in times of severe recession. On the other hand, the principal emphasis of Post-Keynesian (JMK) macroeconomics is on fiscal policy, rejecting many of the mainstream criticisms of fiscal policy as groundless or irrelevant. For as long as mainstream and Post-Keynesian (JMK) economics maintain their entrenched stances, we see little prospect of a meaningful dialogue emerging between them. Rather than sit uncomfortably sandwiched between Scylla and Charybdis,[3] we concentrate on an area in which mainstream economics recognises that fiscal policy, in particular tax policy, has an important, perhaps critical, role to play, namely, the control of greenhouse gas emissions and show how Post-Keynesian (MK) economics may provide common ground on which a useful dialogue may take place In the mainstream view, taxes on greenhouse gases are usually intended to correct for negative externalities by changing relative prices, and, in so doing affect the aggregate level of economic activity. In the Post-Keynesian (MK) approach, greenhouse gas taxes have both short-period and long-period effects that will be considered below.

The paper is in seven parts. In part one we review briefly the current mainstream stance on fiscal policy. In part two we discuss the dominant Post-Keynesian (JMK) approach. In part three we identify the main features of the Post-Keynesian (MK) approach to fiscal policy that distinguish it from the Post-Keynesian (JMK) approach. In part four we discuss the role of taxation in a Kaleckian growth model. In part five, we demonstrate how a Kaleckian approach to the taxation of greenhouse gas emissions can influence the rate of innovation. In part six, we show how policy measures to stimulate innovation may be thwarted by a political innovation cycle. Finally, in part seven, we consider what common ground there may be between mainstream and Post-Keynesian (MK) economics on the interaction between tax policy and innovation.

2. Role of Tax Policy in the Mainstream Fiscal Policy Stance

Contemporary mainstream macroeconomics identifies itself as the New Economic Consensus (NEC) and is an amalgamation of the developments in macroeconomics from the post-war Neoclassical Synthesis to the present day. Its defining characteristic is the claim that choice-theoretic micro-foundations determine

3 In Homer's *The Odyssey*, Odysseus had to navigate between these two natural elements, monster and whirlpool respectively, that threatened the ship. Similarly, we need to navigate between two opposing schools of thought.

macroeconomic outcomes. In order to explain aggregate employment and output, all macroeconomic models must, according to the NEC, incorporate individual inter-temporal decision-making based on rational expectations. Within this framework, however, there are still disagreements as to the role of fiscal policy (Tscherneva 2008).

Having virtually abandoned fiscal policy during its monetarist phase, there are now influential voices within the NEC that recognise it may have a limited role to play (Bernanke et al. 2004, Krugman 2005). This concession stems from recognition that there may be circumstances, for example when the short-term rate of interest falls to zero, under which no further economic stimulus from monetary policy is possible. However, within the NEC coterie, fiscal policy is viewed very much as a measure of last resort to be used only in periods of extreme deflation despite its distortive and inflationary effects. It is now accepted by Bernanke (2003a), among others, that in the short run fiscal authorities may have important reasons for deviating from a balanced budget (or budget surplus) stance when faced with national emergencies or deep recessions (e.g. the 2008 Global Financial Crisis). In the long run, however, the fiscal disciplines of the balanced budget and responsible levels of national debt must be maintained.

An important feature of the emerging NEC stance on fiscal policy is that the Ricardian equivalence hypothesis which had previously precluded fiscal policy effectiveness may not hold. This opens the possibility that wealth effects from deficit spending may affect aggregate demand. Abandonment of Ricardian equivalence raises the fear that governments may lose financial discipline and incur ever-rising debts. Sustainability of a government's budget is a major concern for NEC economists. The NEC overwhelmingly subscribes to the doctrine of 'sound finance' to avoid the distortive and inflationary effects of government spending. The dominant NEC view is that the principal goal for fiscal policy is to avoid an intolerable tax burden on future generations. The inter-temporal budget constraint is an important underlying condition for understanding the role of fiscal policy from an NEC perspective.

There is widespread agreement in the NEC that fiscal policy is inherently inflationary and that its use should be restricted to deflationary conditions. At all other times, monetary policy should dominate and fiscal policy should remain passive and be automatic, transparent, credible and rule-compliant. There is a strong supply-side predilection in the NEC so that if fiscal policy is deemed necessary it should take the form of tax cuts and not increases in government spending.

The final issue we consider is the NEC view of the link between fiscal policy and full employment. The NEC dynamic general equilibrium model does not admit the existence of involuntary unemployment. This marks a complete break from Keynes whose revolutionary *raison d'être* was to find a cure for involuntary unemployment.

This necessarily brief summary of the NEC stance on fiscal policy confirms that except under the direst of circumstances it is to be avoided like the plague, bringing with it as it does all sorts of unwelcome complications such as inflation and resource misallocation. For the NEC 'sound finance' and balanced budgets are the *sine qua non* of responsible macroeconomic fiscal policy. There is, however, one important area in which the NEC sees positive merit in fiscal policy and that is the area of climate change, where the use of taxes is advocated as an important instrument in controlling the levels of greenhouse gases into the atmosphere (Stern 2006). We return to this issue in more detail in part five below.

3. Post-Keynesian (JMK) Stance on Fiscal Policy

The Post-Keynesian (JMK) camp takes a diametrically opposite view of the role of fiscal policy. In terms of achieving macroeconomic coordination and stabilisation objectives, Post Keynesians (JMK) such as Arestis/Sawyer (2004) see fiscal policy as a more potent instrument than monetary policy, although, surprisingly, they give little credit to Kalecki's contribution. Post-Keynesian (JMK) analysis revives Lerner's (1943) functional finance approach in which fiscal policy is to be judged not by ex-post budgetary results but by its real effects on the economy. Governments face no limits to their spending and the role of fiscal policy is to spend as much as is necessary to bring the economy to full employment. Although Arestis/Sawyer identify a number of NEC assumptions that undermine fiscal policy effectiveness, they argue that the Post-Keynesian (JMK) functional finance approach is not necessarily inconsistent with the NEC. They reject crowding out and add to the criticisms of the Ricardian equivalence hypothesis.

The type of fiscal policy advocated by Post Keynesians (JMK) is one that encourages investment and growth. For example, Arestis/Sawyer write:

> Fiscal policy of the 'functional finance' type boosts aggregate demand, and thereby has a stimulating impact on investment, which raises the future productive capacity of the economy... The growth rate may thereby be favourably enhanced by fiscal policy (Arestis/Sawyer 2004: 139).

This version of the Post-Keynesian (JMK) functional finance approach stimulates investment and growth and aims to reduce the demand gap. It is not dependent on any particular type of public spending or investment. These are critical issues to which we return in more detail below. The main virtue of this Post-Keynesian

(JMK) approach is that it always raises aggregate demand, unlike in the NEC where fiscal policy only has demand side effects in non-Ricardian regimes.

For both the NEC and the Post Keynesians (JMK), the barrier to attaining full employment is inflation although the latter have a different interpretation of inflation. Post Keynesians (JMK) see no single NAIRU but rather a fluctuating structuralist inflation barrier whose level depends on a number of factors such as capacity utilisation and the rate of growth of capital stock. With a fluctuating inflation barrier, 'full employment' is given by the employment level when aggregate demand hits this barrier. Thus, a number of levels of full employment exist depending on the level of aggregate demand and the location of the inflation barrier.

The principal feature of the Post Keynesian (JMK) approach is its belief in the effectiveness of fiscal policy, which contrasts with its relative ineffectiveness in the NEC view. The Post-Keynesian (JMK and MK) approaches reject the crowding out effect, Ricardian equivalence, and the fixed supply assumptions of the NEC. Whereas the NEC treats the growth rate as given, in the dynamic Post-Keynesian (JMK) approach as advocated by Arestis/Sawyer, growth rates will change in response to changes in government spending so that fiscal policy need not run into traditional budget constraints. In contrast to the NEC, both Post-Keynesian approaches consider the aggregate income/output and employment effects of broad based taxes, like greenhouse taxes, through channels other than the traditional supply-side channels of NEC.

4. Fiscal Policy: Keynes or Kalecki?

The ghost of Keynes is present at both the NEC and Post-Keynesian (JMK) feasts. The NEC is determined to exorcise it once and for all while Post Keynesians (JMK) are keen to resuscitate it. However, Keynesian fiscal policy is not the only Post-Keynesian game in town. Kalecki has at least as strong a claim as Keynes as the founder of Post-Keynesian economics (Harcourt 2006) and a stronger claim for primacy on the role of tax policy (Asimakopulos 1978). Kalecki (1937) recognised that the publication of Keynes's 'General Theory' required a whole new approach to the study of taxation. He worked through the short-period macroeconomic effects of taxes on commodities, incomes and capital but never explicitly incorporated taxation into his subsequent dynamic analyses. Asimakopulos/Burbidge (1974) published a fully developed short-period Kaleckian model. Laramie/Mair (2000) integrated Kalecki's theories of taxation, income distribution, income determination, investment, business cycle and growth.

There are a number of important, and sometimes subtle, differences between Keynes-based and Kalecki-based (MK) approaches to fiscal policy, which we summarise using five concepts in italics below.

Balanced budget: Both the Post-Keynesian (JMK) and the Post-Keynesian (MK) approaches identify the macroeconomic short-period effects within a balanced budget regime without requiring any changes to aggregate government taxation or spending. In the JMK approach, the effect of a balanced budget tax change, and, therefore, the size of the balanced budget multiplier depends on the relative propensities to save of those being taxed or those receiving transfers. For example, a redistributive balanced-budget tax is a tax on high-income groups (with high propensities to save), balanced against transfers to low-income groups (with low propensities to save). The net effect stimulates aggregate demand.

In the MK approach, the effects of balanced budget changes in taxes on aggregate income/output and employment depend primarily on how the tax change effects aggregate pre-tax profits as national income is pushed up to a level so that pre-tax profits are realised. Kalecki showed that post-tax profits (the sum profits after taxes plus profit taxes) equal the sum of private investment, the government budget deficit, the trade surplus, and consumption out of profits less savings out of wages. Given that the wage share is determined by the degree of monopoly as reflected in price/prime costs markups, *inter alia*, the aggregate level of income is pushed up to the point where pre-tax profits, as described before, are realised, and the wage bill is paid. If changes in wage taxes are shifted, business markups fall, and higher levels of national income and employment are required for aggregate profits to be realised. If changes in profits taxes are shifted, business markups increase, and a lower level of national income is required for aggregate profits to be realised. An increase in the profits tax balanced against a decrease in the wage tax leads to an increase in short-period pre-tax profits, national income and employment.

Note that in the above balanced-budget tax changes, the loss in post-tax profits due to increased profit taxes is completely offset by the increase in wage consumption relative to the wage bill if the marginal propensity to consume out of profits and the marginal propensity to save out of wages are zero. If these propensities are nonzero, then the effects on pre-tax profits, national income and employment are dampened. Similar results are obtained if the increase in the profits tax is balanced against an increase in government purchases. In contrast, an increase in the wage tax, balanced against an increase in government purchases, will stimulate profits, national income and employment, if the marginal propensity to save out of wages is nonzero. As evidenced, the short-period effects of balanced budget tax changes are similar between the JMK and MK approaches. However, the MK approach explicitly links the tax changes to aggregate business profits, which, in turn, lead to long-period effects on investment and growth.

Functional finance and functional distribution of income: Both Post-Keynesian approaches recognise the importance of functional finance. However, unlike the Post-Keynesian (JMK) approach, the Post-Keynesian (MK) approach emphasises the macroeconomic consequences of fiscally-induced changes in the functional distribution of income.

Tax shifting and incidence of taxation: Tax incidence is applied income distribution theory. Therefore, in studying the incidence of taxation it is important to specify on which theory of income distribution it is based. The Post-Keynesian (JMK) approach does not specify its theory of income distribution. The Post-Keynesian (MK) approach is explicitly based on the degree of monopoly theory of income distribution. The importance of tax shifting is recognised in the Post-Keynesian (MK) approach and quite different macroeconomic effects follow depending on whether or not taxes are shifted.

Fiscal policy and growth: Both Post-Keynesian approaches emphasise the role of fiscal policy in promoting a faster rate of growth. In the Post-Keynesian (JMK) approach, the mechanism operates via the impact of functional finance on aggregate demand, which, in turn, stimulates investment and raises the future productive capacity of the economy. The Post-Keynesian (MK) approach uses an investment model to identify the drivers of growth and the channels through which balanced changes in the structure of taxation will have an impact on investment and growth.

Fiscal policy and innovation: The Post-Keynesian (JMK) approach treats the rate of innovation as exogenous and does not identify any role for fiscal policy. The Post-Keynesian (MK) approach recognises that fiscal policy can stimulate innovation and then with a lagged impact on investment demand and growth, although its impact may be limited by a political innovation cycle (see part six below).

Kalecki's original 1937 tax formulation and its subsequent extension by Asimakopulos/Burbidge (1974) are both short-period approaches in which the level of investment is determined by decisions taken in some earlier time period. They must be incorporated in a dynamic model that seeks to identify the dynamic effects of fiscal policy as it impacts on investment, income distribution and growth. This we do in the next section.

In conclusion, both the JMK and MK approaches identify similar short-period effects of taxation. The JMK approach emphasises the effects of taxation on aggregate demand. The MK approach emphasises the effects of taxation on aggregate profits. By explicitly considering the effects of fiscal policy on aggregate profits, the MK approach allows for the dynamic long-period effects of profits to be explicitly considered. This becomes central to the greenhouse gas tax analysis in part five below.

5. Role of Taxation in a Kaleckian Growth Model

Having identified the most important differences between the two Post-Keynesian approaches to fiscal policy, we now proceed to illustrate in more detail how balanced changes in the structure of taxation can impact on the rate of growth in a Kaleckian growth model. In particular, we show how taxation can have an impact on the rate of innovation.

Our starting point is Kalecki's (1971) theory of investment. Recall in the Kaleckian approach, the macroeconomic impact of taxation depends on:

- the relative marginal propensities to consume out of wages and profits
- whether compensating changes exist in the government budget
- the extent to which a tax change is shifted through changes in business markups.

A critical element in the Kaleckian approach is the pricing behaviour of firms as this determines whether or not changes in the taxation of wages or profits result in changes in business markups and in the distribution of income. Kalecki's theory of profits is made dynamic by linking taxation to his theories of profits, national income determination, income distribution, investment and growth. For Kalecki, everything is driven by what happens to investment. Changes in the structure of taxation today can affect investment and, thus, profits, tomorrow.

In Kalecki's theory of investment, taxation affects investment through three channels:

- the level of profits
- the rate of depreciation
- the capacity utilisation rate

In turn, the effect of taxation on the level of profits operates through two channels (ignoring the foreign sector) as described before:

- the impact on the government budget position
- the effect on income distribution

For example, a balanced budget increase in the profits tax, in the manner described above, increases pre-tax profits, leaves after-tax profits unchanged, and increases national income if the marginal propensity to save out of wages is zero and the marginal propensity to consume out of profits is zero. The increase in national income, given the wage share, increases the wage bill and after-tax wages. If the marginal propensity to save out of wages is positive, the increase in after-tax wages increases worker savings and reduces consumption relative to wages. The decline in consumption relative to wages dampens the increase in pre-tax profits and reduces after-tax profits.[4] The reduction in after-tax profits slows down the rate of growth in investment. The dampening effect is reduced if the profits tax is shifted via an increase in business price-costs markups. The increase in the markups reduces the wage share, dampens the increases in the wage bill and in worker savings. By dampening the increase in worker savings, the decrease in after-tax profits is dampened.

In contrast, a balanced budget increase in the wage tax has no effect on pre-tax and post-tax profits and investment if the marginal propensity to save out of wages is zero. If the marginal propensity to save out of wages is positive, the balanced budget increase in the wage tax reduces worker savings, and increases pre-tax and post-tax profits and increases investment. This increase is dampened to the extent that workers are able to shift the tax via a decrease in price-cost markups. The decrease in price costs markups increases national income and the wage bill and increases worker savings (reducing consumption relative to the wage bill) (see Figure 1, Part A).

The rate of depreciation channel operates by altering the relative profitability of existing and new plants and equipment. With technological innovation through time, unit production costs associated with new capital goods decrease. This decrease in unit production costs shifts profits from old capital goods to new capital goods and increases the depreciation (and eventual obsolescence) of old capital goods. Kalecki (1971) illustrates the depreciation effect in a no tax world by assuming that the profits captured by new investment embodied with innovation, lost to existing capital, are proportional to the difference between national income and post-tax profits (the wage bill). In a world with taxes, a balanced budget increase in the profits tax increases national income relative to post-tax profits, and, given the rate of technical progress, increases the profits captured by new investment encouraging investment, and reducing the profits captured by existing capital. This increases the rate of depreciation and obsolescence of existing capital. In contrast, a balanced budget increase in the wage tax, if the tax is not shifted, has no impact on national income relative to post-tax profits and no effect

4 Likewise, if the marginal propensity to consume out of profits is positive, the profits tax reduces consumption out of profits and dampens the increase in pre-tax and post-tax profits.

on depreciation or investment. This result is modified if the wage tax is shifted, via a decrease in the price-cost markup. The decrease in the markup increases the national income relative to post-tax profits, and accelerates the profits captured by innovation, encourages new investment, and decreases the profits captured by existing capital, accelerating its depreciation.

The economy's trend growth rate can be affected by changes in the structure of taxation when both the rate of capacity utilisation and business balance sheets matter in making capital investment decisions (Courvisanos 1996: 103–6). Businesses are assumed to desire a certain rate of capacity utilisation. An increase in the rate of capacity utilisation above the desired level will accelerate expansions and dampen contractions in investment. A decrease in the rate of capacity utilisation below its desired level will dampen expansions and accelerate contractions in investment. As implied above, tax policy—by affecting the level of national income—can change the capacity utilisation rate and impact on investment decisions through this channel. For example, a balanced budget increase in the profits tax, when the marginal propensity to save out of wages is zero and the tax is not shifted, may increase investment by increasing national income and capacity utilisation (as in the JMK approach). Likewise, a balanced budget increase in the wage tax, when the propensity to save out of wages is positive, can also increase national income and capacity utilisation (see Figure 1). Business balance sheets are incorporated by taking into account the firm's gearing ratio (the ratio of total liabilities to net worth) in order to capture the effect of increasing risk associated with investment (Kalecki 1971).

6. Tax Policy and the Rate of Innovation

Having established the channels through which taxation can impact on investment and then through investment to the growth performance of the economy, we now introduce the link from investment to innovation. This will enable us to model the impact of tax policy changes on the rate of innovation and the dynamics of economic growth. The link is through the concept of the margin of obsolescence (Bloch et al. 2007). This concept relates to the decision rule on innovation. Investment in capital equipment that embodies best practice technology is a specific form of innovation. When firms make a decision to invest in plants and equipment that embody new technological knowledge, whether that knowledge is related to products or processes, technological innovation (TI) takes place. Salter (1966) provided a seminal analysis of how technical change comes about through capital accumulation by focusing on the reverse side of innovation, that is, on technological obsolescence (TO).

Salter (1966: 54) defined TO as 'plants which are sufficiently outmoded to be profitably replaced'. At any time, with both new and established knowledge, there is a spectrum of techniques used in production, ranging from 'up to date' to 'outmoded' to 'obsolete'. There are a number of factors that determine investment decisions in addition to TO. There is no inevitability that firms will automatically make investment decisions immediately to order the most up-to-date capital equipment. This may be due to financial constraints, wage costs, industry competitiveness (or lack of) and the level of technological flexibility (or inertia). By defining TO in terms of cost minimisation, Salter provides a method of identifying how and when firms find it profitable to invest in the TI embodied in the newest vintage capital equipment. Thus, technical change through TI becomes endogenous to the investment process.

Salter (1966: 74–5) argued that the 'margin of obsolescence' appears in a particular plant when the unit total (operating plus fixed overheads) costs of production using best-practice capital equipment equals the unit operating (materials plus labour) costs of production of the oldest vintage capital equipment. On the 'margin of obsolescence' the capital stock in a particular plant will be such that the implications, from a cost-minimising perspective, to stay with the existing stock or invest in new equipment are identical. Salter's concept of the 'margin of obsolescence' can be linked to Kalecki's investment function through capacity utilisation on the basis that the 'margin of obsolescence' can be alternatively identified as the point at which the total cost of new capacity equals the operating cost of existing outmoded capacity. Thus, when the total cost of new capacity becomes less than the operating cost of existing capacity, then existing 'marginal' capacity becomes TO. Salter's contribution is a clear decision-based convention or rule for when new TI should be introduced into the investment ordering process, subject to growth in demand.

Kalecki's (1954) degree of monopoly and TI are linked via four potentially quantifiable determinants of the degree of monopoly—the role of giant firms; the development of sales promotion through advertising, selling agents etc.; the influence of changes in the level of overhead costs in relation to prime costs; and the power of trade unions. From a theoretical perspective, TI should be incorporated into investment theory as innovation alters the incentive to invest by 'changing the costs of production' or 'altering product demand' (Bloch et al. 2007:5). This is what Kalecki intended in his formulation of the degree of monopoly. 'Changing the costs of production' is encapsulated in his identification of the 'role of giant firms' (industry concentration and economies of scale), 'changes in the level of overhead costs in relation to prime costs' and 'the power of trade unions' (wage costs); while 'product demand' is encapsulated in 'the development of sales promotion' (product differentiation).

Kalecki's theory of income determination states that profits (capitalists' income) are primarily determined by capitalists' spending (investment) decisions in a previous time period. Businesses, being motivated by technological innovation to improve their degree of monopoly, increase their investment expenditures, and these investment expenditures generate additional aggregate profits. If the result of the innovation-induced investment is an increase in the degree of monopoly, changes in income distribution result. This may, in turn, subsequently affect future investment decisions through the profits, deprecation, or capacity utilisation effects described earlier.

Econometric results obtained by Laramie et al. (2000) show that both 'costs of production' and 'product demand' factors have influenced the degree of monopoly in the UK manufacturing industry in recent years. These results endogenise the effects of technical change on the degree of monopoly. Technical change, in a monopoly-capital scenario, encourages investment and increases profits, the wage bill, and national income. However, if the benefits of technical change are captured exclusively by businesses, business mark-ups increase, the wage share decreases, which further increases the level of profits through a reduction in worker savings, but dampens the investment-induced increase in the wage bill and national income. In addition, by reducing the real costs of production (increasing profits relative to national income), this income redistribution effect of technological change reduces the rate of depreciation and slows down the effect of technical change on new investment. Accordingly, we expect technologically induced changes in investment to move in cycles (for empirical evidence see Courvisanos/Verspagen: 2004). The potential result is a contradiction between technologically induced growth and income distribution, which will give rise to cycles and to trends below the level of full employment.

The Salter/Bloch et al. approach identifies a clear decision rule as to when a firm should adopt the most recent TI and undertake the necessary capital investment. We now consider how the introduction of taxation may influence this decision rule. Two conditions must hold. First, the introduction of taxation must increase the after-tax operating (material and labour) cost of existing capital equipment relative to the after-tax total cost of best-practice capital equipment, or, in the Salter/Bloch et al. terminology, accelerate TO. Second, the introduction of taxation must increase the after-tax profitability of best-practice capital equipment relative to its pre-tax profitability, or, in Kaleckian terminology, increase the rate of depreciation. If these two conditions do not hold, then altering the structure of taxation has no role to play in influencing innovation, obsolescence or the rate of depreciation.

Assuming the two conditions above hold, the decision rule analysis is carried out in a time-dated framework, so that future costs and profits are expressed in discounted values. We begin by assuming that the firm is operating in time period t with existing capital equipment and operating cost, OC_t. The firm has to decide whether to replace this existing equipment in time period $t + \tau$ with best-practice capital equipment with total cost $TC_{t+\tau}$. We assume that the operating and overhead costs of producing with best-practice capital equipment in $t + \tau$ are known with certainty in time period t. The Salter/Bloch et al. decision rule applies when $TC_{t+\tau} = OC_t$. The operating cost of best-practice equipment, $OC_{t+\tau}$, must be less than OC_t, otherwise the decision rule will not be operational, i.e. $OC_{t+\tau} < OC_t$. However, overhead cost, $OHC_{t+\tau}$, will be greater than OHC_t because of higher amortisation charges consequent on investment in best-practice capital equipment, i.e. $OHC_{t+\tau} > OHC_t$, *ceteris paribus*.

The Salter/Bloch et al. rule only relates to firms' costs and does not specify a profit condition. Thus, we specify a net profit (P) condition that $P_{t+\tau} > P_t$. If the firm is applying the Kaleckian markup pricing rule, it follows that the markup, k, in $t + \tau$ has to rise, i.e. $k_{t+\tau} > k_t$. This is because the application of an unchanged markup to the lower operating cost, $OC_{t+\tau}$, (to determine price per unit of output) inevitably means that, with the higher overhead cost, $OHC_{t+\tau}$, profits in $t + \tau$ will be lower, i.e. $P_{t+\tau} < P_t$. Thus, the Salter/Bloch et al. rule may be a necessary condition but it is not a sufficient condition for TO. A necessary condition for TI to result in an increase in profits, thereby encouraging investment, is that the price/cost markup on output associated with new equipment must increase. That is, the rate of depreciation must also be such that $P_{t+\tau} > P_t$. However, as indicated above, a rise in markups has consequences for the distribution of income. The markup-induced decrease in the wage share dampens the effect of TI (TO of existing capital) on depreciation and investment. For this dampening effect to be small, the effect of the technological change on aggregate business markups would have to be small (although perhaps large for some firms or industries).

We now consider how the introduction of taxation affects the above conditions. We illustrate the effect by reference to the introduction of a tax on the emission of greenhouse gases (GHG). We accept all the efficiency arguments in favour of GHG taxes to ensure that GHG emissions are priced to reflect the damage they cause (Stern 2006). We identify two Kaleckian categories of GHG tax (GT). The first is levied on GHG emissions associated with the production of production-goods (GTP), e.g. coal-fired electricity and fleet cars. The second is levied on the GHG emissions associated with the consumption of wage-goods (GTW), e.g. tourist travel and personal (non-luxury) cars.

If there is to be an increase in the TO of high GHG emissions from existing capital, the gap between OC_t and $OC_{t+\tau}$ has to widen. This can only occur in response to an increase in GTP or a shifted increase in GTW. This happens because operating costs (including wage costs and profit taxes), OC_t, are higher than $OC_{t+\tau}$, an increase in GTP and a shifted increase in GTW will have a relatively greater impact on OC_t than on $OC_{t+\tau}$. A tax-induced stimulus to TO will be generated and the real costs associated with existing capital equipment at time period t will rise, thereby stimulating the rate of depreciation. However, GTW shifting implies an inverse relationship between the markup and GTW. Shifting of GTW will, therefore, result in a fall in the markup. With GTW shifting, the wage share increases, and the wage costs of operating existing capital rises relative to costs of operating new equipment. This in turn, will increase the relative profitability of new equipment and reduce the relative profitability of existing equipment, which will thus accelerate its depreciation.

With this modification, we examine first an increase in GTW. The effect of a shifted increase in GTW on the level of profits, P_t, will depend on the extent to which the shifting will increase the wage share, the wage bill, and workers' savings. When workers' savings are zero, a balanced budget tax change will have no effect on post-tax profits, P_t. It is, therefore, not inconceivable that the increase in GTW in time period t would have no effect on P_t although it is more likely that P_t will fall, if GTW is shifted, and workers have a positive propensity to save. An increase in GTP and a shifted increase in GTW in time period t will give a kick-start to TI (and result in existing capital stock gradually becoming obsolete).

We now consider how the firm will respond to this stimulus and how fiscal policy can influence that response. In time period t the firm recognises two consequences of these changes. First, it has a stronger financial incentive to replace its existing capital equipment; and, second, when GTW is shifted, its degree of monopoly has fallen, as witnessed by the fall in its markup. The firm must, therefore, seek to enhance its degree of monopoly, i.e. increase its markup, in order to make investment in TI financially viable in time period $t + \tau$. In either case, the firm attempts to shift these tax effects by accelerating the rate at which it innovates.

From the above analysis we can see that a tension exists between the effects of taxes on GTP and investment, and the effects of taxes on depreciation and investment. Balanced budget increases in GTP, when un-shifted and when workers' propensity to save is zero, have no effect on pre- or after-tax profits, but this increases operating costs and accelerates the margin of obsolescence of existing equipment while stimulating TI. Balanced budget increases in GTW, assuming workers' propensity to save is zero, when shifted, have no effect on after-tax profits, but instead increase national income through an increase in the wage share, and, like GTP, accelerate the margin of obsolescence of existing equipment.

There exists a balanced budget tax change that will accelerate the margin of obsolescence with positive effects on after-tax profits and the level of national income. Note that currently, no GHG taxes exist. Thus, the proposed balanced budget tax change is a combination of (i) an un-shifted increase in GTP and (ii) an un-shifted reduction in existing wage good taxes. Assuming no change in workers' savings and a non-zero positive capacity utilisation reaction coefficient, this tax package is conducive to innovation. Figure 1 summarises the tax change channels of influence to induce low-GHG-emissions technological innovation under specific conditions.

7. Tax Policy and the Political Economy of Innovation

Having established the conditions under which the government can use balanced changes in the structure of taxation to positively influence the margin of obsolescence, the question arises whether it will in fact actually do so. This parallels the question Kalecki posed in relation to the attainment of full employment in 'Political Aspects of Full Employment' (PAFE) (Kalecki, 1943). While he and Keynes had provided the policy tools and techniques that could ensure full employment, Kalecki, from a political economy perspective, recognised that sustained full employment in a capitalist economy would be unattainable. In the context of a capitalist policy solution, Harcourt (2006) refers to this as 'the Kaleckian dilemma'.

Kalecki (1943) identified the fears that capitalists have of full employment—loss of economic control and industrial control. Mair/Laramie (2002) develop this further by arguing that through the process of forming distributional coalitions, business interests can ensure that they do not lose these controls, thereby preventing a permanent and sustained attainment of full employment. Steindl (1979), Bhaduri/Steindl, (1983) and Catley/McFarlane (1981) have provided empirical evidence of a Kaleckian-type political business cycle (PBC) in advanced industrial economies such as the USA, the UK and Australia. Courvisanos (2009) applies Kalecki's PAFE approach to innovation. Whereas in the original formulation of PAFE and its subsequent development, innovation played only a minor role, Courvisanos (2009) argued that analogous to PAFE, the 'political aspects of innovation' (PAI) can also be identified in the recent experience of mature industrial economies.

Analogous to PAFE, the PAI approach identifies three fears that capitalists have with innovation:

- loss of economic control with respect to their individual market power, as innovation encourages new entrants that have the potential to reduce the incumbents' market share and ability to control the market.

To counter this threat, governments are persuaded by business interests to introduce various innovation policies to support incumbents, research and development (R&D) subsidies to support incremental innovations, patent protection and other intellectual property rights.

- loss of policy control as innovation becomes distributed across society through public institutions and public infrastructure that creates the national innovation system.

To counter this threat, governments are persuaded by business interests to develop various strategies that support incumbents to regain some policy control, notably privatisation, public-private infrastructure programmes and public contracting.

- loss of industrial control of the workforce if governments maintain industrial relations policies that reflect the full-employment type, high-union membership structures of the 1950s and 1960s.

To counter this threat, governments are persuaded by business interests to introduce new industrial relations policies in the name of innovation aimed at supporting and encouraging 'flexibility' in the workplace. This flexibility relates to the ability of firms to alter labour costs and structures when they introduce new process innovations that require less (and more flexible) labour.

8. Kaleckian Tax Analysis: A Pathway to Common Ground with the NEC

As we have shown, there are fundamental differences within the Post-Keynesian approaches to fiscal policy. In favour of the Kaleckian approach, it has the major advantage of being a balanced budget approach and, consequently, satisfying the NEC cardinal rule of 'sound finance'. Also, with its emphasis on the revenue side of the budget, the Kaleckian approach of balanced changes in the structure of taxation is more in tune with the supply side orientation of the NEC. Indeed, as we have shown in part five, a Kaleckian GHG tax operates by offering firms a fiscal 'incentive' which under certain conditions will accelerate the obsolescence of existing high GHG emissions plants and equipment and undertake new low GHG emissions technology investment.

The NEC has a morbid fear of inflation. To the extent that this is attributable to increased government spending, this fear is allayed by the balanced budget approach. The mantra of full employment does not arise in the Kaleckian approach. As early as 1943, Kalecki recognised that while full employment might be a technical possibility, the pressure of business interests would ensure it would be a political impossibility. Similarly, as we have shown in part six, while fiscal policy may have a stimulating effect on innovation, again the pressure of business interests will generate a political innovation cycle so that the full economic impact of innovation will never be achieved.[5] NEC economists need not lie awake at night worrying about the inflationary implications of Kaleckian fiscal policy.

A feature of the NEC approach, which finds a resonance in the Kaleckian approach, is 'crowding out'. For the NEC, 'crowding out' is a physical concept in which the demands of the public sector for land, labour and capital elbow out the needs of the private sector, resulting in inflation and resource misallocation. The Kaleckian concept is more subtle and refers to the reaction of the business class to fears of a loss of political and economic control as the state 'crowds out' the private sector by extending its activities into spheres which had been the traditional preserve of the private sector (Kalecki, 1943). But the NEC faces its own dilemma over Ricardian equivalence. Fiscal policy effectiveness can only be realised by abandoning Ricardian equivalence and the strict rationality assumption on which it is based.

Perhaps the most fundamental difference between the NEC and Post-Keynesian (both varieties) approaches to fiscal policy is their stances on fiscal policy and growth. For the NEC, fiscal policy has no contribution to make to growth and, at best, is a short-term palliative to be considered only when the economy is in the grips of serious recession. The Post-Keynesian (JMK) approach recognises that fiscal policy contributes to growth by an expansion of aggregate demand resulting in an increase in investment, productive capacity and growth. But in the Keynesian 'functional finance' approach this increased investment need not be anything more sophisticated than the purchase of shovels for the purpose of digging holes and filling them in again. Again, the Kaleckian approach is more subtle. It specifies the determinants of investment and identifies the channels through which changes in the structure of taxation can have an impact on these determinants. As we have shown in part five, the Kaleckian fiscal approach endogenises innovation so that fiscal policy can, under certain conditions, encourage an acceleration of low emissions technical progress, if the political aspects of innovation can to some extent be nullified.

5 The high public profile of climate change sceptics, notably at a Washington D.C. conference organised by the conservative Heartland Institute in May 2009, provides support for the political innovation cycle. Conservative economists are being recruited by these sceptics to argue that governments pushing GHG reductions result in a loss of economic and social control by the efficient market mechanism.

References

Asimakopulos, A. (1976): Tax incidence, in: Eichner, A. S. (ed), A Guide to Post Keynesian Economics, New York: M. E. Sharpe.

Asimakopulos, A., Burbidge, J. (1974): The short-period incidence of taxation, Economic Journal, 84: 267–288.

Arestis, P., Sawyer, M. (2004): Re-examining Monetary and Fiscal Policies in the Twenty-first Century, Cheltenham: Edward Elgar.

Bernanke, B., Reinhart, V. R., Sack, B. P. (2004): Monetary policy alternatives at the zero bound: an empirical assessment, Brookings Papers on Economic Activity, 2: 1–78.

Bhaduri, A., Steindl, J. (1983): The rise of monetarism as a social doctrine, Thames Papers in Political Economy: Autumn.

Bloch, H., Mangano, M., Courvisanos J. (2007): Innovation and investment: technological obsolescence in Australian manufacturing, Centre for Research in Applied Economics, Curtin University of Technology Working Paper Series 07–02, April.

Catley, R., McFarlane, B. J. (1981): Australian Capitalism in Boom and Depression, Chippendale, NSW: Alternative Publishing Cooperative.

Courvisanos, J. (2009): Political aspects of innovation, Research Policy, available online at: http://dx.doi.org/10.1016/j.respol.2009.04.001. (hard copy forthcoming).

Courvisanos, J., Verspagen, B. (2004): Innovation and investment in capitalist economies 1870–2000: Kaleckian dynamics and evolutionary life cycles, in: Wray, L. R., Forstater, M. (eds), Contemporary Post Keynesian Analysis, Cheltenham: Edward Elgar.

Harcourt, G. C. (2006): The structure of post-Keynesian economics, Cambridge: Cambridge University Press.

Kalecki, M. (1937): A theory of commodity, income and capital taxation, Economic Journal, 47: 444–450.

Kalecki, M. (1943): Political aspects of full employment, Political Quarterly: 347–356.

Kalecki, M. (1954): Theory of Economic Dynamics, London: Unwin University Books.

Kalecki, M. (1962): Observations on the theory of growth, Economic Journal, 72: 134–153.

Kalecki, M. (1971): Entrepreneurial capital and investment, in: Kalecki, M.: Selected Essays on the Dynamics of the Capitalist Economy, Cambridge: Cambridge University Press.

Laramie, A., Mair, D. (2000): A Dynamic Theory of Taxation: Integrating Kalecki into Modern Public Finance, Cheltenham: Edward Elgar.

Lerner, A. P. (1943): Functional finance and the Federal debt, Social Research, 10(1): 38–57.

Mair, D., Laramie A. J. (2002): Full employment: gift horse or Trojan horse? Review of Social Economy, LX (4): 567–594.

Salter, W. E. G. (1966): Productivity and Technical Change, Cambridge: Cambridge University Press.

Steindl, J. (1979): Stagnation theory and stagnation policy, Cambridge Journal of Economics, 3:1–14.

Stern, N. (2006): The Economics of Climate Change, Cambridge: Cambridge University Press.

Tcherneva, P. (2008): The return of fiscal policy: can the new developments in the New Economic Consensus be reconciled with the Post-Keynesian view?, The Levy Economics Institute, Bard College, USA, Working Paper No. 539.

*Figure 1. The Incidence and Effects of Taxation**

Part A. An Increase in Wage Taxes
Short-Period Effects

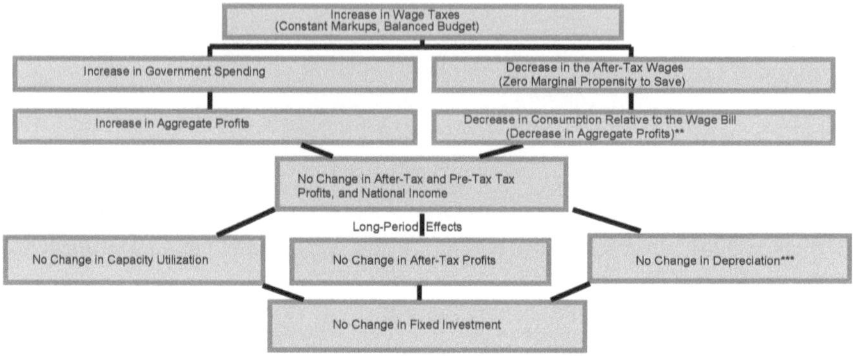

*The short-period incidence and effects of tax changes (where fixed investment expenditures are given by past investment decisions) depends on the government budget stance, the marginal propensity to save of wages, the marginal propensity to consume out of profits, and the degree of tax shifting through changes in business price/cost markups. The long-period incidence and effects of tax changes (where fixed investment expenditures change in response to determinants) incorporates the impact of short-period effects on current period investment decisions and future investment expenditures.

**If the marginal propensity to save out of wages is nonzero, then the decrease in wage consumption relative to the wage bill is dampened. The result is a traditional balanced budget effect where profits and national income rise. The rise in profits, and the increase national income, capacity utilization, increase fixed investment in the long-period.

***If the price/cost markup decreases, as the wage tax is shifted, the wage bill and wage bill's share of national income increases. Through technical progress, the relative real cost of operating existing fixed capital rises and increases the relative rate of depreciation to existing fixed capital, and encourages investment in technological innovation..

Part B. An Increase in Profits Tax
Short-Period Effects

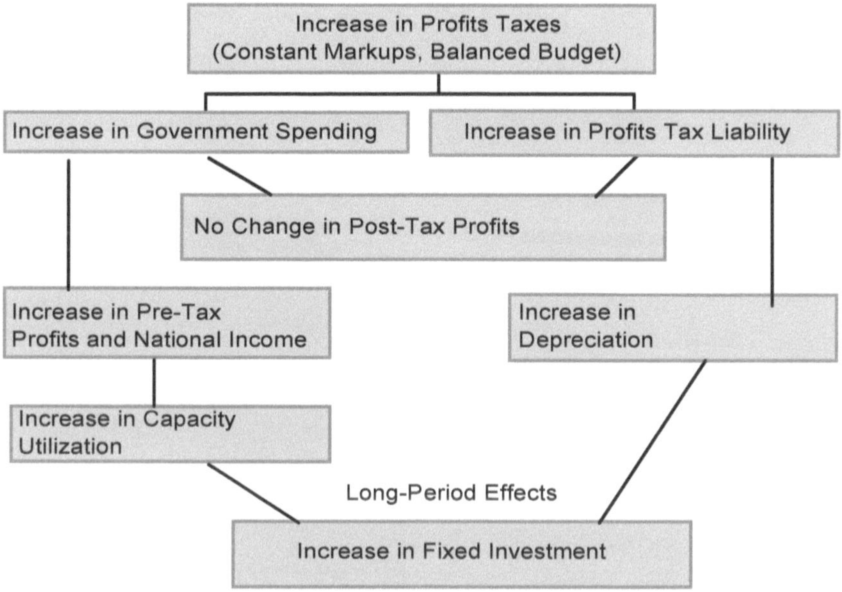

If the propensity to save out of wages is nonzero, the balanced budget increase in the profits tax increases the wage bill, reduces consumption relative to the wage bill, reduces after-tax profits, and dampens the increase in pre-tax profits and national income. If the profits tax is shifted via an increase in price/cost markups, the wage share declines, the relative real cost of operating existing fixed capital declines, and depreciation declines, which discourages innovation.

Anthony J. Laramie, Merrimack College, MA, USA
Douglas Mair, Heriot-Watt University, Edinburgh, UK

Chapter 7: Accounting for Changes in Corporate Profits: 1991 to 2014

Abstract: The US National Income and Product Accounts' gross savings/gross investment identity is used to construct an accounting identity of corporate profits. On the aggregate, corporate profits are largely made up of the sum of gross domestic private investment, net government borrowing, the current account balance, and net dividends less non-corporate savings. US national income data from 1990 to 2014 are examined. The historical record shows that the expansion in corporate profits in the 1990s, and in the pre-Great Recession 2000s was largely investment driven, that the relatively mild recession of 2001 and Great Recession of 2007–2009 led respectively to mild and relatively large breaks in the profits and investment relationship, and that relationship was restored during economic recoveries and expansions. The government budget deficit acts as a "stabilizer," where decreases in the budget deficit dampen the increase in corporate profits during the expansion, and dampen the fall in corporate profits during the contraction. Prior to 2006, increases in the current account deficit move in the same direction as corporate profits. This relationship suggests that other factors, in particular the growth in gross domestic private investment, more than offsets the negative effects of the rising current account deficit on corporate profits. Finally, the growth in corporate profits has been fueled in part by a reduction in compensation to employees' share of gross domestic corporate income.

1. Introduction

In this paper, the National Income and Product Accounts' gross savings/gross investment identity is used to describe changes in corporate profits for the period 1991 to 2014. Our approach is grounded in works of Michal Kalecki. Keynes, as editor of the Economic Journal, published Kalecki's (1971/1937) path-breaking, but often overlooked, paper on tax incidence. Kalecki's approach to taxation can be distinguished from the traditional approaches in two ways: 1) Kalecki views the long period as consisting of a series of short periods as the economy moves through time; and 2) Kalecki gives equal emphasis to macroeconomic and microeconomic foundations. The first distinction implies that full employment does not exist independently of the short-period state, and that the economy does not adjust to full employment via some real balance effect. The second distinction implies that overall macroeconomic conditions influence the spending decisions of businesses and households, while real wage rates and the functional distribution of income are both influenced by the price/cost markup decisions of individual businesses. Kalecki de-emphasized the rigorous maximization problems at the core of traditional approaches to tax incidence, but focused instead on liquidity (cash flow constraints) in explaining spending decisions. In the Kaleckian approach, the effects of tax policy (on aggregate profits and income/output) are largely reflected in spending flows at the macroeconomic level, and in the impact of taxes on business price/cost markups at the microeconomic level (see Laramie and Mair, 2000).

In what follows, Kalecki's famous profit equation is revisited. Its counterpart for corporate profits (see Levy and Levy, 1983) is developed to account for changes in corporate profits and to consider the "sources" of corporate profits over the last 25 years. Corporate profits are largely determined by three sets of factors: 1) private sector effects (for example, the price/cost markup and investment decisions of firms and the savings decisions of households); 2) public sector effects (the government budget stance); and 3) a foreign sector effect, which reflects how changes in the current account balance affect the level of corporate profits of US businesses.

We conclude that: 1) In two periods, from 1991 to 2007 and from 2010 to 2014 corporate profits moved in the same direction as gross domestic private investment; 2) In three periods, 1991 to 2001, 2005 to 2007, and 2010 to 2014, corporate profits and the government budget deficit largely moved in opposite directions; 3) Changes in the government budget deficit have played an important role in dampening changes in corporate profits. In response to the recessions of 1991, 2001 and 2007, the budget deficit increased, and dampened the fall in corporate profits; 4) The recent slow-down in corporate profits can be accounted for, in part, by the decline in the government budget deficit; 5) The deficit in the current account balance typically moved in the same direction as corporate profits, but, in recent years, that relationship seems to breaking down; 6) The relationships between net dividends and corporate profits appear to be roughly stable during the period of 1991 to 2006, but break down thereafter; 7) Personal savings are relatively stable during 1991 to 2005, but with the Great Recession, significant increases in personal savings arise with relatively flat to negative growth in profits, after corporate profits recover with some relatively larges swings in personal savings; and 8) Variations in the statistical discrepancy account for relatively large changes in corporate profits.

The paper is structured as follows. The first section illustrates how Kalecki's famous profit equation is derived and considers briefly Kalecki's theory of national income determination and tax incidence. The second section shows how the National Income and Product Accounts can be adapted to correspond with Kalecki's profit equation in order to account for changes in corporate profits. The third section accounts for the changes in the various right-hand-side variables that have contributed to the change in corporate profits in the US from 1990 to 2014. The fifth section examines recent changes in the distribution of corporate sector income. The sixth section focuses on the long-period effects of changes in the government budget stance. The final section concludes with a summary of the main conclusions.

2. Kalecki's Theories of National Income Determination.

In order to characterize the role of profits in the economy, we follow Kalecki (1968) and Laramie (1991). To start, the pricing decisions of individual firms are considered. Prices are assumed to be a markup over unit costs of production where firms operate with excess capacity, i.e.:

(1) $P = (k)(W + M)/Q$

where P = price, k = markup,[1] W = wage bill, M = materials bill, Q = output. Assuming that j = M/W, and W = wN, where w is the wage rate, and N = units of employment, the price can be rewritten as:

(1') $P = (k)(1+j)[w/(Q/N)]$;

and the real wage rate (as determined in the product market) can be written as:

(2) $w/P = [1/(k)(1+j)](Q/N)$;

and with value added, Y, defined as sales (P times Q) less the materials bill (M), the wage bill's share of value added can be written as:

1 Kalecki (1968) explains that the markup is determined by the degree of monopoly and is influenced by factors such as overheads, the advertising costs to sales ratio, and the degree of unionization. For a fuller discussion, see Laramie, Mair and Reynolds (2004).

(3) $W/Y = 1/[(k-1)(j+1) + 1]$.

Aggregating over all industries and adjusting k and j accordingly, the aggregate wage share in value added is derived. Given that the aggregate wage share is determined by the markup, k, and the ratio of the materials bill to the wage bill, j, and assuming that value added can be defined as the sum of the wage bill, W, overhead labor (salary) bill, β, and pre-tax profits, Π, the aggregate wage share is written as:[2]

(4) $(Y - \beta - \Pi)/Y = \alpha$; where α = the aggregate wage share. Solving for Y yields:

(5) $Y = (\beta + \Pi)/(1- \alpha)$.

Given overhead wages and the wage share (Kalecki's income distribution factors), value added is pushed up to the level where profits are realized.

An expression for profits is easily derived from the National Income and Product Accounts. If value added in terms of expenditures is defined as the sum of household consumption, C, gross domestic private investment, I, government purchases G, and Net Exports, NEX, and if value added in terms income is defined as the sum of the wage bill, W, and pre-tax profits, P, and if wage taxes net of transfers are defined as T_W, the pre-tax profits can be written as:

(6) $\Pi = I + G - T_W + NEX + C - W_N$;

or:

(6') $\Pi = I + G - T_W + NEX + C_\Pi - S_W$;

where W_N equals disposable wages, C_Π equals consumption out profits, C_Π, and S_W equals savings out of wages/salaries. By defining pre-tax profits, Π, as after-tax profits, π, plus profit taxes, T_Π, after-tax profits are written as:

(7) $\pi = I + (G - T_W - T_\Pi) + NEX + C_\Pi - S_W$.[3]

2 See Sawyer (1985, p. 79, 80).

3 Kalecki (1968, pp. 53–56) modifies the profit equation by assuming that consumption out of profits is a lagged function of profits, and given that profits depend on the right-hand-side variables in (7), current profits are a function of the lagged variables on the right-hand side of (7). Weintraub (1979, 1981) simplified Kalecki by introducing a consumption coefficient, a = C/W, which allows profits to be contemporaneously determined with the right-hand-side variables. See (Laramie 1991, Mair, Laramie and Toporowski, 2000, and 2002).

This expression is Kalecki's famous profit equation, where if the government budget is in balance and if net exports are in balance, and workers do not save, then business owners earn what they spend![4] Kalecki, as is well known, concluded that the expression for profits was more than accounting identity, because business owners can plan their spending, but cannot plan their profits, so that the causality flows from right to left.[5]

In addition, with nonzero budget and trade deficits, profits increase "pro tanto" by the size of those deficits (Kalecki 1968, p. 51). Substituting (6') into (5) generates Kalecki's expression for national income.

(8) $$Y = (\beta + I + G - T_W + NEX + C_\Pi - S_W)/(1- \alpha).$$[6]

The above expressions represent the core of Kalecki's short-period model. The model is considered to be short period, because investment expenditures in the current period are determined by investment decisions made in previous periods. To make the model dynamic, explicit consideration has to be given to the determinants of the right-hand-side variables in equations (6'), (7) and (8).

3. Short-Period Government/Budget Stance Incidence

Kalecki's model can be used to illustrate the main issues that influence government budget/tax incidence. To illustrate, assume two taxes, a wage tax and a profits tax. In the short-period, an increase in the wage tax, given the wage bill, reduces the after-tax wage bill, and reduces the after-tax wage bill's income share and the after-tax real wage rate. The increase in the wage tax also reduces business profits (and national income) by reducing consumption relative to the wage bill (which can be reflected as a decrease in the government

---

4 Equation (7) can be modified by adding and subtracting government transfer payments on the right-hand-side of the equation, and by redefining consumption out of profits as non-wage consumption (consumption out of profits plus consumption out of transfers).

5 See Kalecki (1968) and Asimakopulos and Burbidge (1979).

6 As shown in (8), fiscal and monetary policy can affect the level of national income through changing the determinants of pre-tax profits, given the degree of monopoly (which determines the wage share). However, Kalecki was much less optimistic than Keynes, to put it mildly, given existing political and economic institutions, in regard to policy makers' willingness to use such policies. See Sawyer (1985, 184–187), Kalecki (1971/1937), and Mair and Laramie (2003).

budget deficit).[7] In the short period, the effect of the wage tax on the after-tax wage share and the real wage rate can be dampened if the wage tax is shifted through a decrease in business markups. In addition, the negative effect of the wage tax on after-tax profits can be dampened if workers pay for some of the tax by reducing their savings, and if the government uses the tax to finance its purchases (or transfers).

An increase in the profits tax, like the wage tax, reduces after-tax profits (reflected in a decline in the budget deficit), but has no effect on pre-tax profits (and national income) assuming spending out of profits is fixed by decisions made in previous periods. Moreover, the profits tax can be shifted in the short period if the government spends the profit tax receipts, through a balanced budget effect, and if businesses increase their markups, which, in turn, reduces the wage share, the wage bill and personal savings (in effect forcing workers to pay for the profit tax by reducing some of their savings).[8] Kalecki (1971/1937) concluded that the best tax was a tax on the value of capital. Such a tax, if used to finance government spending, has no effect on after-tax corporate profits, and would not be paid for by reducing consumption out of profits, would not result in higher interest rates (because lenders would pay the same tax if 'capital' is lent or not) and would not be shifted on to workers via higher markups.

4. Deriving Corporate Profits from the National Income and Product Accounts of the US

A definition for corporate profits can be derived from the accounting identity that Gross Investment–Gross Savings provided in Table 5.1 of the National Income and Product Accounts. See Table 1 below.[9]

---

7 See Laramie (1993), the wage tax potentially generates a double tax incidence effect: reducing workers' real wages and business profits.

8 **Kalecki** originally assumed a closed economy. With an open economy, the effects and incidence of the wage and profits taxes can be further dampened by changes in the net export balance.

9 For an empirical analysis of the causal relationships between profits and the right-hand-side variables see Giovanni and Paguez (2007).

Table 1: Table 5.1. Saving and Investment by Sector
[Billions of dollars]
Bureau of Economic Analysis
Last Revised on: December 22, 2015 – Next Release Date January 29, 2016

Line		2014
1	**Gross saving**	3266.8
2	**Net saving**	520.1
3	Net private saving	1319.2
4	Domestic business	699
5	Undistributed corporate profits	833.9
6	Inventory valuation adjustment, corporate	-2.9
7	Capital consumption adjustment, corporate	-131.9
8	Households and institutions	620.2
9	Personal saving	620.2
10	Net government saving	-799.2
11	Federal	-631.5
12	State and local	-167.7
13	**Consumption of fixed capital**	2746.7
14	Private	2229.9
15	Domestic business	1775.2
16	Households and institutions	454.8
17	Government	516.8
18	Federal	270.7
19	State and local	246.1
20	**Gross domestic investment, capital account transactions, and net lending, NIPAs**	3054.7
21	**Gross domestic investment**	3455.9
22	Gross private domestic investment	2860
23	Domestic business	2263.8
24	Households and institutions	596.2
25	Gross government investment	595.8
26	Federal	264.6
27	State and local	331.3
28	**Capital account transactions (net) 1**[1*]	0.5

*

Legend / Footnotes:
1. Consists of capital transfers and the acquisition and disposal of nonproduced nonfinancial assets. Prior to 1982, reflects only capital grants paid to the US territories and the Commonwealths of Puerto Rico and Northern Mariana Islands.
2. Consists of damages to fixed assets.

Line		2014
29	Private	5.5
30	Domestic business	4.5
31	Households and institutions	0.9
32	Government	-5
33	Federal	56.1
34	State and local	-61.1
35	**Net lending or net borrowing (-), NIPAs**	-401.6
36	Private	471.6
37	Domestic business	-6.1
38	Households and institutions	477.8
39	Government	-873.2
40	Federal	-681.4
41	State and local	-191.8
42	**Statistical discrepancy**	-212

From Table 1, an expression for corporate profits is derived. Corporate profits are defined as the sum of undistributed corporate profits plus the inventory valuation adjustment plus the capital consumption adjustment plus net dividends plus the corporate consumption of fixed capital. Rearranging term in the NIPA's Table 5.1, and defining the government budget deficit as: gross government investment – net government savings + government net capital account transactions – government consumption of fixed capital; and defining current account balance as net lending plus capital account transactions; and defining the corporate consumption of fixed capital as private capital consumption of fixed capital – non-corporate consumption of fixed capital (i.e. non-corporate business and household and institutions' consumption of fixed capital), allows corporate profits to be defined as in Table 2. In Table 2, corporate profits are defined as gross private domestic investment plus the government budget deficit plus the current account balance less the government capital account transactions (net)[11] plus net dividends less non-corporate consumption of fixed capital less personal savings less the statistical discrepancy

11 To be consistent with the NIPA definitions of Government Net Lending or Borrowing, and the Current Account Balance, the Government Capital Account Transactions (net) had to be double counted on the right-hand-side of the Corporate Profit definition. To correct for the double counting, the government current account balance, net, had to be subtracted out as a separate account.

Table 2. Corporate Profits (2014) – Derived from Table 5.1 (Billions of Dollars, authors' calculations)

line 4, Table 5.1	Domestic business savings	699
line 16, Table 1.12	+Net dividends	860
line 4, Table 7.5	+Corporate business consumption of fixed capital	1467.3
Equals	**=Corporate Profits**[11]	**3026.3**
22, Table 5.1	**Gross private domestic investment**	**2860**
line 25, Table 5.1	Gross government investment	595.8
line 10, Table 5.1	-Net government saving	-799.2
line 32, Table 5.1	+Government current account balance net	-5
line 17, Table 5.1	-Government consumption of fixed capital	516.8
Equals	**=Government Budget Deficit**	**873.2**
line 35, Table 5.1	**Net lending or net borrowing (-), NIPAs**	-401.6
line 28, Table 5.1	+Capital account transactions (net) 1	0.5
Equals	**Current Account Balance**	**-401.1**
line 32, Table 5.1	**Government Capital Account Transactions (net)**	**-5**
line 16, Table 1.12	**Net dividends**	**860**
line 14, Table 5.1	Private Consumption of Fixed Capital	2229.9
line 4, Table 7.5	Corporate business consumption of fixed capital	1467.3
Equals	**Non-corporate Consumption of Fixed Capital**	**762.6**
line 9,Table 5.1	**Personal Saving**	**620.2**
line 42, Table 5.1	**Statistical Discrepancy**	**-212**
Equals	**Corporate Profits** **=Gross private domestic investment** **+Government Budget Deficit** **+Current Account Balance** **-Government Capital Account Transactions (net)** **+Net dividends** **-Non-corporate Consumption of Fixed Capital** **-Personal saving** **-Statistical discrepancy**	**3026.3**

12 This definition is the same as the BEA's Table 1.12 definition of corporate cash flow plus net dividends plus capital transfers (net).

5. Historical Evidence: Accounting for Changes in Corporate Profits 1991 to 2014.

The historical relationships between the level of corporate profits and the major right-hand-side variables: gross domestic private investment, the government budget deficit, the current account balance, the non-corporate consumption of fixed capital, personal savings and the statistical discrepancy are discussed below.

In Figure 1, corporate profits' relationship to gross domestic private investment appears to move in two major cycles: pre-Great Recession and post-Great Recession. Prior to the Great Recession, and prior to the Recession of 2001, corporate profits and gross domestic private investment move very closely with each other, almost along a log linear relationship. During this period, gross domestic investment's share of corporate profits steadily increases (see Table 3) and makes a relatively large contribution to the growth rates in corporate profits. This relationship is altered in 1999 and 2000, when the federal funds rate increased from a low 4.74% in April of 1999 to a high of 6.4% in December of 2000 (FRED DATABASE). The NASDAQ peaked in March of 2000 at 4802.99 and troughed in October of 2002 at 1241. 9 (FRED DATABASE). Following 9/11, with the decline in interest rates and the recovery of the equity markets, the pre-2001 recession relationship seems to be re-established right up 2007, yet gross investment's share of corporate profits trends downward and declines from about 116% of corporate profits to just under 79% of corporate profits in 2009. In addition, gross domestic private investment declines in 2007 and 2009, and accounts for -1.62%, -9.79% and -22.89% of corporate profits' growth rates of -.91%, -2.05% and 6.41%. Since 2009, gross domestic private investment's share of corporate profits has increased but has not come close to the pre-Great Recession levels, while making positive contributions to the growth rate in corporate profits.

In Figure 2, the counter cyclical relationships between corporate profits and the budget deficit is seen. During periods just prior to, during, and just thereafter 'official' recessions, the budget deficit increases as corporate profits increase. For example, in the periods from 2000 to 2003 and from 2006 to 2010, the budget deficit as a percent of corporate profits rises respectively from -5.96% to 39.02% and from 18.67% to 77.35% (see Table 2).

Figure 1. Corporate Profits and Gross Domestic Private Investment (NIPA, Tables 5.1, 1.12 and 7.5, authors' calculations).

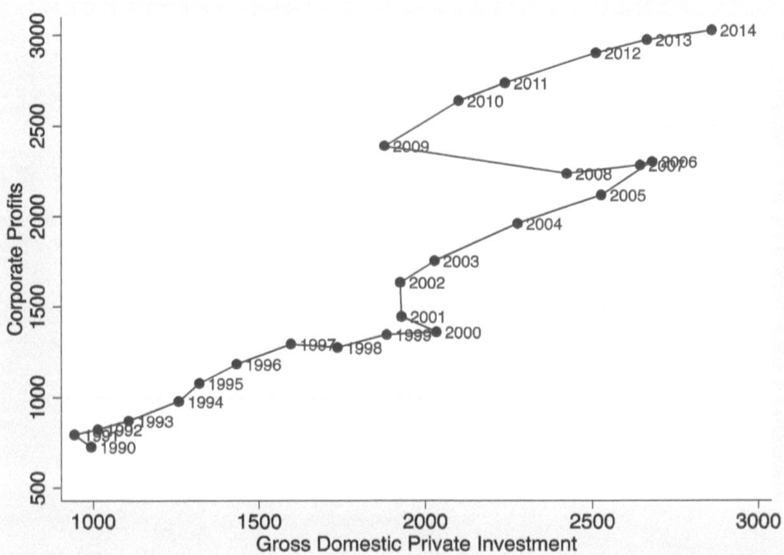

In addition, the budget deficit makes a negative contribution of 6.17% of the growth in corporate profits in 2000, but positive contributions of 15.96% and 22.85% to profits' growth rate in 2001 and 2002, and positive contributions of 23.26% and 33.17% to profits' growth rates in 2008 and 2009. In years of cyclical expansions, the government budget deficit makes negative contributions to profits' growth rate (see Table 3).

This counter cyclical relationship is also seen in Figure 3. As Gross Domestic Private Investment increases, the government budget deficit decreases in three periods: 1991 to 2000, 2003 to 2006, and 2009 to 2014. We suspect that, contrary to the crowding out story the causality runs from investment to the government budget deficit, and the traditional fiscal drag story operates on corporate profits (i.e. gross domestic private investment stimulates corporate profits and gross income, and the government budget deficits react counter-cyclically as an "automatic stabilizer" and through changes in discretionary fiscal policy).

Figure 2. Corporate Profits and the Government Budget Deficit (NIPA, Tables 5.1, 1.12 and 7.5, authors' calculations).

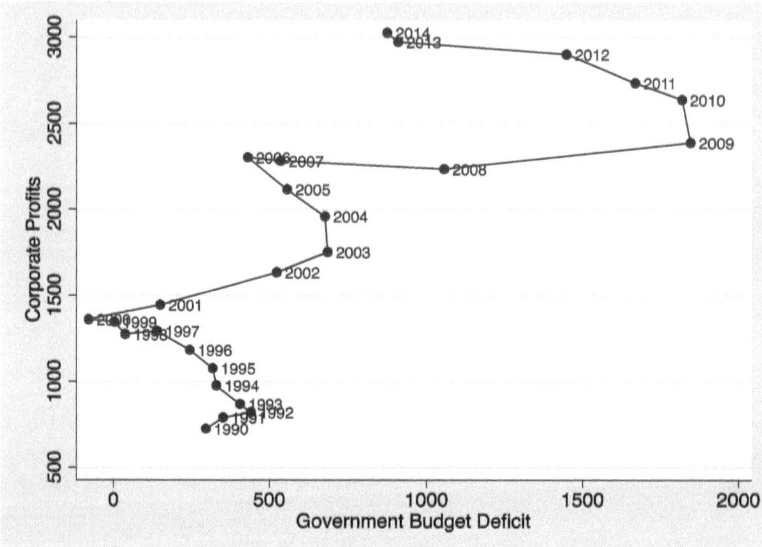

Figure 3. Gross Domestic Private Investment and Government Budget Deficit (NIPA, Tables 5.1, 1.12 and 7.5, authors' calculations).

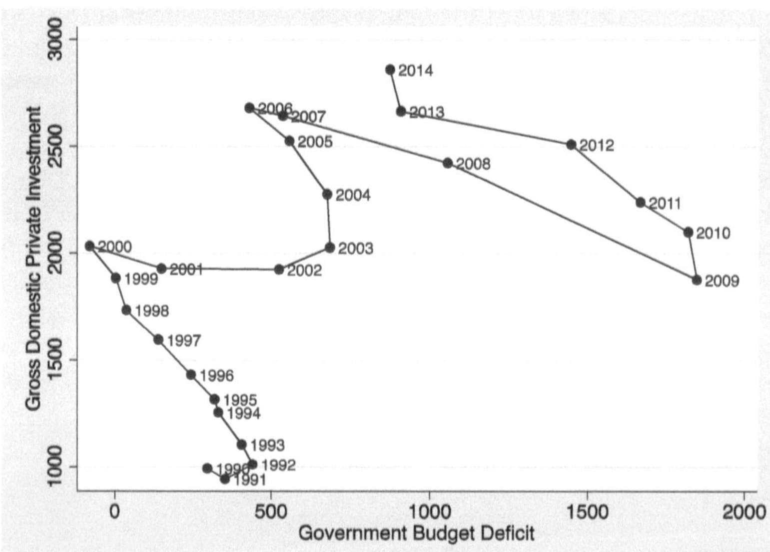

In Figure 4, the accounting relationship between the corporate profits and the current account balance is seen. The current account deficit increases every year, excepting 1991 (Gulf War I payments), and 2001. During the 'official' Great Recession, the Current Account deficit decreases. Post Great Recession, the current account deficit increases through 2011 as the budget deficit falls, and then decreases in 2012 and 2013. The Current Account Balance (deficit) makes a negative contribution to profits and the growth rate in profits in most years. See Tables 3 and 4.

In the 1980s, international crowding out, how the increase in the government budget deficit increased the current account deficit through increases in domestic interest rates and in the dollar exchange rate, was a common theme in macroeconomics. The 1990s appear to show the opposite. With the reduction in the government budget deficit the current account deficit continues to increase. In the period between recessions, 2001 to 2007, as the government budget deficit increases, the current account deficit continues to increase, but, following the recession of 2007, as the government budget deficit increases the current account deficit decreases. From 2009 through to 2014, little change in the current account deficit is seen as the government budget deficit declines. Little stimulus to corporate profits, therefore, can be seen through reductions in the current account deficit as the government budget deficit declines. See Figure 5.

Figure 6 shows the relationship between the current account balance and gross domestic private investment. For most years, gross domestic private investment is increasing as the current account deficit is increasing. Two competing views possibly explain this relationship. The first view is that the current account deficit funds the increase in investment. The second view is that the growth in investment stimulates the economy and contributes to the rise in current account deficit. Given the pro-cyclical response of the current account deficit, the latter view is preferred. Since 2009, the cyclical relationship between the current account deficit appears to have shifted as investment has been increasing and the current account deficit rises and then dips.

In Figure 7, the (lack of) relationship between the current account balance and personal savings is shown. From 1990 to 2006, the current account deficit changes with little movement in personal savings. With the financial crisis, personal savings increase, and the current account deficit decreases. The decrease in the current account deficit is seen as an endogenous response to the slow-down in domestic economic activity.

Figure 4. Corporate Profits and the Current Account Balance (NIPA, Tables 5.1, 1.12 and 7.5, authors' calculations).

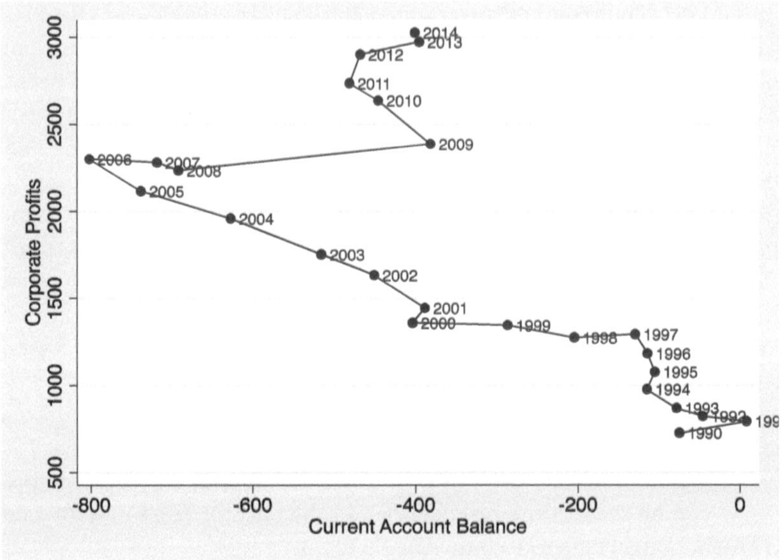

Figure 5. The Current Account Balance and the Government Budget Deficit (NIPA, Tables 5.1, 1.12 and 7.5, authors' calculations).

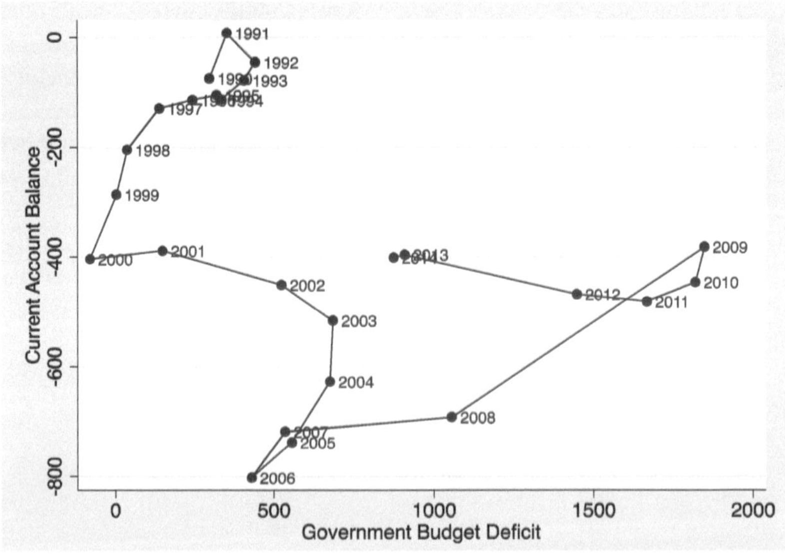

Figure 6. The Current Account Balance and the Government Budget Deficit (NIPA, Tables 5.1, 1.12 and 7.5, authors' calculations).

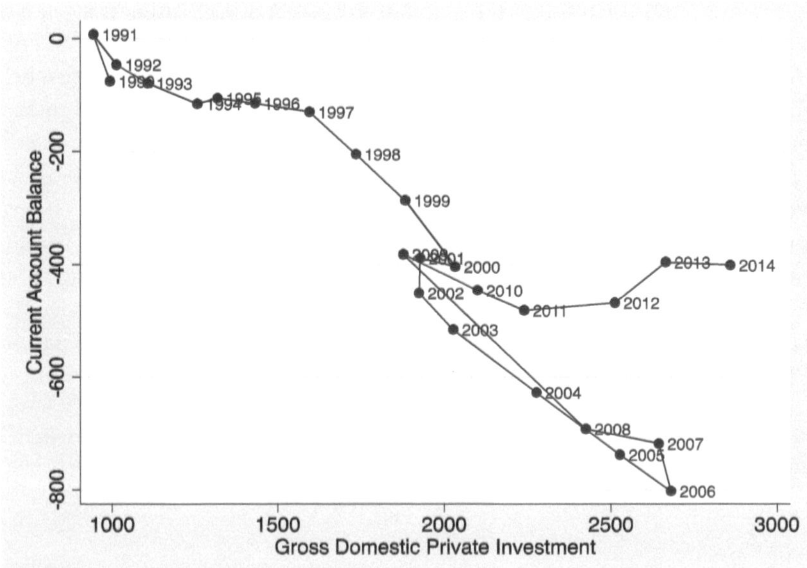

Figure 7. The Current Account Balance and Personal Savings (NIPA Table 5.1).

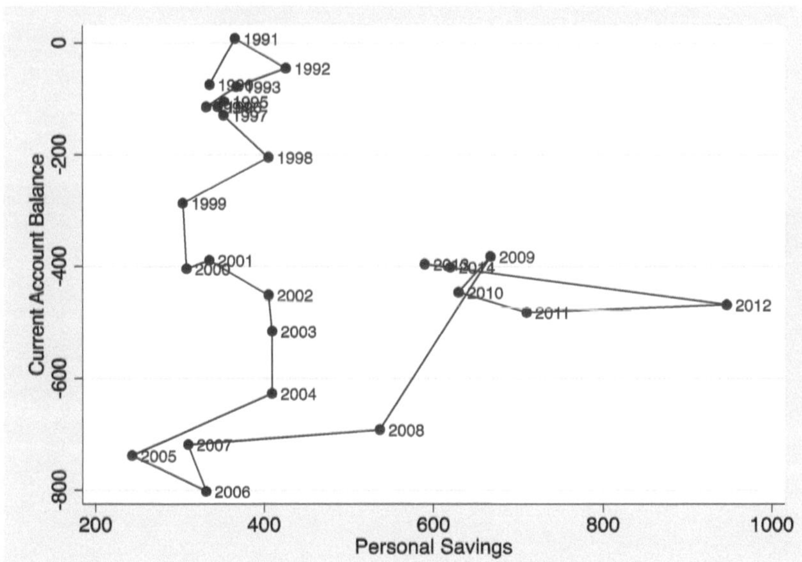

Figure 8 shows the relationship between net dividends and corporate profits. Recognizing that net dividends are determined by corporate management in relationship to the level of corporate profits, a relatively stable relationship exists between net dividends and corporate profits between 1991 and 2001. After 2001, and until 2007, net dividends seem to rise exponentially relative to corporate profits. From 2007 to 2010, net dividends fall relative to profits, and the positive relationship is restored between 2010 and 2013. In 2014, net dividends fell relative to corporate profits. Table 3 shows net dividends' share of corporate profits. Its share is at its lowest level of 21.38% in 2010, and at its highest level of 36.10% in 2008. The average share is about 27% with a standard deviation of about 3.8% (about 14% of the mean). During the period from 1990 to 2003, dividends were on average about 25% of corporate profits, and the standard deviation was about 1.7% (almost 7% of the mean). After 2003, corporate dividends' share was about 29% with a standard deviation of about 4.8% (about 17% of the mean).

Figure 8. Net Dividends and Corporate Profits (NIPA, Tables 5.1, 1.12 and 7.5, authors' calculations).

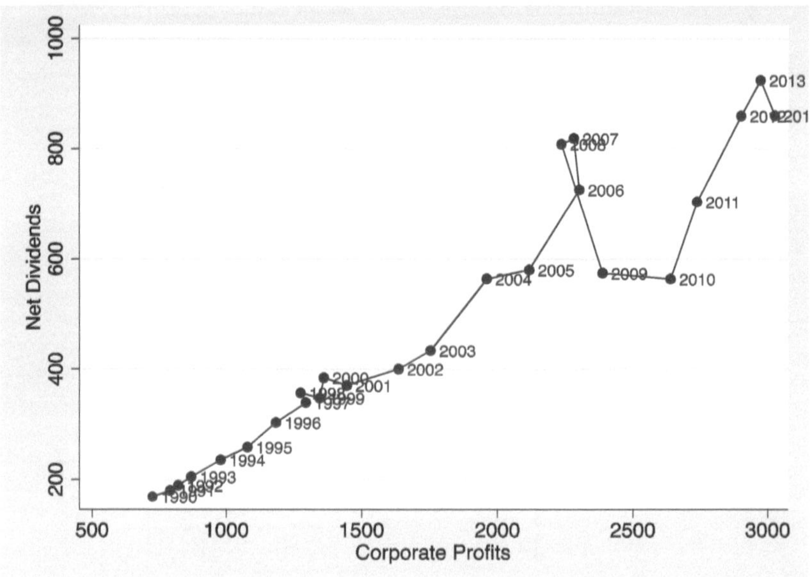

Figure 9 shows the relationship between corporate profits and the non-corporate consumption of fixed capital (defined non-corporate business and household and institutions' consumption of fixed capital). The non-corporate consumption of fixed capital can be considered as (part of gross) personal savings and makes a negative contribution corporate profits. Its average share of corporate profits was 27.42% and the standard deviation was 2.24% (see Table 3). Its average (negative) share of corporate profits growth rate ranged from a low of 23.68% to a high of 32.14%. Its average (negative) contribution to the corporate profits rate (see Table 4) was 1.3%, and its (negative) contribution ranged from a high of 2.7% in 2005 to -.53% in 2009. Figure 10 shows that the non-consumption of fixed capital grew smoothly until the beginning of the Great Recession, dipped during the Great Recession and then recovered. Figure 11 shows that the non-corporate consumption of fixed capital grew almost in tandem with gross domestic private investment in 1991 to 2000 and the 2002 to 2006 expansions. During the Great Recession, due to the decline in gross domestic private investment, the non-corporate consumption of fixed capital rose relative to gross domestic fixed investment. Since 2010, we have seen a recovery of the relationship that we have come to expect to see during economic expansions.

Figure 9. Corporate Profits and Non-corporate Consumption of Fixed Capital (NIPA, Tables 5.1, 1.12 and 7.5, authors' calculations).

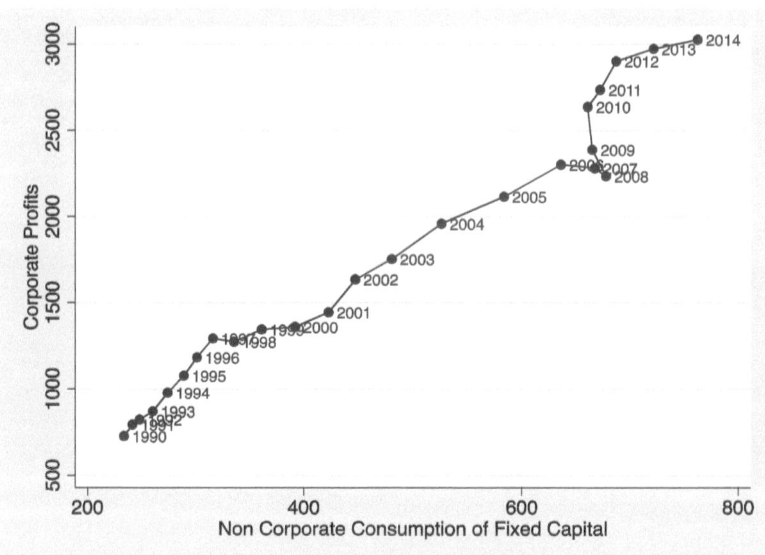

Figure 10. The Non-corporate Consumption of Fixed Capital 1991 to 2014 (NIPA, Tables 5.1, 1.12 and 7.5, authors' calculations).

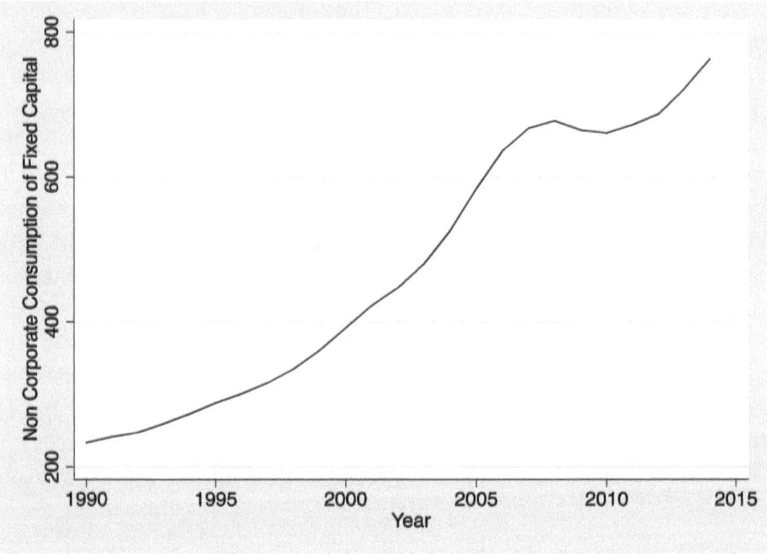

Figure 11. Non-corporate Consumption of Fixed Capital and Gross Domestic Private Investment (NIPA, Tables 5.1, 1.12 and 7.5, authors' calculations).

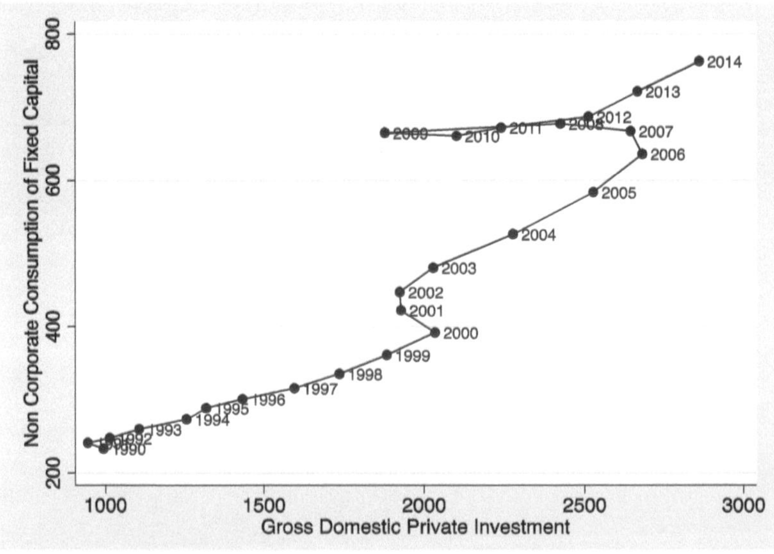

Figure 12 shows the relationship between corporate profits and personal savings. From 1990 to 2007, corporate profits and personal savings seem to have no particular relationship. In 2008, personal savings increase as corporate profits decrease. In 2009, corporate profits increase as personal savings decrease, and from 2010 through 2014, the corporate profits–personal savings relationship begins to move in a pattern similar to that prior to the Great Recession (no particular relationship). Personal savings' average (negative) share of corporate profits was 27.70%, its share standard deviation was 11.48% (about 41.5% of the mean). Its minimum (negative) share was 11.48% in 2005, and its maximum (negative) share was 51.77% in 1992. (see Table 3). Personal savings' average contribution to the corporate profits growth rate was -.64% with a standard deviation of 5.32%. It's minimum (negative) contribution to the corporate profits' growth rate was -12% (its decrease, in other words, contributed twelve percentage points to the corporate profits' growth rate) in 2013, and its (maximum) negative contribution to the corporate profits' growth rate was 10.15% in 2008 (see Table 4).

Figure 13 shows little-to-no stable relationship between personal savings and gross domestic private investment. Figures 14 and 15 show the cyclical relationships in the budget deficit and the current account balance in response to the wide swing in personal savings during and around the Great Recession.

Figure 12. Corporate Profits and Personal Savings (NIPA, Tables 5.1, 1.12 and 7.5, authors' calculations).

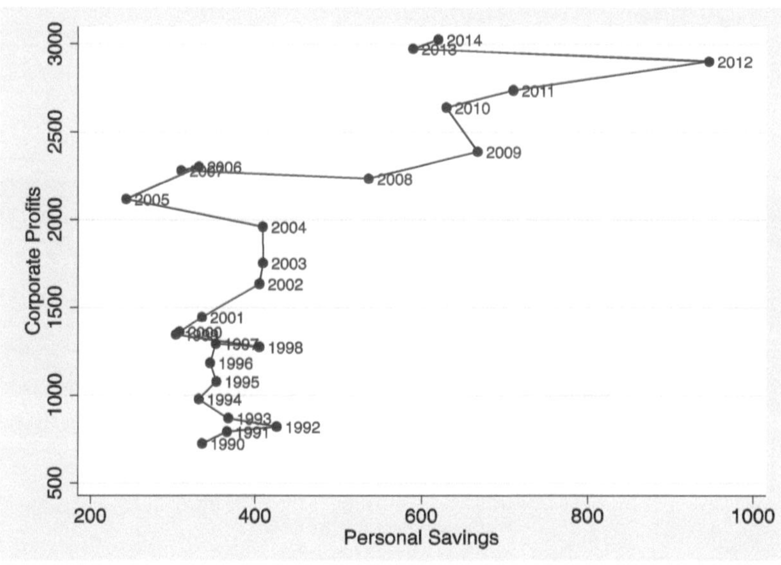

Figure 13. Personal Savings and Gross Domestic Private Investment (NIPA, Tables 5.1, 1.12 and 7.5, authors' calculations).

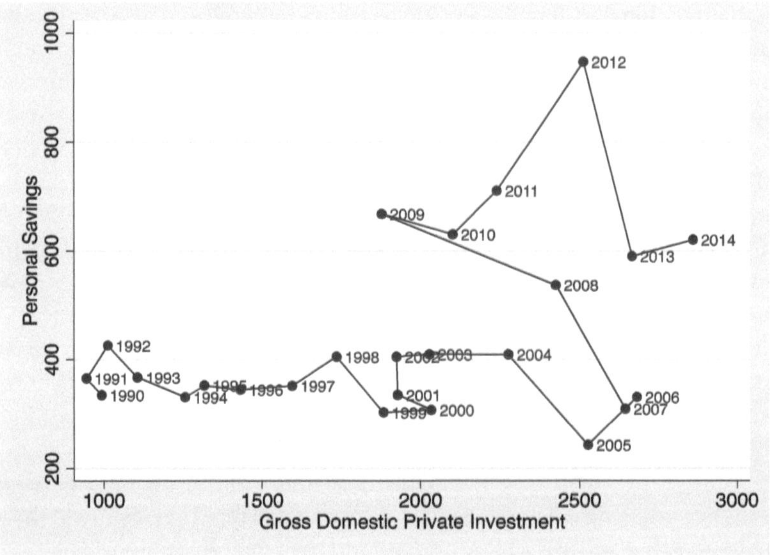

Figure 14. Personal Savings and the Government Budget Deficit (NIPA, Tables 5.1, 1.12 and 7.5, authors' calculations).

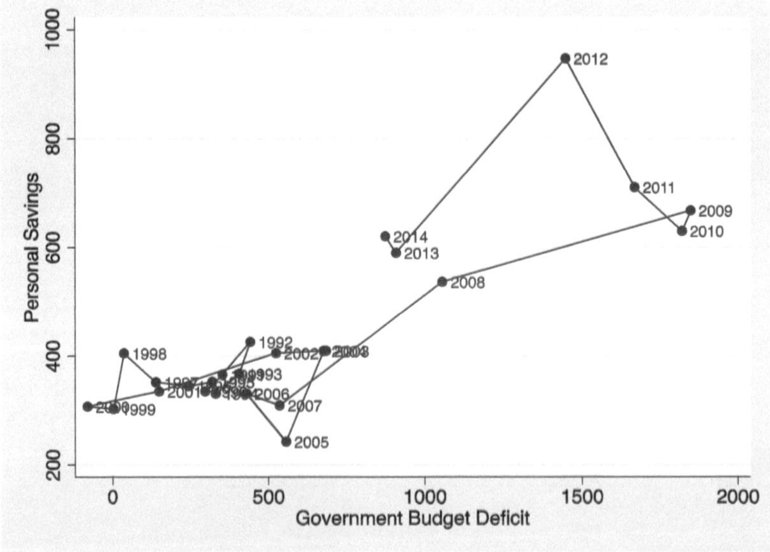

Figure 15. Personal Savings and the Current Account Balance (NIPA, Tables 5.1, 1.12 and 7.5, authors' calculations).

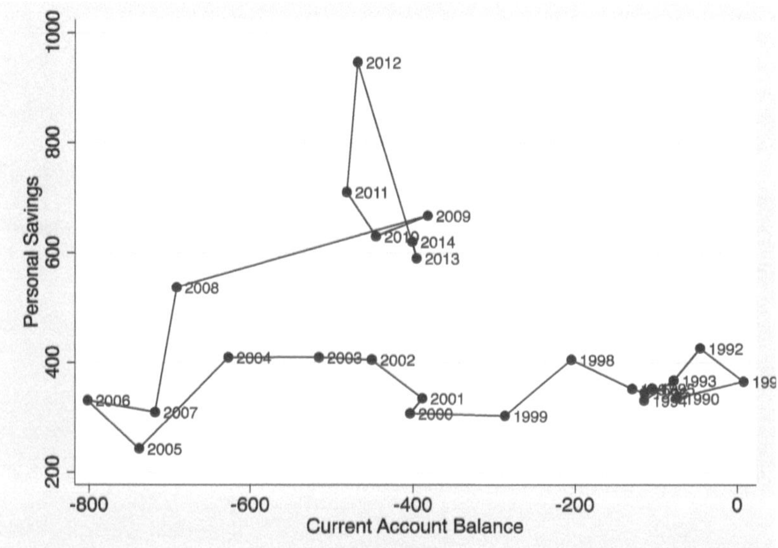

Finally, the statistical discrepancy fluctuates widely (see Figure 17), and in the opposite direction of the investment cycles as depicted in Figure 1. Its average share of profits is only about 1.28% (see Table 3). That share seems to fluctuate rather widely, with its minimum share of profits being -9.44% in 2006, and its maximum share of profits being 17.49% in 1993. Similarly, its average (negative) contribution to the corporate profits' growth rate is -.62%, but it, likewise, fluctuated widely between with its minimum (negative) contribution being -7.90% in 2006 and its maximum (negative) contribution being 10.29% in 2010.

Figure 16. Corporate Profits and the Statistical Discrepancy (NIPA, Tables 5.1, 1.12 and 7.5, authors' calculations).

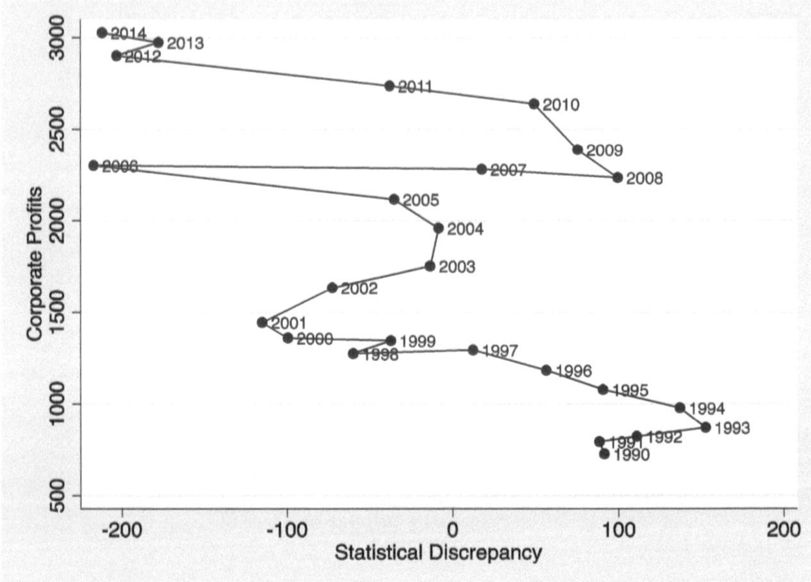

Table 3. Each Account Share of Corporate Profits (Source: NIPA, Tables 1.12, 5.1 and 7.5, author's calculations)

time	Gross Domestic Private Investment	Government Budget Deficit	Current Account Balance	Government Capital Account Transactions (net)	Net Dividends	Noncorporate Consumption of Fixed Capital	Personal Savings	Statistical Discrepancy
1990	136.64%	40.79%	-10.30%	-0.47%	23.26%	32.14%	46.13%	12.57%
1991	118.99%	44.39%	1.00%	-0.54%	22.74%	30.43%	46.11%	11.14%
1992	123.12%	53.62%	-5.54%	-1.15%	23.03%	30.14%	51.77%	13.48%
1993	127.12%	46.69%	-9.02%	-1.24%	23.58%	29.88%	42.22%	17.49%
1994	128.32%	33.80%	-11.71%	-1.30%	24.10%	27.97%	33.84%	13.97%
1995	122.13%	29.58%	-9.74%	-1.93%	24.01%	26.79%	32.71%	8.40%
1996	120.91%	20.63%	-9.63%	-1.83%	25.62%	25.43%	29.15%	4.78%
1997	123.27%	10.78%	-9.99%	-2.28%	26.23%	24.42%	27.21%	0.95%
1998	136.09%	2.93%	-16.04%	-2.40%	28.01%	26.32%	31.79%	-4.71%
1999	139.99%	0.22%	-21.29%	-1.84%	25.85%	26.84%	22.53%	-2.79%
2000	149.48%	-5.96%	-29.68%	-2.01%	28.27%	28.82%	22.62%	-7.31%
2001	133.40%	10.35%	-26.89%	-1.97%	25.63%	29.25%	23.19%	-7.95%
2002	117.71%	32.00%	-27.57%	-1.08%	24.47%	27.36%	24.78%	-4.45%
2003	115.61%	39.02%	-29.40%	-0.02%	24.74%	27.42%	23.35%	-0.78%
2004	116.16%	34.47%	-31.99%	0.10%	28.78%	26.87%	20.89%	-0.44%
2005	119.38%	26.27%	-34.85%	0.85%	27.42%	27.57%	11.48%	-1.68%
2006	116.46%	18.67%	-34.85%	-0.78%	31.54%	27.65%	14.40%	-9.44%
2007	115.90%	23.46%	-31.48%	0.17%	35.90%	29.26%	13.58%	0.77%

time	Gross Domestic Private Investment	Government Budget Deficit	Current Account Balance	Government Capital Account Transactions (net)	Net Dividends	Noncorporate Consumption of Fixed Capital	Personal Savings	Statistical Discrepancy
2008	108.49%	47.20%	-30.94%	2.14%	36.18%	30.32%	24.01%	4.45%
2009	78.64%	77.35%	-15.99%	5.11%	24.06%	27.85%	27.95%	3.15%
2010	79.62%	68.94%	-16.90%	2.24%	21.38%	25.05%	23.88%	1.86%
2011	81.86%	60.91%	-17.60%	1.77%	25.72%	24.57%	25.95%	-1.40%
2012	86.56%	49.87%	-16.14%	0.62%	29.62%	23.68%	32.63%	-7.01%
2013	89.63%	30.54%	-13.31%	-0.21%	31.07%	24.27%	19.84%	-5.97%
2014	94.50%	28.85%	-13.25%	-0.17%	28.42%	25.20%	20.49%	-7.01%
			Summary Statistics					
Obs	25	25	25	25	25	25	25	25
Mean	115.20%	33.01%	-18.92%	-0.33%	26.79%	27.42%	27.70%	1.28%
Std. Dev.	19.62%	20.82%	10.19%	1.75%	3.82%	2.24%	10.22%	7.76%
Min	78.64%	-5.96%	-34.85%	-2.40%	21.38%	23.68%	11.48%	-9.44%
Max	149.48%	77.35%	1.00%	5.11%	36.18%	32.14%	51.77%	17.49%

Table 4. Contributions to the Growth in Corporate Profits in the US[13]

	Gross Domestic Private Investment	Government Budget Deficit	Current Account Balance	Government Capital Account Transactions (Net)	Net Dividends	Noncorporate Consumption of Fixed Capital	Personal Savings	Statistical Discrepancy	Corporate Profits
1991	-6.20%	7.02%	10.43%	-0.11%	1.44%	0.98%	3.84%	-0.38%	8.35%
1992	8.35%	10.80%	-6.50%	-0.63%	1.09%	0.79%	7.30%	2.73%	3.55%
1993	10.77%	-3.99%	-3.78%	-0.15%	1.81%	1.40%	-6.71%	4.75%	5.52%
1994	15.29%	-7.71%	-3.70%	-0.19%	3.14%	1.40%	-3.70%	-1.58%	11.09%
1995	5.65%	-1.10%	0.89%	-0.75%	2.13%	1.40%	1.99%	-4.28%	9.21%
1996	9.68%	-6.32%	-0.76%	-0.08%	3.76%	1.03%	-0.65%	-2.87%	8.92%
1997	12.63%	-8.09%	-1.17%	-0.60%	2.78%	1.15%	0.54%	-3.42%	8.48%
1998	10.96%	-8.02%	-5.90%	-0.09%	1.38%	1.53%	4.16%	-5.68%	-1.51%
1999	11.06%	-2.56%	-6.10%	0.43%	-0.68%	1.91%	-7.58%	1.68%	5.27%
2000	11.00%	-6.17%	-8.61%	-0.18%	2.70%	2.26%	0.32%	-4.56%	1.07%
2001	-7.28%	15.96%	1.04%	-0.08%	-0.98%	2.12%	1.90%	-1.07%	5.88%
2002	-0.22%	22.85%	-3.80%	0.67%	1.81%	1.51%	4.29%	2.58%	11.60%
2003	5.87%	9.18%	-3.70%	0.99%	1.93%	1.90%	0.25%	3.37%	6.77%
2004	12.69%	-0.45%	-5.68%	0.11%	6.64%	2.33%	-0.01%	0.26%	10.52%
2005	11.83%	-5.64%	-5.23%	0.76%	0.77%	2.70%	-7.86%	-1.27%	7.40%
2006	6.67%	-5.50%	-2.80%	-1.56%	6.32%	2.29%	3.84%	-7.90%	8.03%

13 Each variable's contribution to the corporate profit growth rate is measured as the change in the variable divided by the initial value of corporate profits. For example, in 1991, the government budget deficit increased, and therefore, made a positive contribution to the growth in the rate in corporate profits. For 1991, each variable's contribution to the growth in corporate profits is given as: 8.35% = -6.20% + 7.02% +10.43 –(-.11%) +1.44% – .99% + 3.84% – (-.38%).

	Gross Domestic Private Investment	Government Budget Deficit	Current Account Balance	Government Capital Account Transactions (Net)	Net Dividends	Noncorporate Consumption of Fixed Capital	Personal Savings	Statistical Discrepancy	Corporate Profits
2007	-1.62%	4.62%	3.68%	0.96%	4.07%	1.36%	-0.95%	10.29%	-0.91%
2008	-9.79%	23.26%	1.19%	1.96%	-0.46%	0.46%	10.15%	3.66%	-2.05%
2009	-22.89%	33.17%	12.97%	3.11%	-9.80%	-0.53%	5.47%	-1.01%	6.41%
2010	8.44%	-1.07%	-2.43%	-2.38%	-0.40%	-0.16%	-1.42%	-0.99%	9.49%
2011	5.08%	-5.56%	-1.30%	-0.39%	5.11%	0.41%	2.93%	-3.20%	3.58%
2012	9.37%	-7.58%	0.46%	-1.05%	5.37%	0.51%	8.15%	-5.69%	5.69%
2013	5.16%	-18.13%	2.43%	-0.81%	2.17%	1.16%	-12.00%	0.86%	2.42%
2014	6.44%	-1.15%	-0.18%	0.04%	-2.11%	1.35%	1.00%	-1.14%	1.75%
Summary Statistics									
Obs	24	24	24	24	24	24	24	24	24
Mean	4.96%	1.58%	-1.19%	0.00%	1.67%	1.30%	0.64%	-0.62%	5.69%
Std. Dev.	8.91%	12.16%	5.05%	1.11%	3.33%	0.79%	5.32%	3.99%	3.97%
Min	-22.89%	-18.13%	-8.61%	-2.38%	-9.80%	-0.53%	-12.00%	-7.90%	-2.05%
Max	15.29%	33.17%	12.97%	3.11%	6.64%	2.70%	10.15%	10.29%	11.60%

6. Shares of Corporate Domestic Income

As described above, in Kalecki's (1968) theory of income determination, two factors drive the economy profits and distribution requirements to fulfill the level of profits. To illustrate changes in the corporate sector's functional distribution of income, corporate gross domestic income is defined as the sum of corporate national income, line 3-Table 1.13 of the NIPAs, plus corporate profits to the rest of the world, line 62-Table 1.13, and the corporate consumption of fixed capital, as described above. Dividing the corporate sector's compensation to employees, corporate profits, the corporation income tax, corporate net interest, and taxes on production and imports by corporate gross domestic income generates the various shares of corporate sector income. See Table 5 below.

Table 5. Shares or Corporate Sector Gross Domestic Income (NIPA Tables 1.12 and 1.13, authors' calculations).

Year	Compensation to Employees	Corporate Profits	Corporation Income Tax	Net Interest	Taxes on Production and Imports
1990	62.89%	20.46%	4.09%	3.59%	8.96%
1991	62.57%	21.80%	3.81%	2.44%	9.38%
1992	63.30%	21.52%	3.89%	1.88%	9.41%
1993	62.83%	21.75%	4.27%	1.77%	9.38%
1994	61.64%	22.79%	4.49%	1.57%	9.50%
1995	60.91%	23.57%	4.76%	1.54%	9.21%
1996	60.50%	24.26%	4.74%	1.44%	9.06%
1997	60.38%	24.60%	4.66%	1.78%	8.58%
1998	61.69%	22.82%	4.44%	2.40%	8.65%
1999	62.05%	22.67%	4.36%	2.37%	8.55%
2000	62.90%	21.35%	4.16%	2.93%	8.66%
2001	62.78%	22.60%	3.18%	2.66%	8.78%
2002	61.35%	25.25%	2.97%	1.66%	8.77%
2003	60.23%	26.14%	3.63%	1.30%	8.70%
2004	59.13%	27.33%	4.27%	0.55%	8.73%
2005	57.55%	27.41%	5.34%	0.94%	8.76%
2006	56.54%	27.79%	5.72%	1.45%	8.50%
2007	57.28%	26.70%	5.22%	2.02%	8.78%
2008	58.12%	26.30%	3.64%	2.76%	9.19%
2009	56.35%	29.19%	3.29%	1.93%	9.24%

Year	Compensation to Employees	Corporate Profits	Corporation Income Tax	Net Interest	Taxes on Production and Imports
2010	54.54%	30.57%	4.29%	1.50%	9.10%
2011	54.66%	30.29%	4.20%	1.65%	9.20%
2012	54.31%	30.35%	4.68%	2.19%	8.46%
2013	54.26%	30.13%	4.75%	2.19%	8.66%
2014	54.72%	29.36%	4.99%	2.20%	8.74%

Figure 17 shows how the profits share and wage shares of domestic corporation income have fluctuated over time. As is commonly understood, compensation to employees' share has trended down, profit's share has trended upwards.

Figure 17. Compensation to Employees and Corporate Profits Shares of Gross Corporate Domestic Income

Figure 18 shows a scatter of the relationship between the corporate compensation to employees' share and the corporate profits' share. In this diagram, we can see that the only time when compensation to employees' shares was increasing was in the mid to late 1990s and the period around the Great Recession and more recently in 2014.

Figure 18. Compensation to Employees and the Corporate Profits Shares

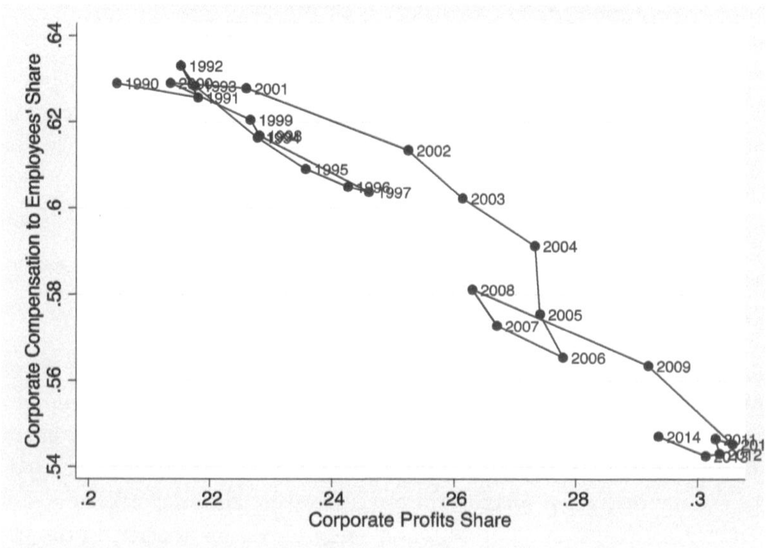

Figure 19. The Corporation Income Tax Share, the Corporate Net Interest Share and the Corporate Taxes on Production and Imports Share

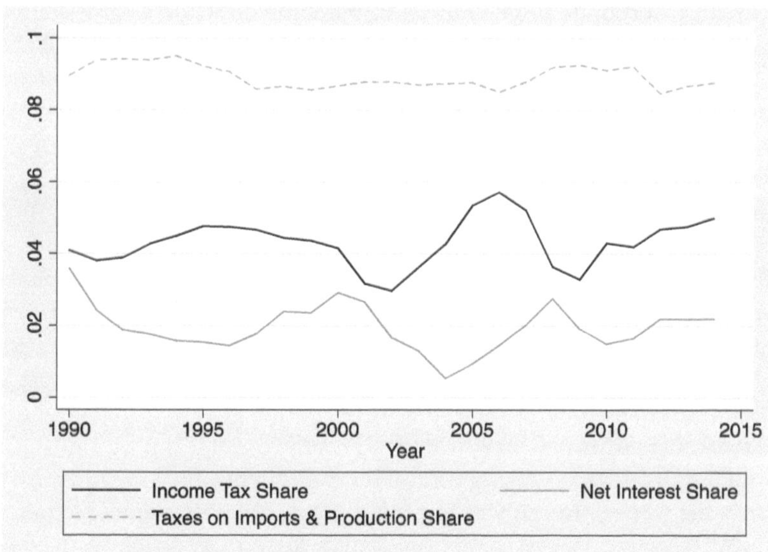

In Figure 19, the corporation production and imports tax share is relatively flat, while the corporation income tax share is pro-cyclical and the corporation net interest share seems to follow interest rate movements.

In the context of our Kaleckian approach, the falling wage share is a dampening factor on economic growth, and limits the effectiveness of countercyclical fiscal policy. When we consider the dampening effects of the falling government budget deficit on the growth in profits with the effects of the falling wage share, we can conclude that economic growth during the continued recovery from the Great Recession will be constrained by these two factors.

7. Conclusion

Ultimately, the importance of explaining corporate profits depends on the extent to which the economy's performance, growth, employment and unemployment can be linked to corporate profits. For the period of 1990 to 2005, while corporate income averaged about 60% of national income, corporate profits averaged over 66% of the net operating surplus, the variables were almost perfectly correlated with each other. Ultimately, growth and unemployment are tied to the performance of the corporate sector, specifically corporate sector profits. What we have attempted to present here is a review of the fluctuations in the variables that account for corporate profits.

Our main conclusions are as follows. First, in two periods, 1991 to 2007 and 2010 to 2014, corporate profits moved in the same direction as gross domestic private investment. Second, in three periods, 1991 to 2001, 2005 to 2007, and 2010 to 2014, corporate profits and the government budget deficit largely moved in opposite directions. Changes in the government budget deficit have played an important role in dampening changes in corporate profits. In response to the recessions of 1991, 2001 and 2007, the budget deficit increased, and dampened the fall in corporate profits. Third, the recent slow-down in corporate profits can be accounted for, in part, by the decline in the government budget deficit. Fourth, the deficit in the current account balance typically moved in the same direction as corporate profits (i.e.: corporate profits and the current account balance are typically moving in the opposite direction—in recent years that relationship seems to be breaking down. Fifth, the relationships between net dividends and corporate profits appears to be roughly stable during the period of 1991 to 2006, but breaks down thereafter. Sixth, personal savings are relatively stable during 1991 to 2005, but with the Great Recession, significant increases in personal savings arise with relatively flat to negative growth in profits, after corporate profits recover with some relatively larges swings in personal savings. Seventh, variations in the statistical discrepancy account for relatively large changes in corporate profits. Finally, the combination of a declining wage share and fiscal drag continue to limit the economic recovery from the Great Recession.

In conclusion, if we consider the long-period effects, where investment in capital goods brings new technologies to market, we expect that the slow-down in profits and incomes (via slack capacity utilizations) will dampen increases in investment and contribute to a secular decline in the economy's growth rate.

References

Asimakopulos, A. and Burbidge, J. B. (1974), "The short-period incidence of taxation." *Economic Journal*, 84, 267–288.

Giovannoni, Oliver and Paguez, Alain (2007), "What drives profits? An income spending model," in *Money, Distribution and Economic Policy*, eds. Hein, Eckhard and Truger, Achiem, North Hampton, MA. Edward Elgar.

Kalecki, M. (1968), *Theory of Economic Dynamics,* New York, Monthly Review Press.

Kalecki, M. (1971/1937), "A theory of commodity, income and capital taxation." *Economic Journal*, 47, 444–450 in *Selected Essays on the Dynamics of the Capitalist Economy,* Cambridge, Cambridge University Press.

Kalecki, M. (1971/1943), "Political aspects of full employment." *Political Quarterly*, in *Selected Essays on the Dynamics of the Capitalist Economy,* Cambridge, Cambridge University Press.

Kalecki, M. (1971/1968), "Trend and business cycles reconsidered," *Economic Journal*, 78, 263–276, in *Selected Essays on the Dynamics of the Capitalist Economy,* Cambridge, Cambridge University Press.

Laramie, A. J. (1991) "Taxation and Kalecki's distribution factors", *Journal of Post Keynesian Economics*, 4, 583–594.

Laramie, A. J. and Mair, D. (2000) *A Dynamic Theory of Taxation,* Northampton, MA, Edward Elgar.

Laramie, A. J., Mair, D., and Reynolds, P. J. (2004) "Kalecki's theory of income distribution: the answer to a maiden's prayer?" in *Contemporary Post Keynesian Analysis*, eds Wray, L. R. and Forstater, M., Northampton, MA, Edward Elgar.

Levy, S. J. and Levy, D. A. (1983) *Profits and the Future of American Society*, New York, Harper and Row.

Mair, Douglas, Laramie, Anthony J. Toporowski, Jan (2000) "Weintraub's consumption coefficient: some economic implications and evidence for the UK," 24, *Cambridge Journal of Economics*, 225–236.

Mair, Douglas, Laramie, Anthony J. Toporowski, Jan (2000) "Weintraub's consumption coefficient," 26, *Cambridge Journal of Economics*, 659–662.

Mair, Douglas, Laramie, Anthony J. (2002) "Full Employment: Gift Horse or Trojan Horse?" Review of Social Economy, LX, 567–593.

Sawyer, M. C. (1985) *The Economics of Michal Kalecki*, London, Macmillan.

Weintraub, Sidney (1979) "Generalizing Kalecki and simplifying macroeconomics," *Journal of Post Keynesian Economics*, 3, 101–106.

Douglas Mair, Heriot-Watt University, Edinburgh, UK
Anthony J. Laramie, Merrimack College, MA, USA

Chapter 8: Kalecki and Fisher: Income and Capital Taxation

Abstract: Both Irving Fisher and Michal Kalecki published seminal articles on tax policy in 1937. Fisher formalized his theories of income and capital and illustrated their practical implications for tax policy. Fisher concluded, after considering charges and credits to various types of capital, that a person's was psychical, and that the best approximation of psychical income, for tax purposes, was consumption. Kalecki explicitly considered the economic incidence and effects of taxes. In doing so, Kalecki showed that all taxes potentially affect the flow of income to capital, and the value of capital, as Fisher defines it. An important implication of Kalecki's analysis is that expenditure taxes on wage goods poses a double incidence: reduces workers' incomes and capital income (and capital values)—a point overlooked by Fisher. Moreover, profits taxes and capital taxes need not affect the aggregate flow of income to capital or capital value if such taxes are used to finance government expenditures—these taxes do affect the distribution of capital flows and capital values between rentiers and capitalists.

1. Introduction

Perhaps it is with some historical irony that Kalecki published his famous paper on "Commodity, Income and Capital Taxation" (1937) the same year as Fisher reformalized his theory of income, capital and taxation ("Income in Theory, Income Taxation in Practice"). Fisher published his fifty-three-page monograph in *Econometrica*, while Kalecki published his seven-page article in the *Economic Journal*. Both Kalecki and Fisher, for better or worse, are rigorous and make explicit assumptions about their theories of income and taxation. Fisher and Kalecki both engage, as Veblen (2002/1908) describes of Fisher, in ratiocination: both lay out exact analysis based on initial premises. Fisher concludes that we can generally deduce incomes from charges and credits to various types of capital, and from an analysis of these various types of charges and credits, various types of income, including psychic, money, and real can be deduced. Fisher's taxonomy of capital and income is clear that capital/property is an asset that produces a future stream of services. Most of these future streams are reflected in money flows. Fisher is quick to point out that any money flow converted into property is capital as it then produces a future stream of income. Any taxation of capital, therefore, is a tax not simply on capital values today, but also a tax on future incomes. Fisher, as a result, was an advocate for exempting savings from taxation (a flow converted into property) as it would result in the "double" taxation of capital/property, and the value of capital, and the reason for investment, would diminish. To avoid this double taxation, Fisher favored a consumption tax, as consumption was the best, theoretically consistent, measure of real income. Kalecki, in contrast to Fisher, explicitly considered the economic incidence of taxation. Kalecki, under the conditions where workers spend what they earn and capitalists earn what they spend, and assuming a balanced government budget constraint, concludes that consumption taxes essentially redistribute income between wage earners and those on the government dole without affecting the aggregate levels of incomes. Kalecki then considers the effect of taxes on profits and capital. Profit taxes essentially have two effects. First, additional profits taxes will raise the rate of interests and expose businesses/borrowers to increasing risks. Second, additional profits taxes will increase government expenditures and increase business revenues sufficiently to offset the negative income effects of the profits tax. The result is that the main drawback of the profits tax is the increase in borrowing costs. Finally, Kalecki analyzed the effects of a capital tax. Kalecki showed that the capital tax essentially has the same effects as the profits tax, with the exception of the first effect. Kalecki, in a striking contrast to Fisher, concluded that the capital tax is the preferred method of taxation. Capital taxation stimulates employment and production without raising the interest rate and borrowing costs, and without reducing after-tax profits. Essentially the difference between Kalecki and Fisher can be summed up in two words: "economic incidence." Fisher, while never explicitly doing so, equates the legal and economic incidence of taxation. Kalecki draws clear distinctions between the two.

In this paper, we review Fisher's theory of income, capital and taxation. We recognize it as the progenitor of the hybrid or dual tax system. We review a sampling of reactions to it. Then we explain Kalecki's theory of consumption, income and capital taxation, and consider some reactions to Kalecki's analysis. Next, we consider the implications of Kalecki's analysis for Fisher theory of income, capital and taxation. We conclude that had Fisher understood or appreciated Kalecki's contributions, Fisher would have understood that all taxes are potentially capital taxes, and that income taxes and capital taxes need not be taxes on capital, as defined by Fisher, at all!

2. Fisher's Income, Capital, and Taxation: Definitions and Assumptions

Fisher's theories of income, capital and taxation have received attention at both the theoretical and practical levels of analysis. The purpose of this section is to review Fisher's theories of income and capital, and then explore implications for income tax policy. In doing so, we largely focus on Fisher's (1937) exposition of the subjects.

Preliminary Definitions and Assumptions: Graves (1939, p. 349) gives a nice summary of Fisher's definitions:

> **Income** is defined as "a flow of services through a period of time," where services are the benefits of wealth.
> "**Capital** as a quantity of wealth existing at a particular instant of time,"
> and consists of material objects owned by human beings.

Income, therefore, necessarily, as explained below, excludes the changes in capital. Changes in capital represent changes in (the expectation) of future income. **Earnings** are defined as capital appreciation plus monetary payments.

To illustrate **monetary payments** from capital, Fisher (1937) introduced Figure 1, p. 9, to illustrate his various concepts that, for example, distinguish between monetary payments and earnings. Instead of repeating Figure 1, we briefly consider a representative numerical example. In our numerical example, a quantity of capital, defined by its present value, produces a stream of services from year zero through year ten (for eleven periods). This capital produces various variable and known monetary payments, M, to its owner in each year. At any given time period, the present value of capital is the present value of the discounted future monetary payments. The presence of capital gains or capital losses is a consequence of the pattern of future monetary payments. Assuming that the capital has a defined life, where monetary payments cease thereafter, the capital gains generated by the asset are transitory. To calculate the present value, a fixed and known discount rate is assumed (see Table 1).

In time period zero, the capital is acquired from "earnings," and, therefore, the capital's value, initial gain, reflects an expenditure of earnings. In each subsequent period, the present value of the asset and the resulting capital gains (loss) is calculated based on the future stream of monetary payments. As shown in Table 1, given that the monetary payments are relatively high in the future, the capital appreciates in value the closer the timing of those payments. However, once the relatively high monetary payments are paid out, the capital loses value. Again, given the defined life of the capital, the capital gains are transitory (add up to zero). Fisher uses this example to illustrate that capital gains, while earnings, are not income but (the expectation of) future income.

Table 1. Illustration of Capital Values, C, Monetary Payments, M, Capital Gains, and Earnings (M + Capital Gains). The discount rate is 10%.

time	M	C	Capital Gains	Earnings
0	$0	$129.58	$129.58	$129.58
1	10	132.53	2.96	12.96
2	12	133.79	1.25	13.25
3	12	135.17	1.38	13.38
4	12	136.68	1.52	13.52
5	16	134.35	-2.33	13.67
6	16	131.79	-2.56	13.44
7	50	94.97	-36.82	13.18
8	40	64.46	-30.50	9.50
9	30	40.91	-23.55	6.45
10	45	0.00	-40.91	4.09
Sum of Capital Gains			0.00	

After this illustration, Fisher (1937) considers a number of special cases including the perpetual annuity, bonds, one period M case, and the savings bank deposit case. Then "The Norms for Money from Investment" are discussed. In accounting practices, the perpetuity is considered the normal case. Accountants, therefore, set up sinking funds, to maintain an investment, or the capital, in perpetuity. For example, as Fisher (1937) describes, a bond sold at premium will not recover the initial capital outlay upon maturity, and a sinking fund is required to maintain the initial capital over the life of the investment. Some of the interest earnings are thus reinvested, via the sinking fund, to maintain the value of the initial investment in perpetuity. The same is true for a mining company, to maintain the value of the initial outlay in perpetuity for the mining resource, a sinking fund, a depletion allowance, is maintained through the earnings of the mining company. In contrast, if a bond is sold at a discount, using the same accounting standard of maintaining the investment in perpetuity, the "bondholder is entitled some of the "income"" in excess of the interest payments, realized for example in selling some of the bond (Fisher 1937, p. 14). In common practice, depleting capital is stigmatized and accumulating capital, for example through the gains described above, is favored. Fisher (1937, pp. 15, 16) stresses that these accounting practices are byproducts of the habitual forms of life. To maintain habitual consumption patterns, steady flows of monetary payments must be maintained.

Next, Fisher (1937, pp. 17–19) considers the "factor of chance." Here Fisher recognizes that the determinants of capital values, for example monetary payments and the discount rates, are subject to chance. Fisher (1937, p. 16) laments at the lack of progress in developing a "realistic and useable… probability factor." Fisher points out that the probability factor makes capital gains and the value of the corporation ambiguous. The corporation will have a book value based on historical costs and market value based on the expectations of the chance factors affecting future monetary payments and earnings. Fisher modifies his calculations of present values, etc., according to an "X" factor, where the X factor is the ratio of the "calculated" (based on the calculations used to determine change) capital value to actual (historic cost) capital value (Fisher, 1937, p 17).

To transition into the definition of income, Fisher discusses money from labor (Fisher, 1937, pp. 19–22). Fisher characterizes calculations of the capital value of labor as "curiosities and [of] little practical applications except possibly as a check sometimes on over-insurance of a person's life" (Fisher, 1937, p. 19). Fisher compares the accounting for salaries and wages with accounting for income from capital. If the accounting standard was to maintain the capital value of labor, in perpetuity, like that of a corporation, only a small part of monetary payments for an elderly person, with a shortened lifespan, could be considered income. A large portion of the monetary payments would need to be sunk into the human capital depletion fund to maintain human capital in perpetuity. Moreover, supporting children with money from labor is a reinvestment of human capital, and accumulated savings of money payments from labor could then be transferred "to keep up, from one generation to the next, the capital value of the family's labor power" (Fisher, 1937, p. 21). Fisher concludes, "savings when taken out of income are no longer income but capital (Fisher 1937, p. 23). This statement sets the stage for defining income as the summation of the flow of services generated by various assets.

Defining Income(s). Fisher (1937, pp. 23, 24) defines a person's income, I, as the sum of services generated by a person's assets. He defines income, for a given time period, assuming all components can be expressed in money terms, as:

$$I = (\Sigma Mr - \Sigma Md) + (\Sigma Mw - \Sigma Yn) + (\Sigma R - \Sigma Ms) + (\Sigma Yp - \Sigma R) + m + U; \tag{1}$$

where (see Graves, 1939, p. 350):

ΣMr = money received from investment property (including proceeds from sales)

ΣMd = money disbursed on investment property (including purchases of investments)

ΣMw = money received from work
ΣYn = negative psychical services associated with work
ΣR = money value of "real" services of consumption goods
ΣMs = money spent on consumption goods.
ΣYp = positive psychical services generated by consumption goods
$m = \Sigma Mcr - \Sigma Mdb$ = money spent from cash assets, ΣMcr, less money added to cash assets, ΣMdb
U = unclassified

The first term in brackets represents the monetary services generated by capital investments. The second term represents the services generated by work, the third term represents the real value of consumption goods, the fourth term is psychical satisfactions generated by the consumption goods, the fifth term, m, is the "net value received from all cash assets" (using cash, the credit to the cash account, is a positive service provided by cash, holding cash, the debit to the cash account, is a negative service provided by cash), and the sixth term U consists of many self cancelling items, like the net value of self-done work (Fisher, 1937, pp. 25, 26).

Assuming $U = 0$, and given that $\Sigma Mdb = \Sigma Mr + \Sigma Mw$, and $\Sigma Mcr = Md + Ms$, equation (1), the expression for income, reduces to:

(1') $I = \Sigma Yp - \Sigma Yn$.[1]

In other words, as Graves (1939, p. 350) writes "income becomes ipso facto the algebraic sum of psychical services." The trick then is to come up with some measure of the value of these psychical services.

Graves (1939, p. 350) provides a nice summary of how the trick is achieved. Assume psychical services are measureable, the value of negative psychical services is zero, positive psychical services correspond one-to-one with the money value of real services generated by consumption goods, the value ΣYp is the value of SR, and the money value of the service equals the money spent on the services. As Graves sums up:

(2) $I = \Sigma Yp - \Sigma Yn = I = \Sigma Yp = \Sigma R = \Sigma Ms$.

From this definition of income, Fisher (1937, p. 36) develops a best approximation of income for tax purposes; i.e.:

(3) $Iba = \Sigma Ms + c$;

1 Notice that Fisher does not attribute any current psychical income to the value of capital owned by a person, and to the security and status it provides.

where ΣMs = (ΣMr – ΣMd) + ΣMw + m, and c = use-cost discrepancy.[2] The use-cost discrepancy is the difference between the value of the good consumed in the period and the costs of the good. Fisher concludes that the use-cost discrepancy matters mostly for three goods—housing, automobiles, and household fixtures and appliances (and other goods, for practical purposes) can be ignored.

Fisher (1937) contends that this definition of income provides four basic benefits:

1) It is easy to administer and enforce. Putting aside use-cost discrepancy, a person's accounting records easily reveal net investment receipts and money receipts from labor. These receipts plus the change in the cash balance gives total spending.

2) It avoids the double taxation of savings caused by the income tax. Fisher illustrates that the income tax taxes savings when earned and then taxes the earnings from savings. Fisher (1937, pp. 47 and 48) uses the example of three brothers each who receive $100,000 in lump sum. Assuming an interest rate of 5% and a tax rate of 1%, Brother A spends only the interest. Brother A earns $5000 in interest, spends $5000 per year, and pays a tax of $50 per year. In perpetuity, the present value of the tax is $1000 (=$50/.05). Brother B has zero spending for fourteen years. As a result, the principal doubles in value to $200,000. Thereafter, from year fifteen on, in perpetuity, Brother B spends the interest on $200,000 ($10,000), and pays taxes of $100 per year. The present value of the Brother B's taxes at the end of year fourteen is $2000 (100/.05), while the present value of those year fifteen-plus taxes in year zero is $1000. While the present value of taxes paid in years zero to fourteen is $750. Brother B, despite having the same present value of income, because he saves some interest income in the early years, has a higher present value of taxation than Brother A. Brother C spends $20,000 each year exhausting the $100,000 in six years. Brother C's consumption lowers his interest income and taxation, and, therefore, Brother C, with the same initial capital of Brothers A and B, pays less in taxes.

By implication, Fisher concludes that the double taxation of savings violates the criteria for lifetime horizontal equity—where persons with the same lifetime incomes pay different lifetime income taxes. Fisher illustrates that had taxable income been defined as his measure of 'real' income (i.e. consumption), then each of the brothers would have the same present value of taxation of $1000. Moreover, income taxation encourages consumption and discourages savings.

---

2 Fisher (1937, p. 35) defines five different types of income: 1) Psychical income: I = ΣYp – ΣYn; 2) Real Income = ΣR; 3) Total Spending ΣMs = (ΣMr – ΣMd) + ΣMw + m; 4) Money Income = (ΣMr – ΣMd) + ΣMw, and 5) Best Approximation of Real Income = ΣMs = (ΣMr – ΣMd) + ΣMw + m + c.

3) It avoids the capitalization of the income tax that results in a decline in the value of capital. To illustrate, consider the case of a perpetuity that generates annual monetary payments of M, and the discount rate is i, its present value use is $C_o = M/i$. Now introduce the income tax, where t_m is the tax rate applied to M. The present value of capital is now reduced to: $C'_o = M(1-t_m)/i$ or $C'o = M/(i/1-t_m))$— the tax rate increases the effective discount rate and reduces the value of capital.[3]

4) It eliminates the triple and quadruple effects of taxation of corporate income when corporate profits, dividends and capital gains are taxed. As has been well written elsewhere (for example, see Shoven and Walley (2005)), the taxation of corporation income coupled with taxes on dividends, when saved, produces three levels of taxation: taxation of the corporation income, taxation of the future earnings of the savings, and taxation of the dividends.[4] The fourth level of taxation is the taxation of capital gains.

3. Some Reactions to Fisher's Theory of Income and Capital Taxation

The reactions to Fisher's theory of income and capital taxation are varied. Here we limit our brief survey to Graves (1939), Veblen (2002/1908), Tobin (2005), Shoven and Whalley (2005), Auerbach (2005), and Graetz (2005).

Graves (1939) raises a number of important issues. First, why is negative psychical income, Yn, ignored? It can't be any harder to measure than positive psychical income, Yp. Moreover, the exclusion of savings and capital gains from the definition of income is "contrary to the social objectives of personal income taxes" (Graves, 1939, p. 351). Second, Graves considers the issue of double taxation of savings quite literally, in the sense that savings are taxed at a rate that is 200% of the consumption tax (as opposed savings being taxed twice, once when earned and again when the savings, once invested, earn income). Savings are taxed double the income tax rate when savings are never spent, the income tax rate remains constant, and the expenditure tax remains zero. Graves then shows that Fisher's

---

3 The income tax, as described below, also increases the risk of failure as Kalecki (1937) and Kaldor (1958, p. 102, fn) describe.

4 Fisher (1937, p. 52) also explained the effects of taxation on corporate retained earnings. A tax of 50% on undistributed profits of $100,000 reduces the funds to be reinvested in the business to $50,000. With less funds for reinvestment, less profits are earned and retained. The result is that government continuously takes 50% of a smaller and smaller pool of profits, until corporations "will be merely holding property to earn taxes for the government."

conclusion, that an expenditure tax avoids the double taxation of savings, is a special case where the expenditure tax rate remains constant over time, and savings are never spent. The spending of savings, some years in the future, reduces the relative tax rate of saving (to the tax rate on expenditures) to a factor less than two. Furthermore, if savings are never spent, and no income tax exists, but if the consumption tax rate varies over time, the effective tax rates on savings (capital) varies. If consumption tax rate increases over time, the effective tax rate on capital rises. Finally, Graves (1939, p. 354) does not show that double taxation of savings represents an "impediment to progress… the validity of [which] is a function of one's views regarding possible patterns of progress."

Veblen (2002/1908) recognized Fisher's (2011/1906) work as contributing to the taxonomy of capital and income, but criticizes the work for being little more than that, while simultaneously, failing on other fronts. In particular, """immaterial wealth" or intangible assets"" are excluded from Fisher's definition of capital (Veblen, 2002/1908: p. 3).[5] The presence of immaterial wealth or intangible assets give rise to more than one measure capital, as is common in business practices. For example, the value of a firm can be both measured at book value and at market value. The blending of tangible and intangible assets into the capitalization of wealth creates claims of ownership, serves as the basis for credit extensions, and increases the aggregate claims of creditors beyond the ability debtors to satisfy those claims during times of economic declines and wide-scale liquidations. Capital gains, therefore, do not simply reflect actual future earnings, but reflect guesses of expected future earnings, where winners and losers necessarily result. In short, Veblen presages some of the Keynesian criticisms of financial theory, for example, as described by Davidson (1982–83), where the value of capital cannot be reduced to a certain outcome or to a deterministic outcome of some probabilistic process.

Stepping back from Veblen, Tobin (2005) cites Schumpeter's praise of Fisher's *Theory of Income and Capital* (1906) as one of his three great works. In contrast to Veblen, Fisher's is more than about classification, but also creates new economic theory with its significant achievement being "the distinction between stocks and flows" (Tobin, 2005, p. 209). For example, as evidenced by Adam Smith's title *The Wealth of Nations*, is wealth a stock or a flow? In addition, Smith conflates stocks and flows in the text where "part of the "stock" is invested to yield profits, while

---

5 According to Veblen (1908/2002, p. 3); "… various immaterial items of wealth classed as intangible assets counts for more and more in the conduct of affairs; and any theory that aims to deal with the actualities of modern businesses will have to make its peace with the term or terms by which these elements of capital are called, however wrong-headed a habit it may be conceived to be."

another part pays wages (Tobin, 2005, p. 210). Tobin recognizes Fisher's contribution to the study risk preferences, "coefficients of caution" but that he did not integrate his theory of risk into his theory of capital valuations. Tobin explains that Fisher, through double entry bookkeeping, defines social capital—the net worth of all individuals once intermediary claims are washed out—and that the income from social capital is income (albeit psychical income). Finally, Tobin questions Fisher's measure of psychical income as consumption—"the implication being "that a wealthy household or society has a low income in periods when it chooses to live frugally and accumulate capital and a high income in periods when it is depleting its capital, is difficult to swallow" (Tobin, 2005, p. 212). For that reason, an alternative definition of income gained wider acceptance for tax purposes—that being the Haig-Marshall concept of income (consumption consistent with maintaining capital intact).

Shoven and Whalley (2005) give a more typical modern day presentation of Fisher. To that end, Shoven and Walley are concerned about economic distortions generated by the double, triple and even quadruple taxation of corporation income through the taxation of savings, corporate profits, dividends and capital gains. Moreover, once we become concerned about equity in taxation, the relevant tax period has to be considered. To promote horizontal equity, taxpayers with equal (present values of income) lifetime incomes should pay equal taxes. Assuming each taxpayer consumes all of his or her lifetime income, then the best way to ensure equal lifetime taxes, and promote horizontal equity, is to tax lifetime consumption. Taxing consumption promotes economic efficiency and promotes horizontal equity. Taxing consumption is best achieved with a spending tax or a net cash flow tax—where net cash flow is the sum of net cash receipts from businesses (dividends, rents, net interest receipts, receipts from loan repayments less lendings, borrowings less repayments from loans, cash received from sales of investments less cash paid out in purchases of investments, cash from windfalls, net cash from other sources), net cash receipts from work plus the decline in the cash balance, less certain deductions (for example, other taxes paid, certain insurance premiums, certain health care costs, etc.) (Shoven and Whalley, 2005, pp. 221, 222).

Shoven and Whalley (2005, p. 223) term the early reactions to Fisher as "strange," while ignoring Veblen (2002/1908) and Graves (1939), reporting that the reactions either ignored the substance of Fisher's proposal (Simon, 1938; Vickery 1939) or misunderstood the logic of Fisher's argument (Musgrave, 1939; Slitor 1973). Shoven and Whalley (2005) mention that public finance economists were interested in broadening the tax base to lower tax rates, and exempting savings from taxation was viewed as counter-productive to that goal.

Shoven and Whalley (2005) recognize that Kaldor (1955) embraced an expenditure tax. Kaldor saw the consumption tax as a means to cut through the fog of defining a reasonable measure of taxable capacity. Kaldor, for example, mentions the difficulties in taxing accruals, or taxing capital gains, the differential tax treatment of different types of savings, the incentive to save, and the incentive for entrepreneurship. The consumption tax allows individuals to reveal their taxable capacity. Without expressing a particular macro theory, Kaldor argues that high consumption tax rates, for example on capitalist consumption, will encourage capital investment and savings (the causal order of which is not discussed). Jacoby (1957, pp. 518, 519), while appreciating the logic of Kaldor, cites in detail the aforementioned concerns of Simon (1938): 1) The problems of measuring current income will be compounded by having to measure net savings; 2) The tax base would be too narrow; 3) Problems coordinating inheritance and spending taxes; and 4) Obtaining the progressivity of the income tax system would require surtaxes on high levels of consumption in excess of 100%.

Auerbach (2005) summarizes the efficiency, distributional and savings effects of the consumption tax. First, consumption taxes are seen as contributing to economic efficiency, but the efficiency and distribution effects are inter-related. The introduction of a consumption tax increases the relative tax burden of the elderly (who spend a larger percent of their money receipts). Auerbach (2005, p. 239) reports that his simulations with Kotlikoff (Auerbach and Kotlikoff 1987) show that adopting a consumption tax "while maintaining the same degree of progressivity… and protecting asset values in the transition" will cause a loss in the potential efficiency gains of the tax. Auerbach mentions the importance of the tax period in defining the ability to pay (one period vs. several periods). He also mentions implicitly the role of psychic income associated with capital accumulation. Wealth accumulation can lead to more than future income, which is covered by future consumption taxes. It also leads to psychic income, status, which is untaxed, and it can lead to tax avoidance schemes. Fisher, as Auerbach describes, favored inheritance or estate taxes to achieve progressivity, but these taxes remain politically unpopular. As an alternative to achieve progressivity, large consumption tax exemptions could be utilized.

Finally, Auerbach (2005, p. 240) recognizes that many prefer the consumption tax as a means to encourage national savings, but it is not clear that "this should be an end in itself." The resulting substitution effect shifts the tax burden from savers to consumers, rich to poor, young to old. Moreover, if the consumption tax places all forms of savings on equal footing (for example discretionary savings and defined contribution plans), then what effect will the consumption tax have on the overall level of savings?

Graetz (2005) considers the contributions of Fisher (being ahead of his time in articulating rationale for and the implementation of the consumption tax) and examines some problematic issues (tax treatments covered by social insurance protections, other politically favored tax treatments, and defining the relevant tax period, given the short-term aspects of the political process). Graetz (2005) tells a nice anecdote about fairness indicating that the public's view of tax fairness is quite universal. People with the same (pre-savings) income should pay the same taxes, and that persons with higher incomes should not only pay higher taxes, but also pay higher tax rates. The result is that consumption tax proposals will be considered unfair and politically unfeasible.

Given the political unfeasibility of the consumption tax, those who advocate consumption taxes will sell their tax proposals as "income" tax proposals. Doing so, of course, has lowered tax rates on income from capital (lowered tax rates on capital gains and dividends, for example as seen in Economic Growth and Tax Reconciliation Act of 2001, The Jobs and Growth Tax Reconciliation Act of 2003, and The American Tax Payer Relief Act of 2012), and has created what has now been commonly referred to as the "dual tax" system (where labor income is taxed a higher rate than capital income). Fisher's ideas continue to seep into the tax system through "reforms" and through "economic growth" and "job creation" acts.

4. Kalecki's Theory of Commodity, Income and Capital Taxation

Kalecki (1937) and Fisher (1937) share one thing in common: the ability to articulate a clear argument based on an initial set of assumptions, but that is where the similarities between the two end. The main differences between Kalecki and Fisher are fourfold: 1) Kalecki uses far fewer words than Fisher; 2) In all of Fisher's discussion, (and in much of the discussion of others that follows his work) there is little or no mention of the economic incidence of taxation. Fisher and others seem to conflate the legal incidence and economic incidence of taxes. 3) Kalecki, while writing in the context of the Great Depression, acknowledges the significance of Keynes, while Fisher does not. As Veblen (2002/1908) recognizes, Fisher continues to write in the Austrian tradition; and 4) Fisher's work has gained a much wider influence on the development of tax policy. This influence is evidenced in development of the dual systems and the preferred tax treatment given to income from capital.

In this section, we consider the implications of Kalecki's theory of the incidence and effects of taxation on Fisher's theory of income, capital and taxation. We will first review Kalecki's (1937) paper, and then we discuss how various taxes, in light of Kalecki's work, affect capital values.

5. Kalecki's (1937) "A theory of commodity, income and capital taxation"

Kalecki (1937, p. 344) begins his theory by first acknowledging the significance of Keynes' *General Theory* "for the inquiry into the theory of taxation." If an economy operates with excess capacity, and prices are determined by unit costs and (fixed) price-cost markups, then income effects explain the economic incidence and effects of taxation. Kalecki illustrates these effects under a restrictive set of assumptions. Maintaining the excess capacity assumptions while relaxing, for example, the price assumptions, still gives prominence to the income effects in explaining the role of taxation in the economy (see, for example, Laramie and Mair, 2000).

Vecchi (2008, pp. 167, 168), who refers to Kalecki's work as "pioneering," spells out Kalecki's (1937) assumptions (which we paraphrase here):

1) Consumption taxes and income taxes are levied on wage goods and on capitalist income respectively.
2) Money wage rates are given and workers do not save.
3) The economic system is closed with surpluses of all types of labor and equipment.
4) The money supply is elastic.
5) Capitalists do not consume wage goods, and their consumption is unaffected by changes in current income.
6) Investment is fixed by past investment decisions.

In addition to these assumptions, Kalecki assumes that all tax revenues are used to finance the doles of the unemployed, maintaining a balanced budget constraint, and that the economy is closed. Under these circumstances, aggregate gross (of depreciation) business profits are the sum of business investment expenditures and capitalist consumption, i.e.: $P = I_g + Csp$,[6] where I_g = gross investment expenditures and Csp = capitalist consumption.

---

6 Kalecki derives this expression from the National Income and Product Accounts. To simplify, assume $Y = E$, where Y = GDP expressed in income, and E = GDP expressed in expenditures, and that $Y = W + Tw + P + Tp$, and $E = Cs + I_g + G + Ex - IM$, where Cs = personal consumption, I_g = gross investment expenditures, G = government

Given these assumptions, the effect of consumption taxes on wage goods is to redistribute income from employed workers to unemployed workers without affecting the wage bill or the levels of spending and incomes. Taxes on capitalist incomes, profits, increase the consumption of the unemployed while increasing business revenues, leaving profits unchanged. The drawback to taxing profits, as explained by Kalecki, is that lenders in response to the income tax will require a higher yield in compensation for the income tax. The higher cost of funds exposes businesses to increasing risk of failure, which, in turn dampens investment.[7] In contrast, a capital tax "on every type of capital owned" (Kalecki, 1937, p.449) has the same effect as the profits tax but does not increase the rate of interest, because the same tax is paid, to quote Kalecki (1937, pp. 449, 450):

> if someone borrows money [or ventures by his own means] and builds a factory, he does not increase his own capital by this action and does not pay a greater capital tax… In the same way, everybody is willing to lend at the current rate of interest; for whether he lends money or not does not affect the capital tax he pays.

Kalecki (1937, p. 450) concludes that a capital tax:

is perhaps the best way to stimulate employment. It has all the merits of financing the State expenditures by borrowings, but it is distinguished from borrowings by the advantage of the State not becoming indebted.

6. Refinements and Extensions to Kalecki

Kalecki's theory of income and capital taxation received little attention until Asimakopulos (1975). Asimakopulos (1975) utilized a Keynesian, as opposed to a Kaleckian, model of income determination with different price assumptions, flexible vs. inflexible, with different supply assumptions, fixed and variable. Laramie

---

purchases, Ex = exports, and Im = imports. Solving for P and adding and subtracting government transfer payments, Tr, on the right-hand side yields: $P = I_g + [G+Tr - Tw - Tp] + [Ex\text{-}IM] + [C - Tw - Tr]$. Defining C = Csp + Csw + Cstr, where Csp = capitalist consumption, Csw = worker consumption, and Cstr = consumption of transfer payments. Further assuming the balance budget constraint, a closed economy and that W =Csw and Tr – Cstr, yields: $P = I_g + Csp$. As Kalecki (1965) explains, the profit equation is more than identity, it is a causal equation, with causality moving from right to left, because capitalists cannot determine how much in profits they earn, but they can determine their expenditures.

7 If the interest rate is initially 3%, and a 20% tax rate is imposed, a lender's after-tax return is 3% -.20*3% = 2. 4%. If the **lender** wants to keep the after-tax rate of return at 3%, then the lender must raise the lending rate to 3.75 to maintain the 3% yield.

and Mair (2000) integrate Kalecki (1937) into Kalecki's theories of income determination, pricing, investment, and long-term economic growth, for different government budget constraints. In doing so, Laramie and Mair (2000) refined and extended Kalecki's conclusions. Laramie and Mair (2000) explain that, in a closed economy, or with an economy with a balance of trade, maintaining the assumption that investment is fixed by past decisions, the effects of taxation depend on four sets of effects: 1) changes in the composition and level of the government budget stance in reaction to the taxation; 2) the extent to which a tax affects consumption out of profits, capitalist consumption; 3) the extent to which a tax affects savings out of wages, worker savings; and 4) the extent to which the tax is shifted through a change in business price-cost markups. We briefly consider their story for each of the taxes, wage goods tax, profits tax and a capital tax. To simplify, we will assume that each tax increase is used to reduce the government budget deficit.

An increase in the tax on wage goods, unshifted, reduces workers' disposable income and reduces workers' spending, and decreases business revenues and profits. The reduction in profits, via an income multiplier, reduces national income and employment. If the tax is completely financed by a reduction in workers' consumption, then, in the short-period (when investment is fixed by past expenditures), business profits decline, as worker consumption declines relative to the wage bill, by the full amount of the tax. The result is *a double incidence of the tax* where both owners of capital and labor bear the burden of the tax! Fisher ignored, and mainstream economists have continued to ignore, the double incidence of expenditure taxes. If workers finance some of the tax by reducing their savings, the negative effects of the tax are dampened. However, with the assumption that the propensity to save out wages is low, this dampening effect is expected to be quite small. If workers shift the tax, for example, by seeking higher pre-tax wage rates, two possible effects can result: 1) Prices will increase, and the real spending of workers will be unaffected by the higher money wage rates; and 2) Price-cost markups will decrease, and real spending of workers will increase, dampening the negative effects of the wage tax increase. If the market power of workers is small, the decrease in the price-cost markup and the dampening effects are likely to be quite small. These small dampening effects, through the change in disposable income's effect on worker savings or the effects of changes in business price-cost markups on worker savings, reinforce Kalecki's (1937) original conclusion that the effects of taxes on wage goods largely depend on the government budget stance.

An increase in the profits tax or a capital tax to reduce a budget deficit reduces business after-tax profits, assuming investment is given in the short-period, and capitalist consumption is unaffected by the reduction in after-tax profits, national income and workers' income are unaffected by the tax. Under these conditions, the profits tax or capital tax generate a single, as opposed to a double, tax incidence. These short-term effects are modified to the extent to which: 1) capitalist consumption responds to changes in the profits tax; and 2) businesses increase their price-costs markups to shift the tax. If capitalist consumption falls, the effects of the profits or capital taxes become negative, and national income and workers' incomes decrease. If capitalists are able to shift the profits or capital tax, business price-cost markups increase and workers' real income, consumption and savings decrease, dampening the fall in after-tax profits, while decreasing national income and employment. If capitalist consumption and price-cost markups are largely insensitive to changes in the profits or capital tax, then, the insights derived from Kalecki's original (1937) work are largely correct. However, we note, as Laramie and Mair (2000) show, the longer-period effects play out as the change in profits affects businesses' investment decisions, giving rise to dynamic tax incidence effects.

7. Kalecki's Implications for Fisher's Theory of Income, Capital and Taxation

We appreciate Fisher's (1937) logical development of the theory of income, capital and taxation. However, Fisher's logical developments hinge on two assertions: the first explicit and the second implicit. The explicit assumption is that psychical income, as Graves (1939) mentions, is best reflected in consumption, Fisher's measure of real income, and not money income. Fisher ignores that savings, the accumulation of financial and real capital, provide two other very important "goods", social status (see Auerbach, 2005) and security that are both important parts of psychical income. Second, Fisher never addresses the incidence of taxation. The discussion of the real economic burden of taxation never seems to arise. When we consider Kalecki's theory of taxation, all taxes (commodity or expenditure, income and capital) potentially affect income to capital, and, therefore, are capitalized. If we logically extend Fisher's argument that savings should not be taxed because it will result in the double (or some multiple levels of) taxation, then taxation of expenditures also potentially leads to multiple levels of taxation of income from capital in ways unforeseen by Fisher. Moreover, the taxation of capital potentially has no effect on the value of capital while stimulating the economy—it depends, as described above, on the government budget stance. In this section, we consider some examples as to how expenditure taxes, income taxes, and capital taxes affect the value of capital.

Commodity Taxation and the Value of Capital. Suppose, as Fisher describes, that we use the accounting norm of a perpetuity to describe the value of capital, so that capital's value is:

(4) $C_o = M/i.$

Now further suppose that an expenditure tax on wage goods, T_w, is introduced to reduce the government budget deficit. If we adopt Kalecki's original assumptions, which to us seem a good approximation of what results, the expenditure tax reduces the value of monetary payments and the value of capital, so that value of capital in (4) can be rewritten as:

(4') $C_o = (M-T_w)/i.$

These results can be modified if we recognize that some owners of capital are preferred claimants, rentiers or lenders (bondholders, mortgage holders and preferred stock holders) earning fixed monetary payments regardless of earnings. In this circumstance, rentiers' incomes are unaffected by expenditures tax, but residual claimants' (stockholders) incomes fall by more than the expenditure tax, because of their contractual commitments to rentiers.[8] These financial commitments result in a decline in the capital of residual claimants that is greater than the capitalized value of the expenditure tax.

If the commodity tax is used to finance an increase in government expenditures, for example to increase the dole of the unemployed, as Kalecki described, the value of capital remains unchanged, as described in (4).

Taxation of Capital Income (and the Double Taxation of Savings). Fisher (1937) concluded that capital income taxes reduce the flows of income that are capitalized in the value of capital, and that capital income taxes are, therefore, capital taxes. Capital income taxes are an example of the double taxation of income. However, as Kalecki (1937) shows, the taxation of capital income only reduces monetary payments to capital if the capital income taxes are used to reduce the budget deficit. In the first case, where the capital income tax reduces the budget deficit, the tax is capitalized as:

(5) $C_o = M(1\text{-}t_p)/i;$

8 For example, suppose, because of debt contracts and the like, that preferred claimants share or monetary payments are fixed by contract at Mp. If the sum of monetary payments to capital is M = Mp + Mrd, where Mrd = monetary payments to residual claimants, and Mp/M = z, and Mrd/M = 1 – z. The expenditure tax reduces M, but given Mp, z must increase, Mrd must decrease.

where t_p = profits tax rate. If we suppose that the profits tax is used to increase government expenditures, then monetary payments to capital increase by the amount of the tax so that equation (5) reduces back to (4) or:

(4") $C_o = M/i = M(1-t_p)/i + t_p M/i.$

If we introduce rentiers, fixed income claimants, then the capital income tax, coupled with an increase in government spending, redistributes capital income from rentiers, fixed income claimants, to capitalist, residual income claimants. The capital income tax, with the increase in government spending, increases the pre-tax flow of income without affecting contractual debt service obligations. As Kalecki (1937) explains, as rentiers find their after-tax monetary payments reduced by the income tax, the lending rate of interest potentially increase as lenders attempt to shift the income tax.

Taxation of Corporation Income and Double/Triple Taxation. As Fisher and others have explained, the taxation of corporation income when earned and then distributed results in triple taxation of income to capital. As the story goes, the original investment was financed out of income that was taxed (taxation in the first instance), the corporation income (a capital flow that determines the value of capital) is then taxed (taxation in the second instance), and then dividends are taxed (taxation in the third instance). These additional two layers of taxation, as the story goes (see for example Harberger (1962)), disproportionately increase the tax burden on corporate capital, reduce incentives and misallocate capital.

If we follow Kalecki's line of reason, the multiple layers of taxation on capital reduce capital income flows when the taxation is used to reduce the budget deficit. If the multiple layers of taxation on capital income are coupled with increases in government spending, then the same effects result as in the case of the capital income tax: capital income flows to residual claimants, capitalists, are likely to increase at the expense of rentiers.

Taxation of Capital Gains (Another layer of taxation). A fourth instance of taxation of capital income is the capital gains tax. Fisher logically describes the source of capital gains: getting closer to the realization of planned (expected) future monetary payments. However, we know that capital gains results from a variety sources, for example Fisher's "X-factors."

Like the other taxes, the capital gains tax, if used to finance government expenditures, is likely to redistribute the flows of capital income rather than alter the level of capital income. If for example, capital gains are the consequence of speculative financial transactions, the capital gains tax will redistribute capital income away from financial capitalists (those engaged in the production and distribution of financial products) to industrial capitalists (those engaged in the production and distribution of "goods"). Given the redistributive nature of capital gains taxes, not all capital gains taxes are alike. The government can use the capital gains tax, therefore, to discourage certain types of speculative activities and to encourage other types of productive activities.

Capital Taxes. Fisher (1937) views capital taxes as, in effect, a tax on future monetary payments. Kalecki (1937) shows that when the incidence of taxes is considered, capital taxes, on aggregate, when spent to finance government expenditures, potentially do not affect the flow of monetary payments, but the distribution of the flow. Like for the other cases, the flow of monetary payments to capital will be redistributed from rentiers to capitalists.

For Fisher (1937), if a capital tax on a perpetuity is introduced in time period 1, and the value of perpetuity is given in equation (4), the capital value of the perpetuity after the tax is:

(6) $C_1 = (M/i) - t_c(C_0/i);$

where t_c = capital tax rate, or in the general case:

(6') $C_t = (M/i) - t_c(C_{t-1}/i),$

Equation (6') is a first order difference equation that converges to:

(7) $C_t = M/(i+t_c),$

assuming $i > t_c$. As seen in (7), the capital tax is negatively capitalized in the value of capital.

For Kalecki (1937), monetary payments, M, increase by the amount of the capital tax so that equation (6) can be rewritten as:

(7') $C_1 = (M/i) + t_c(C_0/i) - t_c(C_0/i) = M/i.$

Once again, Fisher ignored the incidence of taxation in considering the effects of taxation on capital values. Again, rentiers will pay higher capital taxes and lose capital values, but capitalists, as residual claimants, will see their share of profits rise, and see the value of their capital increase.

Kalecki (1937), as quoted above, concluded that capital taxes were preferred to income taxes, because the tax would be the same if the funds were lent or not. However, we can see here that rentiers are squeezed by the capital tax, and that rentiers are likely to react to the situation by requiring higher "risk" premiums and interest rates, reducing capital values in general. This situation could be mitigated by Central Bank policy but, central bankers being "bankers" are like to object to a capital tax in the first instance. Given that all taxes are capital taxes, we find such an objection questionable.

8. Conclusion

Irving Fisher logically defines income, capital, capital gains, and earnings. Based on his logical definitions, Fisher applies accounting theory, in the form of double-entry bookkeeping, to derive at a measure of income. This measure of income is a monetary measure of the net flow of services generated by various types of capital, and the net flow of services is reflected as the psychical income. Psychical income is the net flow of services to the mind-body capital asset. From this definition of income, other types of income can be deduced, such as real income measuring the real consumption of goods, and money income reflecting net monetary payments to capital and labor. Fisher applies his theory of income to the practical problem of taxation. Fisher starts from the perspective that, in practice, the tax base should best approximate psychical income. To develop a practical measure of psychical income, Fisher makes some explicit and implicit assumptions. Fisher assumes that negative psychical income, for example the disutility caused by work, is zero. He also assumes that positive psychical income is best reflected in consumption, and that the monetary value of consumption, approximated in part through the application of accounting theory (for durable goods such as automobiles household appliances and homes), provides a best approximation of psychical income, and, therefore, the tax base. Fisher reminds readers that income once set aside as savings is no longer income, the savings are an addition to capital, and capital is future income, not current income. In making the assumption that psychical income is best reflected in some measure of consumption, Fisher seems to ignore that the additions to capital generate two very important social goods that are part of psychical income: security and social status.

Fisher concludes that his tax base, consumption, has practical advantages over the income tax base. The consumption tax base avoids complicated definitions of income, and is easier to administer than the income tax base. The consumption tax base promotes lifetime horizontal equity. In promoting lifetime horizontal equity, the consumption-based tax system encourages two goods: individual responsibility, and savings induced economic growth. The practical advantages are based upon some implicit assumptions.

First, Fisher implicitly assumes a pre-Keynesian economic system where savings determine investment, and output is fixed by supply constraints. Second, Fisher implicitly assumes that the legal incidence and economic incidence of taxation are the same, and, therefore, none of his "practical" proposals consider any separate economic incidence effects, and especially aggregate demand effects, on the national economy.

A brief sampling of the literature reflects early concerns (Veblen, 2002/1908, and Grave, 1939) over Fisher's theory that were ignored, that Fisher continues to have strong supporters (Shoven and Walley, 2005, and Kaldor, 1958), that others, notably Tobin (2005), Auerbach (2005) and Graetz (2005) have theoretical and practical concerns about the consumption tax. For example, Graetz explains that the progressive income tax (in Fisher's terminology, "pre-savings income" tax) is universally accepted as fair, and that any attempt to undermine that tax, for example vis-à-vis a consumption tax, is politically unacceptable, maybe even another "third rail" in politics. The political infeasibility of the consumption tax has caused Fisher's consumption tax to creep into the income tax system by giving preferential tax treatment to various types of savings and, in recent years, to various types of capital income. The result of this "creep" is the hybridization of the tax system and the development of the dual tax system.

In our judgment, Fisher would have benefited from Kalecki's early insights into the tax system. Kalecki explicitly considered the economic incidence and effects of taxation. Kalecki shows that if taxes are used to reduce the government budget deficits that those taxes, regardless of the tax base, reduce the flow of income to capital. Consumption taxes reduce the flow of income to capital, and consumption taxes are negatively capitalized in the value of capital goods. As consumption taxes increase, and the flow of income to capital decreases, fixed income claimants' share of capital income increases. Consumption taxes used to reduce budget deficits and the like, and increase rentiers' shares of capital income. We recall that Keynes was interested in the euthanasia of the rentier. Moreover, income and capital taxes used to fund government expenditures have little effect on the flows of income to capital and little effect on the value of capital, but such taxes do redistribute income away from fixed income claimants, like rentiers, to capitalists. We conclude that the shift in tax policy towards consumptions taxes, for example at the state and local government levels, results in a double negative incidence, reducing the income of workers and the flow of capital to capitalists. We also conclude that Fisher was wrong about (state and local) consumption taxes not being capitalized in the value of capital; they are, and that national taxes on capitalist incomes, or on capital directly, would adversely reflect capital values; they don't.

Finally, from reading Fisher and his proponents, who like to emphasize the double, triple or quadrupling of taxes when the tax base is (pre-savings) corporation income, one would wonder why businesses would ever choose to incorporate in the first place. The success of the corporation as a form of business is so prevalent that Kalecki's tax shifting mechanisms must be clearly in place. To understand tax policy, and its connection to moral goods, such as economic growth, we need to understand Kalecki's tax shifting mechanisms.

References

Asimakopulos, A. (1975). "A Kaleckian theory of income distribution." *Canadian Journal of Economics*, 8, 3, 313–333.

Auerbach, Alan J. (2005). "Comments on John. B. Shoven and John Whalley's "Irving Fisher's Spendings (Consumption) Tax in Retrospect." *American Journal of Economics and Sociology*, 64, 1, 237–243.

Auerbach, Alan J., and Kotlikoff, Laurence J. (1987). *Dynamic Fiscal Policy.* Cambridge: Cambridge University Press.

Davidson, P. (1982–83). "Rational expectations: a fallacious foundation for studying crucial decision-making processes." *Journal of Post Keynesian Economics*, 5, 2, 182–197.

De Vecchi, Nicolo (2008). "Keynes on Kalecki's Theory of Taxation: Contents Approved, Method Question." *History of Political Economy*, 40, 1, 164–182.

Fisher, Irving (1937). "Income in Theory and Income Taxation in Practice." *Econometrica*, 5, 1, 1–55. Fisher, Irving (2011/1906). *The Nature of Capital and Income.* ThaiSunset Publications.

Graetz, Michael J. (2005). "Comments on John B. Shoven and John Whalley. "Irving Fisher's Spendings (Consumption) Tax in Retrospect." *American Journal of Economics and Sociology*, 64, 1, 245–256.

Graves, Clyde H. (1939). "A Note on Irving Fisher's Concept of Income." *Econometrica*, 7, 4, 349–356.

Harberger, A.C. (1962). "The incidence of the corporation income tax." *Journal of Political Economy*, 70, 215.

Jacoby, Neil H. (1958). "Review of *An Expenditure Tax*." *The Yale Law of Journal*, 67, 3, 516–51. Kaldor, Nicholas (1955). *An Expenditure Tax.* Allen and Unwin.

Kalecki, Michal (1937). "A Theory of Commodity, Income and Capital Taxation." *The Economic Journal*, 47, 187, 444–450.

Laramie, Anthony J., and Mair, Douglas (2000). *A Dynamic Theory of Taxation.* Edward Elgar.

Musgrave, Richard A. (1939). "A Further Note on the Double Taxation of Savings." *American Economic Review*, September, 549–550.

Simons, H. C. (1928). *Personal Income Taxation.* Chicago: University of Chicago Press.

Slitor, R. E. (1938). Administrative Aspects of Expenditure Taxation." In *Broad-Based*

Taxes: New Options and Sources, ed. R. A. Musgrave. New York, John Hopkins University Press.

Tobin, James (2005). "Fisher's *The Nature of Capital and Income*." *American Journal of Economics and Sociology*, 64, 1, 207–214.

Shoven, John B. and Whalley, John (2005). "Irving Fisher's Spendings (Consumption) Tax in Retrospect." American Journal of Economics and Sociology, 64, 1, 215–235.

Evangelos N. Charos, Merrimack College, MA, USA
Hossein Kazemi, Stonehill College, MA, USA
Anthony J. Laramie, Merrimack College, MA, USA
Douglas Mair, Heriot-Watt University, Edinburgh, UK

Chapter 9: The Susceptibility Cycle: A New Approach to our Kaleckian Study of New Orders of Non-Defense Capital Goods in the USA: 1992–2013

Abstract: The paper follows Kalecki's 'golden rules' under which historical materialism and econometrics can be reconciled, provided that changes in the superstructure are not of such a magnitude as to invalidate the use of econometrics to estimate the relationships between the economic variables in the sector of productive activity and that productive relations are explicitly included in the model. Econometric estimates of the determinants of non-farm, non-financial (non-defense) capital goods in the USA 1992–2013 are presented. Statistically significant relationships are found between investment orders and net cash flows (or "profits"), the net increase in financial liabilities, the net increase in financial assets, manufacturing capacity utilisation, manufacturing sales the interest rate spread, and national defense spending as a share of GDP.

1. Introduction

Downward (2003) identifies a tension in Post Keynesian economics between philosophical pronouncement and practice over the role of econometrics. Critical realists, such as Lawson, maintain that there will be a plurality of partial regularities and processes underlying events that are either not predictable or are not universal event-regularities, thereby rendering econometric inference inherently problematic. This view is shared by Davidson who argues that Post Keynesians embrace a non-ergodic and transmutable-reality view of the world in which probabilities, and thus econometric inference, are not reliable guides to the future. Only Dow's 'Babylonian' approach allows for the possibility of some limited econometric testing. Herein lies the rub for Post-Keynesian economics, how to reconcile its philosophical rejection of 'empirical realism' with a practical need for empirical analysis.

Kalecki (1965) was also aware of the tension between the historical materialist foundations of Post-Keynesian economics and econometrics. Econometric models, he recognised, are based on functional relationships over time between econometric variables which are assumed to be given and not subject to change. Historical materialism considers the development of society as the interaction between the spheres of productive forces and productive relations (the base), and the spheres of natural resources and of government, culture, science and technology (the superstructure). The base and the superstructure interact with each other. Econometric modeling can only be properly applied in the sphere of productive forces if the relationships between the economic variables remain stable. But Kalecki recognised that the complexity of the relationships between the base and the superstructure raises doubts over the legitimacy of econometric modeling.

His historical materialist vision of the development of society would, therefore, appear to lead Kalecki to the same negative conclusion on the role of econometrics as Post Keynesians generally. But he goes on to argue that... "the two approaches [historical materialism and econometrics] do not seem to be irreconcilable" (ibid: 233). He emphasises (ibid: 236) that the basic postulate of historical materialism is that autonomous changes in the superstructure are of lesser importance when compared with the effect upon it of productive forces and changes in productive relations.

Kalecki (ibid: 236) defines three 'golden rules' under which econometric estimation of productive forces can be justified.

Rule #1: there are no autonomous changes in the spheres other than strictly economic conditions or if they do not affect significantly the pattern of economic development; and

Rule # 2: there is no significant feedback effect involved in the impact of economic development upon the other spheres of the system.

Rule # 3: What is, however, totally inadmissible is to construct an econometric model of future economic development postulating tacitly non-existent productive relations.

Kalecki justifies rules #1 and #2 in the following manner. He defines a function, f, which stands for the aggregate of the relationships between and within the base and the superstructure. He assumes f to be invariable, an assumption he recognises as 'rather far-reaching' (ibid: 234), but is justifiable as a useful tool of analysis if its limitations are kept in mind. Kalecki (ibid: 236) accepts that the basic assumption of the econometric model that the function, f, which stands for all the relationships between the economic variables past and present, is not subject to change cannot be maintained, but concludes nevertheless (ibid: 237):

It may be therefore concluded that f is normally a function of such a type that small changes in its shape do not lead to major changes in the economic variables (authors' emphasis).

For Kalecki, therefore, the impact of the superstructure on the spheres of production forces and productive relations is an empirical issue.

In our present study of the determinants of new orders for non-defense capital goods in the USA, we justify our use of econometrics by following Kalecki's 'golden rules'. We examine specifically whether changes that may have taken place in the superstructure in the USA over the period of our study have not been of such a magnitude as to have had a significant impact on the behaviour of the economic variables in the sphere of productive activity. This is not the same as assuming 'ceteris paribus'. We pay close attention to the residuals in our reported equations for evidence of mis-specification, which might suggest evidence of changes in the superstructure. We explicitly include a measure of the wage share as a variable in our model to capture some of the influence of the sphere of productive relations on the sphere of productive forces.

The remainder of the paper is structured as follows. First, we discuss Kalecki's theory of investment as refined and updated by Courvisanos (1996). We then develop an updated version of Kalecki's model of new orders of capital goods new orders, the empirical categories of which we define in Appendix 2. In the next section, we present and discuss the various statistical tests of the model, the details of which are given in Appendix 1. Finally, we present our conclusions and consider their implications.

2. Kalecki's theory of investment updated

Following the publication of Keynes' *General Theory* (1936), understanding the determinants of business fixed investment expenditures has been an important focus in understanding cyclical volatility and long-period economic growth. Alongside Keynes, Kalecki (1954) developed an alternative theory of investment that links profits, risk, and income distribution to the determination of decisions to place new orders of investment goods. Kalecki's analysis links the macro-economic and micro-economic foundations of investment in explaining short-period fluctuations in investment and longer-period trends in production and employment.

Courvisanos (1996) has refined and extended Kalecki's theory of investment by combining Kalecki's 'objective' and Keynes' (and others') 'subjective' determinants of investment. The synthesis of these elements results in what Courvisanos terms the susceptibility cycle. The susceptibility cycle seeks to explain the fragility of fixed investment decisions. Fragility is the result of tensions that investment decisions create concerning firms' future profitability and viability. These tensions are a function of exposure to risk and uncertainty over time and lead to the emergence of a cycle. It is this susceptibility cycle of investment orders that drives the investment expenditure cycle and plays a significant role in the shape and intensity of the business cycle.[1]

By identifying these tensions, or behavioral elements, Courvisanos provides a link between Kalecki's (1971a/1968) rather mechanical theory of the business cycle and Keynes's views on the role of conventions or rules of thumb (event-regularities) in the investment decision process. The tangible, quantifiable, behavioral elements of this Kalecki-Courvisanos (K-C) susceptibility cycle are reflected in profits, the gearing (debt to equity) ratio and in the level of capacity utilisation.

Recognition of the latent behaviouralist foundations of Kalecki's investment theory is a major step in confirming his contemporary relevance in a global economy that has changed significantly since he wrote about it from the 1930s to the 1960s (Courvisanos, 2004). Essentially, Kalecki was a child of the second industrial revolution based on the widespread use of electrical power and the application of 'Fordist' mass production techniques. Since his death, a major revolution has occurred resulting in the emergence of what is generally described as The New Economy based on the widespread use of micro-electronics and computer-based networks. Information and communication technologies (ICT) have resulted in knowledge becoming the key engine of economic growth. For Kalecki to remain relevant to 21st century economics, he must be understood and applied from a new perspective. This can be achieved if the latent behaviouralist foundations of his original writings are brought into the open. Interpreting Kalecki from a behaviouralist perspective allows his basic insights to be linked with recent research in evolutionary economics.

If Kalecki is to be re-interpreted as a behavioural economist, then it has to be demonstrated that the K-C susceptibility cycle model is capable of being measured empirically. Laramie, et al. (2007) report the results of their attempt at estimating the K-C susceptibility cycle for the United Kingdom over the period 1980Q1 to

1 We thank Jerry Courvisanos for this clarification.

1996Q4. From that study, they conclude that such tangible Kaleckian manifestations of business susceptibility as profitability, risk and capacity utilisation have played a significant role in explaining investment behaviour in the UK through the 1980s and early 1990s.

However, time has moved on since that UK study and the transition to The New Economy has proceeded apace. The present paper presents an updated version of the K-C susceptibility cycle, for a different economy, the USA, for a more recent time period, 1992Q3–2013Q4, using a different econometric approach.

3. Kalecki's model of new orders updated

We now proceed to consider the determinants of new orders of non-defense capital goods of non-financial corporations in the USA over the last three decades. New orders of capital goods lead investment expenditures over the business cycle and can be used to predict business fixed investment expenditures. Kalecki (1954, 1971/1968) explained new orders as being dependent upon entrepreneurial savings, the change in business profits and the change in the capital stock. Given these determinants, new orders lead investment expenditures subject to a construction/production time lag. In order to develop his susceptibility cycle, Courvisanos (1996) builds on the work of Kalecki and Zarnowitz (1973) by blending in ideas from Keynes (1936), Minsky (1982), Loasby (1967) and Shackle (1970). By so doing, he considers the psychological tensions that build up over a cumulative investment process. These psychological factors manifest themselves in new orders of investment goods, and reflect semi-autonomous factors, like cash flows, capacity utilisation, and debt-to-equity (or gearing) ratios, (some of which reflect the sphere of productive activity) and "exogenous" factors, for example, innovations and political instability (the superstructure) (Courvisanos 1996, pp. 164–189). The one important feature not present in Courvisanos's formulation of the susceptibility cycle, however, is a reference to productive relations.

4. The model and statistical tests

In Courvisanos's basic specification, investment orders, D_t, depend on P_t = the level of profits; $\Delta P = P_t - P_{t-1}$, an actual increment in profit levels; g_t = the gearing ratio; c_t = the capacity utilisation rate; i. e.:

(1) $D_t = f(P_t, \Delta P_t, g_t, c_t)$.[2]

We update Courvisanos's investment equation to include the following:

- an interest rate spread, s (between Moody's Aaa Corporate Bond Yield and the Federal Funds Rate) as an additional measure of risk and cash commitments,
- a sales accelerator, sa,
- the wage share, w, to satisfy Kalecki's third golden rule,
- a defense spending variable, nd, to capture the superstructure

and we drop the change in profits term (as we expect the capacity utilisation rate variable and the sales accelerator to pick up this effect).

We rewrite Courvisanos's basic investment equation to read:

(1') $D_t = f(P_t, s_t, sa_t, g_t, c_t, w, nd)$.

We now consider the relationship between the right-hand-side variables and the level of investment orders.

Profits: We expect the profits coefficient to be positive. In the various versions of his investment theory, Kalecki included a profits variable to capture the effects of 'entrepreneurial' savings on investment and changes in profitability as affecting the prerequisites for re-investment of 'entrepreneurial' savings. Zarnowitz (1973), Fazzari and Mott (1986–1987), have used net internal cash flows as a proxy for profits in explaining investment expenditures. We modify their approach by also considering the effects of increasing liabilities or acquiring additional financial assets on investment orders. Businesses can acquire financial liabilities to place orders to purchase capital goods, and businesses can use internal funds or the funds raised through the increase in liabilities to acquire financial assets instead of placing orders to purchase capital goods.[3]

Gearing ratio: According to Kalecki's principle of increasing risk, a rising gearing ratio (an increase in debt relative to equity) generates a higher risk of failure

2 Courvisanos (1996, p. 161) lags the right-hand-side variables by one period. Kalecki (1954, p. 98) has investment orders and the right-hand-side variables as contemporaneously determined. We adopt Kalecki's approach here.

3 As described below in Appendix 2, our data on cash flows, the net increase in liabilities and the acquisition of financial assets are derived from US flow of funds accounts. In these accounts, Capital Expenditures = Total Internal Funds (plus the Inventory Valuation Adjustment) plus the Net Increase in Liabilities minus the Net Acquisition of Financial Assets plus the Statistical Discrepancy. Again, we do not expect problems of simultaneity as investment orders lead investment expenditures.

if expected profits from investment plans are not realised. We expect the gearing ratio and new orders to be inversely related.

The interest rate spread: Minsky (1975) modified the effects of the gearing ratio on investment by explicitly considering the effects of cash commitments, such as interest payments. In our approach, we use the interest rate spread to proxy for the effects of cash commitments, and risk and liquidity premium on investment. Moreover, Gertler, et. al. (1991) use an interest rate spread as a proxy to measure the agency costs associated with external finance. A rising interest rate spread increases cash commitments and risk, and reduces new orders.

Capacity utilization: We expect the coefficient on capacity utilisation, *c*, to be positive as rising capacity utilisation is expected to encourage future investment orders. If businesses maintain excess capacity over the business cycle as Kalecki (1971) has asserted (see White 1999), then we expect the capacity utilisation effects to be weak.

Sales Accelerator: A number of capital stock adjustment models link changes in the capital stock, and, therefore, new orders to changes in sales (Zarnowitz 1973, p. 468). Since we are using Census of Manufacturing data, we use manufacturing sales to capture the accelerator effect.[4]

Wage Share: The wage share variable is included to satisfy Kalecki's golden rule that it is inadmissible to postulate tacitly non-existent productive relations.

Defense Spending: Courvisanos (1996) considers defense or military spending (the superstructure) as an exogenous factor influencing investment orders, and he considers the possibility that defense spending can crowd in, that is encourage, non-defense orders of capital goods. The effects of military spending on non-defense new orders of capital goods can be indirect, effected through changes in the other determinants of new orders, or indirect, effected through changes in military spending. Here we simply test for direct effects.

All the nominal data levels were deflated as described in Appendix 2. The data were converted to natural logs, except for the net acquisition of financial assets and the net increase in financial liabilities. During and around the recessions of 2001 and 2007–2009, these series took on negative values. In an attempt to reduce the scale difference between the dependent variable and the explanatory variables, these two variables were divided by real GDP.

4 Sawyer (1986, pp. 51–52) explains the analogous relationship between sales and profits in the investment equation.

Stationarity tests were performed on all the variables for both levels and first differences. The stationarity test statistics are provided in Appendix 1. The test statistics were generated using two methods: the Dickey-Fuller Generalized Least Squares and the Phillips-Perron approaches. The test results with respect to levels is mixed with some levels, such as the net acquisition of financial assets, the net increase in financial liabilities, and the interest rate spread, showing evidence of stationarity (being I(0)). All the first differenced levels show strong evidence of being stationary.

The summary statistics of the variables levels, first-differenced levels are provided in Appendix 1. The empirical definitions of the variables are provided in Appendix 2. A number of variants of the model were tested. We summarise a sample of our results. The estimates were generated using STATA's Prais-Winsten auto-correlation correction technique. The estimates without the constant generated the lowest RMSEs and are illustrated below.

Table 1 shows that all the variables, with the exception of the gearing ratio and the wage share, are statistically significant. All the variables have the expected sign. The coefficient on the national defense share GDP is negative—indicative of a direct crowding out effect. The coefficient on the profits variables indicates that a 1% increase in profits in times t and t-1 increase investment orders by approximately .346% and .198%. A one-percentage point increase in the net acquisition of financial assets reduces investment orders by about .74%, and a one percentage point increase in the net acquisition of liabilities increases investment orders by about .96%. A one percent increase in the manufacturing capacity utilisation rate increases investment orders by about 1.13%, and an increase in manufacturing sales increases investment orders by approximately .81%.[5] A one percent increase in the interest rate spread reduces investment orders by about .02%, and a one percent increase in national defense spending's share of GDP, lagged one quarter, reduces new orders by about .316%. The gearing ratio and the wage share variables are both statistically insignificant. Both of these variables are probably at too high a level of aggregation to pick up.

---

5 Adding manufacturing sales, lagged on period, does not significantly alter the equation. While the lagged variables do have the negative expected sign (their value is -.1944), the coefficient is not statistically different from zero.

Table 1. New Orders of Non-Defense Investment Goods: 1992Q3 to 2013Q4.

Prais-Winsten AR(1) regression -- iterated estimates

Source	SS	df	MS
Model	.320812489	10	.032081249
Residual	.095798932	75	.001277319
Total	.416611421	85	.004901311

Number of obs =	85
F(10, 75) =	25.12
Prob > F =	0.0000
R-squared =	0.7701
Adj R-squared =	0.7394
Root MSE =	.03574

ΔD_t	Coef.	Std. Err.	t	P>|t|	[95% Conf. Interval]	
ΔP_t	.3463605	.1327088	2.61	0.011	.081991	.61073
ΔP_{t-1}	.1982764	.0960539	2.06	0.042	.0069272	.3896256
$\Delta nafY_t$	-.7442393	.2789923	-2.67	0.009	-1.30002	-.1884581
$\Delta nilY_t$	.959292	.3738125	2.57	0.012	.2146193	1.703965
Δc_t	1.127687	.4764282	2.37	0.021	.1785936	2.076781
Δsa_t	.8069462	.3674734	2.20	0.031	.0749017	1.538991
Δs_t	-.0209673	.0099047	-2.12	0.038	-.0406985	-.0012361
Δg_t	.0037397	.0510492	0.07	0.942	-.0979556	.105435
Δw_t	.3220218	.6794165	0.47	0.637	-1.031445	1.675489
Δnd_{t-1}	-.3164188	.1572542	-2.01	0.048	-.6296852	-.0031524
rho	-.3552888					

Durbin-Watson statistic (original) 2.548020
Durbin-Watson statistic (transformed) 2.045225

The transformed value of the Durbin-Watson statistic lies within the prescribed range of values confirming that the error terms are uncorrelated. We take this as confirmation that we have no grounds for not proceeding with our econometric analysis.

We also test the model for two sub-sample periods: 1) 1992Q3 to 2001Q3; and 2) 2001Q 4 to 2013Q4.[6] These results are summarised in Tables 2 and 3. The stationarity tests were repeated for these sub-sample periods, and are reported in Appendix 1. The evidence suggests that for both sample periods that the first differences are I(0).

In estimating the model for the first time-period, we considered a number of the model's variants, including: 1) the model as estimated in Table 1 above; and 2) that same model excluding the variables whose coefficients are statistically insignificant. The second variant generated the smallest RMSE, and the results are presented in Table 2.

6 These two periods basically cover the last two business cycles as defined by the NBER Business Cycle Dating Committee.

Table 2. New Orders of Non-Defense Investment Goods: 1992Q3 to 2001Q3

Prais-Winsten AR(1) regression -- iterated estimates

Source	SS	df	MS
Model	.045418327	3	.015139442
Residual	.027895996	33	.000845333
Total	.073314323	36	.002036509

Number of obs =	36
F(3, 33) =	17.91
Prob > F =	0.0000
R-squared =	0.6195
Adj R-squared =	0.5849
Root MSE =	.02907

ΔD_t	Coef.	Std. Err.	t	P>|t|	[95% Conf.	Interval]
Δsa_t	1.388973	.2833026	4.90	0.000	.8125899	1.965357
Δs_t	-.0241963	.0143548	-1.69	0.101	-.0534014	.0050087
Δnd_{t-1}	-.5804141	.1801764	-3.22	0.003	-.9469858	-.2138424
rho	-.2269584					

Durbin-Watson statistic (original) 2.240190
Durbin-Watson statistic (transformed) 1.938091

For the second time-period, we find that investment orders are essentially driven by two factors: manufacturing sales and defense spending's share of GDP.[7] Recall that for this time period, national defense spending's share of GDP steadily declined.

For the third sub-sample period, 2001Q4 to 2013Q4, our results, see Table 3, are qualitatively similar to those reported in Table 1. In Table 3, we exclude the gearing ratio and the wage share, and the national defense share of GDP isn't lagged.[8] Two noticeably different results emerge for the third sample period in comparison to the first. First, the statistical significance of the capacity utilisation rate coefficient is lost. This finding is not surprising given that manufacturing was operating with slack capacity: the mean capacity utilisation rate was about 75%, fluctuating between a low of about 64% in 2009Q2 and a high of around 79% in 2007Q2. Second, the spread's coefficient is no longer statistically significant. Beginning in 2004Q3, the Federal Funds rate increased from around 1% to about 5.25 in 2007Q3, and the spread decreased from 4.63% to .5%. Prior to the Fed's

7 To consider whether or not national defense share of GDP coefficient was picking up some macro-cyclical effects, we included the first difference of the natural log of real GDP as an explanatory variable. With this inclusion, the real GDP coefficient was statistically insignificant, and the standard errors of spread and national defense coefficients slightly decreased.

8 The lagging national defense share of GDP one period increases the standard error of the estimate and causes the coefficient to be statistically different from zero at the 90% critical value.

tightening in 2004, the average spread was around 4.4% with a standard deviation of about 10% the mean. Following the Fed's easing in 2009, the spread returned to 4.1% with a standard deviation of about 23% of the mean. Given that the average spread during the time period was around 3.5% with a standard deviation of 44%, much of the variation in the spread came from policy changes associated with the Federal Funds rate.

Table 3. New Orders of Non-Defense Investment Goods: 2001Q4 to 2013Q4

Prais-Winsten AR(1) regression -- iterated estimates

Source	SS	df	MS		
Model	.292443709	9	.032493745	Number of obs =	49
Residual	.057152228	40	.001428806	F(9, 40) =	22.74
				Prob > F =	0.0000
				R-squared =	0.8365
				Adj R-squared =	0.7997
Total	.349595936	49	.007134611	Root MSE =	.0378

ΔD	Coef.	Std. Err.	t	P>|t|	[95% Conf. Interval]	
ΔP_t	.3997705	.1287455	3.11	0.003	.1395662	.6599748
ΔP_{t-1}	.2731093	.1317621	2.07	0.045	.0068083	.5394104
Δnaf_t.	-1.10709	.3389705	-3.27	0.002	-1.792175	-.422005
Δnil_t	.9794215	.440463	2.22	0.032	.0892126	1.86963
Δc_t	1.022472	.7123653	1.44	0.159	-.4172723	2.462216
Δsa_t	1.370372	.5603653	2.45	0.019	.2378319	2.502913
Δsa_{t-1}	-.6974323	.3184553	-2.19	0.034	-1.341055	-.0538101
Δs_t	-.0153227	.0125877	-1.22	0.231	-.0407634	.010118
Δnd_t	-.4785189	.2338092	-2.05	0.047	-.951065	-.0059729
rho	-.4179211					

Durbin-Watson statistic (original) 2.737541
Durbin-Watson statistic (transformed) 2.068951

Figure 1. The Spread: The difference between Moody's Aaa Corporate Bond Yield and the Federal Funds Rate, 2001Q4 to 2013Q4 (Source: Federal Reserve Bank of St. Louis, FRED DATABASE).

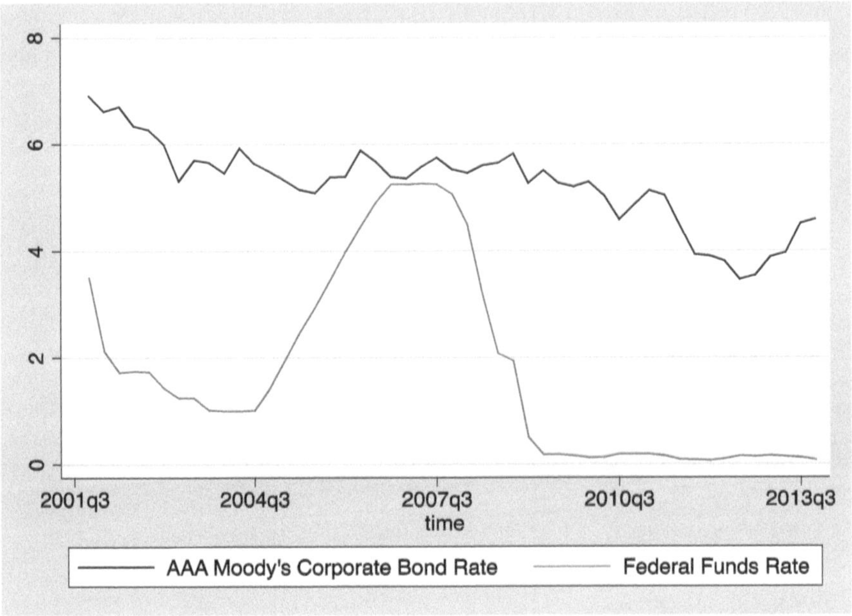

None of the estimates show any relationship between the wage share and new orders. We believe that this result does not violate Kalecki's third 'golden rule' for two related reasons. First, the wage share was calculated at a higher level of aggregation that what is needed to capture economic class relationships. Our definition of the wage share is non-financial sector corporation compensation to employees divided by value added. This measure includes overhead salaries (including executives' compensation). Second for all three sample periods, the wage share is relatively stable with standard deviations of less than 3% of the mean. Changes in the wage share effect on investment decisions, we suspect, is a slower secular process affecting trend investment decisions.

5. Conclusion

As Post Keynesians, we are conscious of the need to exercise caution in the use of econometrics to explain business investment behaviour. We think that it is counter-productive for Post Keynesians to retreat into empirical nihilism. We have explicitly adopted a Kaleckian approach in this paper as this appears to us to offer a course by which Post Keynesians may plot a hazardous voyage between the Scylla of theoretical integrity and the Charybdis of empirical testing.

We had three objectives in this paper. First, we wished to test whether it is appropriate to attempt to estimate econometrically a Post-Keynesian model of fixed capital investment decisions. Our results suggest that provided Kalecki's 'golden rules' are observed it is possible to do so. It is necessary to check whether the structure of the equations is such as to justify the assumption that the superstructure of the economy has remained sufficiently stable to permit econometric modeling of the base. In the equations we report above, we see no evidence that precludes us from drawing that conclusion.

Second, we attempt to estimate an updated behaviouralist version of Kalecki's investment theory. This we do by extending Courvisanos's Kaleckian interpretation of the susceptibility cycle. We find that new orders of capital non-defense goods are largely explained by six variables which impact on business susceptibility: 1) business profits (cash flows); 2) net cash flow as modified by the net increase in financial liabilities and net acquisition of financial asset; 3); the manufacturing capacity utilisation rate; 4) manufacturing sales; 5) the interest rate spread; and 6) national defense's share of GDP. The gearing ratio, the debt-to-equity ratio, which we might have expected to influence business susceptibility, had no statistically significant effect on new orders. We believe our study to be unique in seeking to estimate ex ante business susceptibility as manifested in new orders for non-defense capital goods instead of the more conventional ex post measure of actual capital expenditures.

Third, we believe our study to be unique in explicitly including the wage share as an explanatory variable. However, as Kalecki (1954, 1971/1968) indicates, and is borne out by the evidence here, the wage share is a slowly evolving variable and should be treated as a parameter in cyclical studies of investment.

The results we report in this paper, when taken in conjunction with the earlier results for the UK (Laramie, et al., 2004a), lead us to conclude that, on a behavioralist interpretation, Kalecki's investment theory provides a relevant 21st century explanation of investment volatility. To the best of our knowledge, ours are the only two studies that have recognised the importance of studying investment behavior *ex ante*, incorporating the behavioural and institutional influences that impact on business investment decision-making and explicitly recognising the potential influence of productive relations.

Appendix 1

Table 1A. Summary Statistics (Data sources are described below.)

Variable	Obs	Mean	Std. Dev.	Min	Max
D	87	174.8677	44.6418	91.14934	251.1632
P	87	1114.629	457.4706	419.7128	2019.83
naf	87	493.4621	438.8687	-932.2855	1343.737
nil	87	498.1355	426.7266	-783.7058	1443.118
c	87	.7725632	.045156	.639	.8419999
sa	87	713.5234	54.19265	593.4122	804.7954
s	87	.0306379	.0153328	.0011	.0533
w	87	.6146624	.0270823	.5678809	.6628107
g	87	.5023793	.1003123	.294	.844
nd	87	.047592	.0060876	.0377268	.0624155

Variable	Obs	Mean	Std. Dev.	Min	Max
ΔlnD	86	.0111608	.0596238	-.2574372	.1573067
ΔlnP	86	.0182697	.0378657	-.1365118	.1270461
ΔrnafY	86	.0007324	.0208259	-.1006386	.0564644
ΔrnilY	86	.000637	.0177709	-.0569616	.0464633
Δlnc	86	-.0004153	.0149297	-.063678	.0343873
Δlnsa	86	.0026761	.0201138	-.1029134	.0319486
Δlns	86	.0006631	.3482412	-1.704749	1.067838
Δlnw	86	-.0015085	.0079907	-.0196817	.0168445
Δlng	86	-.004609	.0891479	-.1997702	.2364772
Δlnnd	86	-.0039701	.0254398	-.0662053	.059566

Table 2A. Stationarity Tests#

1992Q2 to 2013Q4

Variable	t_μ	t_τ	n_μ	n_τ
D	-0.132	-2.206	-4.531	-10.43
ΔD	-3.878*	-4.263*	-65.791*	-66.136*
P	-2.179**	-2.173	-1.025	-12.738
ΔP	-11.115*	-2.551**	-98.104*	-97.558*
naf	-2.568**	-3.193**	-23.158	*-23.628**
Δnaf	-5.438*	-5.137*	-92.047*	-92.05*
nil	-2.994***	-2.216**	-17.728**	-18.26***

Δnil	-9.833*	-9.882*	-95.458*	-95.469*
c	-2.089***	-3.77*	-6.801	-10.703
Δc	-4.461*	-4.48*	-27.924*	-27.981*
sa	-1.215	-2.455	-8.464	-9.081
Δsa	-4.57*	-4.6*	-35.396*	-36.076*
s	-3.053*	-3.326**	-12.944***	-13.007
Ds	-3.98*	-4.001*	-45.402*	-45.529*
w	0.026	-1.86	-0.732	-4.878
Dw	-2.41**	-3.056**	-101.86*	-101.95*
nd	-0.953	-1.869	-4.441	-4.588
Dnd	-1.189	-1.456	-92.835*	-95.827*
g	-1.461	-1.897	-10.955***	-11.231
Dg	-8.417*	-8.594*	-79.853*	-80.128*

1992Q2 to 2001Q3

Variable	t_μ	t_τ	n_μ	n_τ
D	-6.06	-0.956	-1.595	2.908
ΔD	-1.679	-4.6262*	-29.643*	-30.422*
P	-0.309	-1.388	-0.833	-3.999
ΔP	-2.166***	-3.97*	-35.558*	-34.673*
naf	-1.884	-2.266	-9.476	-12.125
Δnaf	-4.318*	-7.001*	-40.911*	-41.84*
nil	-1.485	-2.289	-7.217	-7.451
Δnil	-5.681*	-5.967*	-37.221*	-38.311*
c	-1.32	-0.932	-4.446	2.169
Δc	-2.298***	-3.419**	-11.236***	-19.196**
sa	-1.561	-1.73	-2.584	3.259
Δsa	-3.852*	-2.899**	-24.765*	-29.876*
s	-2.377	-3.481**	-7.775	-12.211
Δs	-3.779*	-3.894*	-20.875*	-21.005*
w	-0.764	-1.879	-2.369	-2.684
Δw	-4.475*	-4.831*	-27.807*	-29.018*
nd	-494	-0.384	-1.582	-1.003
Δnd	-1.411	-1.628	-41.524*	-39.169*
g	-1.158	-2.04	-4.134	-2.88
Δg	-5.848*	-6.2*	-44.046*	-45.282*

2001Q4 to 2013Q4

Variable	t_{μ}	t_{τ}	n_{μ}	n_{τ}
D	-1.284	-2.115	-5.89	-8.594
ΔD	-4.791*	-5.05*	-36.904*	-36.982*
P	0.452	-3.013***	-1.08	-17.344***
ΔP	-7.417*	-8.046*	-57.755*	-57.603*
naf	-2.236	-2.493	-13.376*	-14.203*
Δnaf	-4.451*	-4.385*	-51.912*	-51.9*
nil	-1.816	-2.216	-10.145	-10.635
Δnil	-7.744*	-7.796*	-57.072*	-56.924*
c	-1.902	-2.109	-6.945	-6.949
Δc	-3.122*	-3.424*	-17.124*	-17.016*
sa	-1.896	-2.01	-7.45	-7.434
Δsa	-4.061*	-4.067*	-17.806*	-17.808*
s	-2.885*	-2.962***	-6.446	-6.491
Δs	-2.766*	-2.939***	-24.612*	-24.403**
w	-0.013	-2.213	-2.393	-10.078
Δw	-2.797*	-8.517*	-62.953*	-62.541*
nd	-1.527	-1.799	-4.145	1.309
Δnd	-.621	-1.019	-52.134*	-59.311*
g	-2.447**	-2.575	-9.825	-9.783
Δg	-4.528*	-5.177*	-41.429*	-41.605*

#The tests statistics were derived from data expressed in natural logs (except for naf and nil) and were generated using the Dickey-Fuller Generalized Least Squares, the t_{τ} and t_{μ} columns, and the Phillips-Perron unit root methods, the n_{τ} and n_{μ} columns. Stationarity tests were performed assuming a constant, and no trend (see the τ test statistics), and a constant and a trend (see the μ test statistics). *, **, and ***, indicate statistical significance at the 99%, 95% and 90% critical values. For the Dickey-Fuller test, the lag was constrained to four and the optimal lag was chosen to minimise the root mean squared error. For the Phillips-Perron test, the lag was constrained to three by the Newey-West criteria.

Appendix 2: Empirical Definitions

Our data are derived from four main sources: 1) The US Census of Manufacturers (*Manufacturer's Shipments, Inventories, and Orders: Historic Timeseries Accounts (NAICS Based)*; 2) The Federal Reserve's *Flow of Funds Accounts*; 3) *The National*

Income and Product Accounts of the US; and 4) The Federal Reserve Economic Data (FRED database) provided by the St. Louis Federal Reserve Bank.

Investment orders (D): For the dependent variable, investment orders of non-defense new capital goods, as published by the Census Bureau, was used. The Census Bureau provides monthly data. The monthly data were converted into quarterly data by summing up the three months of data. We used the NAICS time series. This series is available from 1992, second quarter to date. Investment orders were deflated by the Non-residential Business Fixed Investment Equipment price index as provided by BEA in Table 1.1.4, line 11.

Profits (P): For the profit variable, total internal funds plus the inventory valuation adjustment of non-farm non-financial corporations (which excluded dividends) is used. This series is found in the *Federal Reserve's Flow of Funds Accounts*, Table F1.02, line 9. In addition to the profits variable, we consider the effects of the net increase in liabilities (*nil*) and the net acquisition of financial assets (*naf*) on new orders. The net acquisition of financial assets minus the net increase in financial liabilities equals net lending, if positive, or net borrowing, if negative. These data are provided by the Federal Reserve, in the *Flow of Funds Accounts*, Table F.102, lines 16 and 37. These data also deflated using the equipment price index.

Gearing (or leverage) ratio (g): Two measures of the gearing ratio were considered: 1) Debt to Net Worth; and 2) Debt to Equity. Neither series generated statistically significant results. We report our findings using the debt to equity ratio. These data are found in the *Federal Reserve Flow of Funds Accounts*, Table B.102, lines 36 and 37.

Capacity utilisation (c): We considered two empirical definitions of the capacity utilization rate: 1) Total Industrial Capacity Utilisation provided by FRED; 2) Manufacturing Capacity Utilisation, also provided by FRED. Total Industrial Capacity Utilisation and the cyclical variation in output variables were highly correlated.

The interest rate spread (s): The interest rate spread is calculated as the difference between the yield on Moody's Seasoned Aaa Corporate Bond Yield and the Federal Funds Rate as provided by FRED. Other measures of the spread, such as the difference between Moody's Aaa Corporate Bond Yield and the Ten-Year Treasury Rate were used, but this spread measure was statistically insignificant.

The Sales Accelerator (sa): The sales accelerator is seasonally adjusted manufacturing sales provided by the Census of Manufacturing. Monthly data were summed to derive quarterly data. The quarterly data we deflated by the producer price index found as provided by FRED.

The wage share (w): The wage share is calculated as non-financial corporations' compensation to employees divided by the respective value added and this series is provided in Table 1.14 in the National Income and Product Accounts.

Defense Spending (nd): The defense spending variable is measured as the ratio of National Defense and Consumption Expenditures and Gross Investment (Table 3.11.5 of the NIPA) to Nominal GDP.

References

Courvisanos, J. 1996. *Investment Cycles in Capitalist Economies: A Kaleckian Behavioural Contribution*, Cheltenham, Edward Elgar.

Downward, P. 2003. "Econometrics" in King, J. E. ed. *The Elgar Companion to Post Keynesian Economics*, Cheltenham, Edward Elgar.

Fazzari, S. M. and Mott, T. L. 1986–87. Investment theories of Kalecki and Keynes, *Journal of Post Keynesian Economics*, Vol. IX, No. 2, 171–187.

Gertler, R., Hubbard, R. Glenn, and Kashyap, Anil, "Interest Rate Spreads, Credit Constraints, and Investment Fluctuations: An Empirical Investigation," in Financial Markets and Financial Crises, ed. R. Glenn Hubbard, University of Chicago Press, 1991.

Kalecki, M. (1943), Political Aspects of Full Employment, *Political Quarterly*, pp. 347–356.

Kalecki, M. 1954. *Theory of Economic Dynamics*, London, Unwin University Books.

Kalecki, M. 1965. "Econometric Model and Historical Materialism in On Political Economy and Econometrics: Essays in Honour of Oskar Lange, Warsaw, Polish Scientific Publishers.

Kalecki, M. 1971/1968. Trend and the business cycle, *Selected Essays on the Dynamics of the Capitalist Economy*, Cambridge, Cambridge University Press.

Keynes, John Maynard 1936. *The General Theory of Employment, Interest and Money*, New York, Harbinger,

Laramie, A. J., Mair, D. and Miller, A.G. 2004a. 'Kalecki's investment theory reconsidered', in Sadowski, Z. L. and Szeworski, A. (eds) *Kalecki's Economics Today*, London, Routledge.

Laramie, A. J., Mair, D. and Reynolds, P. J. 2004b. 'Kalecki's theory of income distribution: the answer to a maiden's prayer?' in Wray, L. R. and Forstater, M. (eds) Contemporary Post Keynesian Analysis, Cheltenham, Edward Elgar.

Laramie, A. J., Mair, D. and Miller, A. G. 2007. 'Kalecki's investment theory: a critical realist approach', in Holt, R. P. F. and Pressman, S. (eds) *Empirical Studies in Post Keynesian Economics*, New York, M. E. Sharpe.

Laramie, A. J., Mair, D. 2010. "The Kalecki-Courvisanos Susceptibility Cycle: Does it Exist?" unpublished.

Loasby, B. J. (1967), "Long-Range Formal Planning in Perspective," *Journal of Management Studies*, 4, pp. 300–308.

Minsky, H. P. 1975. *John Maynard Keynes*, New York: Columbia University Press.

Minsky, H. P. 1982. *Can it Happen Again?*, Armonk, New York, M. E. Sharpe.

Shackle, G. L. S., 1970. Expectations, Enterprise and Profits: The Theory of the Firm, 2nd ed., Cambridge, Cambridge University Press.

White, G. 1999. 'Rethinking Kalecki on the Trend and Cycle', *Review of Political Economy*, Volume 11, Number 3, pp. 341–353.

Zarnowitz, Victor 1973, *Orders, Production and Investment – a Cyclical and Structural Analysis*, National Bureau of Economic Research, New York, Columbia University Press.

Douglas Mair, Heriot-Watt University, Edinburgh, UK
Evangelos N. Charos, Merrimack College, MA, USA
Hossein Kazemi, Stonehill College, MA, USA
Anthony J. Laramie, Merrimack College, MA, USA

Chapter 10: New Orders of Non-Defense Capital Goods and Its Relationship to Business Fixed Investment Expenditures: 1992 to 2013

Abstract: The determinants of non-farm non-financial corporation orders of non-defense capital goods (as generated by the Census Bureau) is reviewed and modeled during the period of 1992 to 2013. A statistically significant relationship between investment orders and profits (cash flows), capacity utilization, sales, the interest rate spread, and other variables is found. New orders of capital goods are used to explain, subject to a lag, shipments of investment goods. A statistically significant relationship is found between investment expenditures and new orders, subject to modifications by changes in contemporaneous economic conditions (largely reflected in cyclical changes in financial conditions). In addition to autocorrelation corrected regression equation, a vector error correction model is developed to show that a long-term relationship exists between *current* shipments and *current* new orders of investment goods. The "error correction" part of the model is shown to be statistically insignificant.

1. Introduction

This chapter extends the work of the last chapter to consider the relationship between the susceptibility cycle (the new investment orders cycle) and the investment expenditure cycle. To extend the work, we revisit the determinants of new orders of non-defense capital goods of non-financial corporations during the last two-plus decades, we consider the lagged relationship between the two cylces, and we consider the factors that impact on that lagged relationship.[1]

1 Non-financial corporations' new orders of non-defense capital goods series is provided by the US Census Bureau. This series includes new orders of: small arms and ordnance; farm machinery and equipment; construction machinery; mining, oil, and gas field machinery; industrial machinery; vending, laundry, and other machinery; photographic equipment; metalworking machinery; turbines and generators; other power transmission equipment; pumps and compressors; material handling equipment; all other machinery; electronic computers; computer storage devices; other computer

New orders of capital goods lead investment expenditures over the business cycle and can be used to predict business fixed investment expenditures. Kalecki (1954, 1971/1968) explained new orders as being dependent upon entrepreneurial savings, the change in business profits and the change in the capital stock. Given these determinants, new orders lead investment expenditures subject to a construction time lag. Likewise, Zarnowitz (1973, p. 413) states: "Investment decisions are necessarily the antecedent and are treated as the proximate "cause" of investment spending." Zarnowitz (1973, pp. 442–463) estimates investment expenditures as a distributive lag depending on past levels of investment orders. In order to develop his susceptibility cycle, Courvisanos (1996) builds on the work of Kalecki and Zarnowitz by blending in the work of Keynes (1936), Minsky (1982), Loasby (1967) and Shackle (1970), and, by so doing, considers the psychological tensions that build up over a cumulative investment process. These psychological factors manifest themselves in new orders of investment goods, and reflect semi-autonomous factors, like cash flows, capacity utilization, and debt-to-equity (or gearing) ratios, and exogenous factors, like innovations and political instability (the superstructure) inter alia (see Courvisanos 1996, pp. 164–189). Laramie, Mair and Miller (2004 and 2007) provide evidence of the susceptibility cycle using UK data. Laramie and Mair (2010) looked for further evidence of the susceptibility cycle in the US and made comparisons to the findings for the UK.

This paper refines the econometrics of Laramie, Mair and Miller (2004 and 2007). We use new empirical definitions of the dependent and explanatory variables, and include the interest rate spread (between the Ten-Year Treasury Note and the Federal Funds Rate) as an additional measure of risk and cash commitments. We explicitly follow Kalecki's "golden rule" by testing for the effects of the "wage share" and military spending (the superstructure) on investment orders, and we relate investment orders to capital expenditures, subject to the production lag and modifications.

The major conclusions of the paper are as follows. First, new orders of nondefense capital goods are largely explained by five factors: 1) Profits (cash flows); 2) Changes in business net asset position (acquisition of net financial assets

peripheral equipment; communications equipment; search and navigation equipment; electromedical, measuring, and control instruments; electrical equipment; other electrical equipment, appliances, and components; heavy duty trucks; aircraft; railroad rolling stock; ships and boats; office and institutional furniture; and medical equipment and supplies (http://www.census.gov/manufacturing/m3/adv/pdf/table1a.pdf).

less the increase in net financial liabilities); 3) The capacity utilisation rate; and 4) Manufacturing sales; 5) The interest rate spread. The gearing (leverage) ratio and the wage share are not shown to be statistically significant in explaining new orders. Moreover, national defense's spending share is inversely related to new orders. Second, as can be expected, the relationship between shipments of capital goods (investment expenditures) and new orders is shown to be statistically significant, subject to a lag, using both quarterly and monthly data. Third, the lag is subject to adjustments, given changes in the debt-to-equity ratio (and changes in other "economic" conditions). Specifically, an increase in the debt-to-equity ratio reduces capital goods shipments relative to new orders. In addition, dummies were used to capture shifts in intercept and slope relationships. An intercept dummy was used to capture a shift in the post 9/11 intercept, and a slope dummy was used to capture the affects of the "Great Recession" on the relationship between shipments and new orders (the coefficients of both dummy variables were statistically significant with negative signs).

This paper is structured as follows. First, the capital goods new orders model is developed. Then, the empirical categories are defined. Next, various statistical tests are presented and discussed. Finally, the conclusions are summarised.

2. The Model: New Orders of Non-Defense Capital Goods

In Courvisanos's basic specification, investment orders, D_t, depend on P_t = the level of profits; $\Delta P = P_t - P_{t-1}$, an actual increment in profit levels; g_t = the gearing ratio; c_t = the capacity utilisation rate; i.e.:

(1) $D_t = f(P_t, \Delta P_t, g_t, c_t)$.[2]

We update Courvisanos's investment equation to include the following:

- an interest rate spread, s (between Moody's Aaa Corporate Bond Yield and the Federal Funds Rate) as an additional measure of risk and cash commitments,
- a sales accelerator, sa,
- the wage share, w, to satisfy Kalecki's third golden rule,
- a defense spending variable, d, to capture the superstructure

and we drop the change in profits term (as we expect the capacity utilisation rate variable and the sales accelerator to pick up this effect).

2 Courvisanos (1996, p. 161) lags the right-hand-side variables by one period. Kalecki (1954, p. 98) has investment orders and the right-hand-side variables as contemporaneously determined. We adopt Kalecki's approach here.

We rewrite Courvisanos's basic investment equation to read:

(1') $D_t = f(P_t, s_t, sa_t, g_t, c_t, w, d).$

We now consider the relationship between the right-hand-side variables and the level of investment orders.

Profits: We expect the profits coefficient to be positive. In the various versions of his investment theory, Kalecki included a profits variable to capture the effects of 'entrepreneurial' savings on investment and changes in profitability as affecting the prerequisites for re-investment of 'entrepreneurial' savings. Zarnowitz (1973), Fazzari and Mott (1986–1987), have used net internal cash flows as a proxy for profits in explaining investment expenditures. We modify their approach by also considering the effects of increasing liabilities or acquiring additional financial assets on investment orders. Businesses can acquire financial liabilities to place orders to purchase capital goods, and business can use internal funds or the funds raised through the increase in liabilities to acquire financial assets instead of placing orders to purchase capital goods.[3]

Gearing ratio: According to Kalecki's principle of increasing risk, a rising gearing ratio (an increase in debt relative to equity) generates higher risk of failure, if expected profits from investment plans are not realised. We expect the gearing ratio and new orders to be inversely related.

The interest rate spread: Minsky (1975) modified the effects of the gearing ratio on investment by explicitly considering the effects of cash commitments, such as interest payments. In our approach, we use the interest rate spread to proxy for the effects of cash commitments on investment. Moreover, Gertler, et. al. (1991) use an interest rate spread as a proxy to measure the agency costs associated with external finance. A rising interest rate spread increases cash commitments and risk, and reduces new orders.

Capacity utilisation: We expect the coefficient on capacity utilisation, *c*, to be positive as rising capacity utilisation is expected to encourage future investment orders. If businesses maintain excess capacity over the business cycle as Kalecki (1971) has asserted (see White 1999), then we expect the capacity utilisation effects to be weak.

---

3 As described below in Appendix 2, our data on cash flows, the net increase in liabilities and the acquisition of financial assets are derived from US flow of funds accounts. In these accounts, Capital Expenditures = Total Internal Funds (plus the Inventory Valuation Adjustment) plus the Net Increase in Liabilities minus the Net Acquisition of Financial Assets plus the Statistical Discrepancy. Again, we do not expect problems of simultaneity as investment orders lead investment expenditures.

Sales Accelerator: A number of capital stock adjustment models link changes in the capital stock, and, therefore, new orders to changes in sales (Zarnowitz 1973, p. 468). Since we are using Census of Manufacturing data, we use manufacturing sales to capture the accelerator effect.[4]

Wage Share: The wage share variable is included to satisfy Kalecki's golden rule that it is inadmissible to postulate tacitly non-existent productive relations.

Defense Spending: Courvisanos (1996) considers defense or military spending (the superstructure) as an exogenous factor influencing investment orders, and he considers the possibility that defense spending can crowd in, that is encourage, non-defense orders of capital goods. The effects of military spending on non-defense new orders of capital goods can be indirect, effected through changes in the other determinants of new orders, or indirect, effected through changes in military spending. Here we simply test for direct effects.

All the nominal data levels were deflated as described in Appendix 2. The data were converted to natural logs, except for the net acquisition of financial assets and the net increase in financial liabilities. During and around the recessions of 2001 and 2007–2009, these series took on negative values. In an attempt to reduce the scale difference between the dependent variable and the explanatory variables, these two variables were divided by real GDP.

Stationarity tests were performed on all the variables for both levels and first differences. The stationarity test statistics are provided in Appendix 1. The test statistics were generated using two methods: The Dickey-Fuller Generalized Least Squares and the Phillips-Perron approaches. The test results with respect to levels is mixed with some levels, such as the net acquisition of financial assets, the net increase in financial liabilities, and the interest rate spread, showing evidence of stationarity (being I(0)). All the first differenced levels show strong evidence of being stationary.

The summary statistics of the variables' levels and first-differenced levels are provided in Appendix 1. The empirical definitions of the variables are provided in Appendix 2. A number of variants of the model were tested. We summarise a sample of our results. The estimates were generated using STATA's Prais-Winsten auto-correlation correction technique. The estimates without the constant generated the lowest RMSEs and are illustrated below.

---

4 Sawyer (1986, pp. 51–52) explains the analogous relationship between sales and profits in the investment equation.

Table 1 shows that all the variables, with the exception of the gearing ratio and the wage share, are statistically significant. All the variables have the expected sign. The coefficient on the national defense share GDP is negative—indicative of a direct crowding out effect. The coefficient on the profits variables indicates that a 1% increase in profits in times t and t-1 increase investment orders by approximately .346% and .198%. A one percentage point increase in the net acquisition of financial assets reduces investment orders by about .74%, and a one percentage point increase in the net acquisition of liabilities increases investment orders by about .96%. A one percent increase in the manufacturing capacity utilisation rate increases investment orders by about 1.13%, and an increase in manufacturing sales increases investment orders by approximately .81%.[5] A one percent increase in the interest rate spread reduces investment orders by about .02%, and a one percent increase in national defense spending's share of GDP, lagged one quarter, reduces new orders by about .316%.

The gearing ratio and the wage share variables are both statistically insignificant. An intercept dummy variable and a various slope dummies were used to test for any post-9/11 effects or Great Recession effects. None of theses variables' coefficients were statistically significant.

5 Adding manufacturing sales, lagged on period, does not significantly alter the equation. While the lagged variables do have the negative expected sign (its value is -.1944), the coefficient is not statistically different from zero.

Table 1. New Orders of Non-Defense Investment Goods: 1992Q3 to 2013Q4.

Prais-Winsten AR(1) regression -- iterated estimates

Source	SS	df	MS
Model	.320812489	10	.032081249
Residual	.095798932	75	.001277319
Total	.416611421	85	.004901311

Number of obs	=	85
F(10, 75)	=	25.12
Prob > F	=	0.0000
R-squared	=	0.7701
Adj R-squared	=	0.7394
Root MSE	=	.03574

ΔD_t	Coef.	Std. Err.	t	P>|t|	[95% Conf.	Interval]
ΔP_t	.3463605	.1327088	2.61	0.011	.081991	.61073
ΔP_{t-1}	.1982764	.0960539	2.06	0.042	.0069272	.3896256
$\Delta nafY_t$	-.7442393	.2789923	-2.67	0.009	-1.30002	-.1884581
$\Delta nilY_t$	.959292	.3738125	2.57	0.012	.2146193	1.703965
$\Delta c_t 1$	.127687	.4764282	2.37	0.021	.1785936	2.076781
Δsa_t	.8069462	.3674734	2.20	0.031	.0749017	1.538991
Δs_t	-.0209673	.0099047	-2.12	0.038	-.0406985	-.0012361
Δg_t	.0037397	.0510492	0.07	0.942	-.0979556	.105435
Δw_t	.3220218	.6794165	0.47	0.637	-1.031445	1.675489
Δnd_{t-1}	-.3164188	.1572542	-2.01	0.048	-.6296852	-.0031524
rho	-.3552888					

Durbin-Watson statistic (original) 2.548020
Durbin-Watson statistic (transformed) 2.045225

The transformed value of the Durbin-Watson statistic lies within the prescribed range of values confirming that the error terms are uncorrelated. We take this as confirmation that we have no grounds for not proceeding with our econometric analysis.

3. Statistical Results: Non-Farm Non-Financial Corporate Fixed Investment

In this section, we attempt to explain the relationship between non-farm non-financial corporate fixed investment expenditures (as reflected in manufactures shipments), and new orders of investment goods. The new orders and shipments data series are provided by the Census Bureau.

To begin, like Kalecki (1971) and Zarnowitz (1973), investment expenditures are a lagged function of investment orders; i.e.:

(2) $I_{t+\tau} = f(D_t)$.

Courvisanos' susceptibility (investment orders) cycle and investment expenditure (shipments) cycle is illustrated using quarterly data in Figure 1 below. As shown in Figure 1, during the expansion of the 1990s orders and shipments followed each quite closely. With the expansion coming to an end in 2001, shipments initially increased relative new orders, and, then, with the contraction, shipments fell relative to new orders. With recovery of 2003 to 2007, shipments exceeded new orders and with the Great Recession, shipments dramatically fell relative to new orders. Since the 'recovery' from the Great Recession, shipments have risen relative to new orders. The post-9/11 relationship between shipments and orders seems to be much 'looser' when compared to the pre-9/11 shipments.

Figure 1 illustrates that new orders can be cancelled or otherwise modified, as discussed by Courvisanos (1996), in the lag between orders and deliveries. As a result, we modify the investment equation as:

(3) $I_{t+\tau} = f(D_t, \text{Modifiers}_t).$

Figure 1. The Susceptibility Cylce: US, 1992Q2 to 2013Q4.

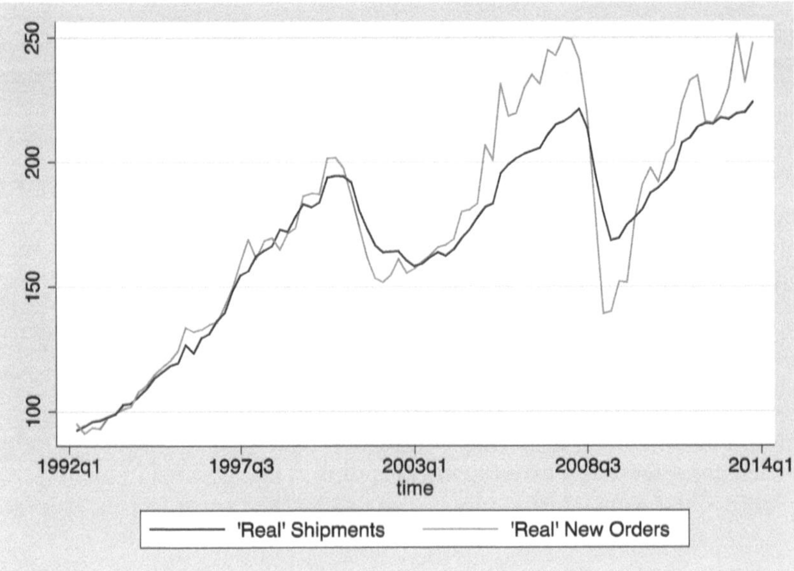

Source: Census of Manufactures. Nominal Data were deflated using the BEA's Equipment Price Deflator (as described in the Appendix).

Various "modifiers" were tested, and three modifiers proved to have statistically significant coefficients: the debt-to-equity ratio, the post-9/11 intercept dummy, and the "Great Recession" slope dummy, which will be discussed below.

To illustrate this model, we utilised two sets of techniques for different sets of data. First, we illustrate the model using autocorrelated regressions for both quarterly and monthly data, and then we consider a vector error correction model, again, using quarterly and monthly data. All the data are converted natural logs. The stationarity tests for the shipment (investment expenditure) series is provided in the Appendix with the other stationarity tests. The investment series in levels is non-stationary (I(0)), and its first differences are stationary (I(1)).

Table 2 illustrates our estimates without the modifiers. The lags were chosen to minimise the root mean squared error of the regression. Table 2 shows that investment expenditures are determined by contemporaneous and one-and-two-quarter lagged levels of new orders. A 1% increase in new orders in times t-2, t-1 and t generate increases in shipments of about .124%, .141% and .256%. The constant, given that the data are first differenced, reflects the trend level of shipments. The constant has the expected sign and is statistically significant.

Table 2: The Relationship between Shipments and Orders, 1993Q1 to 2013Q4: Without Modifiers, quarterly data.

Prais-Winsten AR(1) regression -- iterated estimates

Source	SS	df	MS		
				Number of obs =	84
				F(3, 80) =	58.69
Model	.049975134	3	.016658378	Prob > F =	0.0000
Residual	.022707716	80	.000283846	R-squared =	0.6876
				Adj R-squared =	0.6759
Total	.07268285	83	.000875697	Root MSE =	.01685

D.lnrndeship	Coef.	Std. Err.	t	P>|t|	[95% Conf.	Interval]
lnrndeno						
D1.	.255891	.0323669	7.91	0.000	.1914788	.3203033
LD.	.1410125	.034352	4.10	0.000	.07265	.2093751
L2D.	.1237046	.0328741	3.76	0.000	.058283	.1891262
_cons	.0041484	.0017269	2.40	0.019	.0007117	.0075851
rho	-.105701					

Durbin-Watson statistic (original) 2.194274
Durbin-Watson statistic (transformed) 1.992537

Next, we consider the effects of including modifiers. The first modifier we include is the debt-to-equity ratio. In addition, we consider the possibility that the trend is non-linear and include time as an additional RHS variable. The two-quarter lagged debt-to-equity ratio's coefficient has a negative sign and is statistically significant at the 90% confidence level. A one percent increase in the debt-to-equity ratio decreases shipments by .04%. In addition, the coefficient on the time variable is small (and statistically significant), indicating that the trend is non-linear (see Table 3).

Table 3: The Relationship between Shipments and Orders, 1993Q1 to 2013Q4: With the Debt-to-Equity Ratio, Non-linear trend.

Prais-Winsten AR(1) regression -- iterated estimates

Source	SS	df	MS
Model	.055681104	5	.011136221
Residual	.020913548	78	.000268122
Total	.076594651	83	.000922827

Number of obs	=	84
F(5, 78)	=	41.53
Prob > F	=	0.0000
R-squared	=	0.7270
Adj R-squared	=	0.7095
Root MSE	=	.01637

D.lnrndeship	Coef.	Std. Err.	t	P>|t|	[95% Conf.	Interval]
lnrndeno						
D1.	.244678	.0322004	7.60	0.000	.1805719	.3087841
LD.	.1158811	.0356863	3.25	0.002	.0448352	.186927
L2D.	.1179994	.0319768	3.69	0.000	.0543385	.1816604
time	-.000123	.0000647	-1.90	0.061	-.0002519	5.92e-06
lndebtequity						
L2D.	-.0399975	.0225212	-1.78	0.080	-.0848338	.0048388
_cons	.0258246	.0113973	2.27	0.026	.0031344	.0485149
rho	-.1525499					

Durbin-Watson statistic (original) 2.282638
Durbin-Watson statistic (transformed) 2.001409

Next, we modify our results by including a shift dummy to reflect the post-9/11 era, and a slope dummy to reflect the effects of the Great Recession on the relationship between orders and shipments (see Table 4). In Table 4, the intercept dummy's and the time's coefficients are not statistically different from zero, neither is the constant. The slope coefficient on the slope dummy is statistically different from zero and negative. Its coefficient indicates that, with a two-quarter lag, the "Great Recession" reduced the new coefficient from about .184 to about .042 (= .184 – .142). Given that the time variable and intercept DUM are highly correlated (simple correlation coefficient = .84), we drop the time variable, retain the constant and re-estimate the model.

Table 4: The Relationship between Shipments and Orders, 1993Q1 to 2013Q4: With the Debt-to-Equity Ratio, Non-linear trend, Intercept and Slope Dummies.

Prais-Winsten AR(1) regression -- iterated estimates

Source	SS	df	MS		
				Number of obs =	84
				F(7, 76) =	34.03
Model	.061113152	7	.00873045	Prob > F =	0.0000
Residual	.019499687	76	.000256575	R-squared =	0.7581
				Adj R-squared =	0.7358
Total	.08061284	83	.000971239	Root MSE =	.01602

D.lnrndeship	Coef.	Std. Err.	t	P>|t|	[95% Conf.	Interval]
lnrndeno						
D1.	.2375789	.0320371	7.42	0.000	.1737716	.3013862
LD.	.1322943	.0362812	3.65	0.000	.0600341	.2045545
L2D.	.1843882	.0444772	4.15	0.000	.0958041	.2729723
dum	-.0031128	.0058852	-0.53	0.598	-.0148342	.0086087
dum2dlnrnd~o						
L2.	-.1418083	.0635622	-2.23	0.029	-.2684033	-.0152133
time	-.0000739	.0001194	-0.62	0.538	-.0003117	.0001639
lndebtequity						
L2D.	-.0505618	.022557	-2.24	0.028	-.095488	-.0056356
_cons	.0176417	.0178526	0.99	0.326	-.0179148	.0531981
rho	-.1974655					

Durbin-Watson statistic (original) 2.370548
Durbin-Watson statistic (transformed) 2.034110

Table 5: The Relationship between Shipments and Orders, 1993Q1 to 2013Q4: With the Debt-to-Equity Ratio, Intercept and Slope Dummies.

Prais-Winsten AR(1) regression -- iterated estimates

Source	SS	df	MS
Model	.060661675	6	.010110279
Residual	.019597747	77	.000254516
Total	.080259422	83	.000966981

Number of obs	= 84
F(6, 77)	= 39.72
Prob > F	= 0.0000
R-squared	= 0.7558
Adj R-squared	= 0.7368
Root MSE	= .01595

D.lnrndeship	Coef.	Std. Err.	t	P>|t|	[95% Conf.	Interval]
lnrndeno						
D1.	.2392541	.0317546	7.53	0.000	.1760226	.3024856
LD.	.1326707	.0360938	3.68	0.000	.0607988	.2045426
L2D.	.1799147	.0437428	4.11	0.000	.0928117	.2670178
dum	-.006244	.0030081	-2.08	0.041	-.0122339	-.000254
dum2dlnrnd~o						
L2.	-.1365163	.0628443	-2.17	0.033	-.2616553	-.0113772
lndebtequity						
L2D.	-.0497922	.02244	-2.22	0.029	-.0944758	-.0051085
_cons	.0066984	.0024713	2.71	0.008	.0017775	.0116194
rho	-.1936294					

Durbin-Watson statistic (original) 2.362587
Durbin-Watson statistic (transformed) 2.032529

In Table 5, we can see all the coefficients are statistically different from zero. The inclusion of the intercept-dummy variable indicates that the trend in shipments shifted towards zero (.00067 – .00062 = .00005) in the post-9/11 era.

Next, we consider whether or not income distribution plays any role in affecting the relationship between orders and shipments. As a "rough" measure of income distribution, we utilise compensation-to-employees' share of non-financial sector corporation income. The wage share's coefficient is positive and statistically significant at the 90% confidence level. This result provides further evidence that the falling wage share is contributing to the stagnation of shipments. However, the inclusion of this variable increases the standard errors of the dummy coefficients. We find that the wage share and intercept dummy are correlated (a simple correlation coefficient of .72), and we conclude that the intercept dummy is to some degree picking up the effects of rising income inequality on shipments of capital goods (see Table 6)

Table 6: The Relationship between Shipments and Orders, 1993Q1 to 2013Q4: With the Debt-to-Equity Ratio, Intercept and Slope Dummies, and the Wage Share.

Prais-Winsten AR(1) regression -- iterated estimates

Source	SS	df	MS
Model	.064398523	7	.009199789
Residual	.018795052	76	.000247303
Total	.083193574	83	.001002332

Number of obs	=	84
F(7, 76)	=	37.20
Prob > F	=	0.0000
R-squared	=	0.7741
Adj R-squared	=	0.7533
Root MSE	=	.01573

D.lnrndeship	Coef.	Std. Err.	t	P>|t|	[95% Conf.	Interval]
lnrndeno						
D1.	.2471581	.0315018	7.85	0.000	.1844168	.3098995
LD.	.1405174	.0362366	3.88	0.000	.068346	.2126889
L2D.	.1639394	.0438443	3.74	0.000	.0766159	.2512628
dum	-.004894	.0029847	-1.64	0.105	-.0108386	.0010505
dum2dlnrnd~o						
L2.	-.1133628	.0625773	-1.81	0.074	-.2379963	.0112708
lndebtequity						
L2D.	-.0475272	.0220955	-2.15	0.035	-.0915342	-.0035202
lnwageshare1						
LD.	.4207069	.2308512	1.82	0.072	-.0390731	.8804868
_cons	.0066745	.0023793	2.81	0.006	.0019356	.0114133
rho	-.2248733					

Durbin-Watson statistic (original) 2.414260
Durbin-Watson statistic (transformed) 2.022640

In building the above models, we aggregated the Census Bureau's monthly new orders and shipment series into quarterly data. Now we examine the model using their monthly data. The stationarity tests for the monthly data are similar to the quarterly data and provided in the Appendix. To use monthly data, we had to impute monthly data from quarterly data for the debt-to-equity ratio and for the wage share.[6]

Table 5 shows our estimates with the modifiers included. Our modifiers are the current period's cyclical variation in output and the interest rate spread. These modifiers are expected to be simultaneously determined with investment expenditures. Like before, we used two-stage least squares to estimate equation (3), where

6 The monthly series was derived as follows. Defining Y_0 as the previous quarter's value of Y, and Y_t as the current quarter's value of Y, the value of $Y_i = Y_0 (1+g)^i$, where i = 1, 2, and 3, Y_i = the value of Y in month i, and $g = (.5*(Y_t/Y_0) -1)$.

in the first stage, new investment orders, the cyclical variation in output and the interest rate spread depend on the variables depicted in Table 1. In the second stage, investment expenditures depend on the fitted values of investment orders, the cyclical variation in output, and the interest rate spread. The results are similar to those in Table 4—where the lagged values of new orders retain their statistical significance with the expected signs. However, the inclusion of the modifiers improves the goodness of fit while allowing us to accept the null hypothesis that instruments are uncorrelated with the error term. The cyclical variation in output coefficient is statistically different from zero, and is positively related to investment expenditures. The interest rate spread coefficient has the expected sign, and it is statistically different from zero at the 90% level. These results suggest that the interest rate spread does affect the relationship between new orders and investment expenditures.

Table 5. Investment Expenditures and New Orders: 1994Q1 to 2010Q4: With Modifiers

Instrumental variables (2SLS) regression

Number of obs	=	66
Wald chi2(10)	=	204.70
Prob > chi2	=	0.0000
R-squared	=	0.7608
Root MSE	=	.00098

ΔI_t	Coef.	Std. Err.	z	P>|z|	[95% Conf.	Interval]
ΔD_{t-1}.	1.627684	.5986736	2.72	0.007	.4543051	2.801063
ΔD_{t-2}.	1.395098	.5169306	2.70	0.007	.3819325	2.408263
ΔD_{t-3}.	1.997984	.521553	3.83	0.000	.9757592	3.020209
ΔD_{t-4}.	.7066289	.4911141	1.44	0.150	-.255937	1.669195
ΔD_{t-5}.	.0690834	.5151413	0.13	0.893	-.9405751	1.078742
ΔD_{t-6}.	-.2621003	.5236337	-0.50	0.617	-1.288403	.7642029
ΔD_{t-7}.	.7731969	.507639	1.52	0.128	-.2217572	1.768151
ΔD_{t-8}.	.1τ□144444	.5536809	0.21	0.836	-.9707501	1.199639
Δc_t.	.136787	.0253796	5.39	0.000	.0870439	.18653
Δs_t.	-.0005583	.0003044	-1.83	0.067	-.0011549	.0000384
_cons	.0002969	.0001234	2.41	0.016	.0000552	.0005387

Instrumented: ΔD_{t-i}, i = 1 - 8; Δc_t; Δs_t

Instruments: ΔP_{t-i}, i = 1 - 8
Δc_{t-i}, i = 1 - 8
Δs_{t-i}, i = 1 - 8
Δnil_{t-i}, i = 1 - 8
$\Delta nafa_{t-i}$, i = 1 - 8
Δsa_{t-i}, i = 1 - 8

Tests of overidentifying restrictions:

Sargan (score) chi2(38) = 45.2115 (p = 0.1962)
Basmann chi2(38) = 36.9722 (p = 0.5168)

We also examined equation (3), with and without modifiers for our two sub-sample periods. For the first sample period, 1992 to 2001, the lagged orders' coefficients were statistically different from zero, but the equation's goodness of fit left much room for improvement. When the modifiers were included, the new orders' coefficients lost their statistical significance, and the cyclical variation in output coefficient was statistically significant. The interest rate spread coefficient was not statistically different from zero. These results are available upon request.

For the second sample period, 2001Q4 to 2010Q4, we present our results in Table 6. In this illustration, we lag new orders over four quarters. The coefficients on the first, third and fourth lags are statistically different from zero at the 95% confidence level or higher. The coefficient on the second lagged variable is not statistically different from zero. Like in Table 5, the cyclical variation in output appears to modify investment expenditure, but, in contrast to Table 5, the interest rate spread does not.

Table 6. Investment Expenditures and New Orders: 2001Q4 to 2010Q4: With Modifiers

Instrumental variables (2SLS) regression

Number of obs	= 37
Wald chi2(6)	= 221.23
Prob > chi2	= 0.0000
R-squared	= 0.8473
Root MSE	= .00088

ΔI_t	Coef.	Std. Err.	z	P>|z|	[95% Conf.	Interval]
ΔD_{t-1}.	1.480338	.7014244	2.11	0.035	.1055711	2.855104
ΔD_{t-2}.	.8460939	.5416572	1.56	0.118	-.2155347	1.907722
ΔD_{t-3}.	1.93845	.5087059	3.81	0.000	.9414043	2.935495
ΔD_{t-4}.	1.007792	.495108	2.04	0.042	.0373985	1.978186
Δc_t.	.2210133	.0339548	6.51	0.000	.1544632	.2875634
Δs_t.	.0000588	.0004472	0.13	0.895	-.0008177	.0009353
_cons	.0002919	.000159	1.84	0.066	-.0000198	.0006035

Instrumented: ΔD_{t-i}, i = 1 - 4; Δc_t; Δs_t

Instruments: ΔP_{t-i}, i = 1 - 4
Δc_{t-i}, i = 1 - 4
Δs_{t-i}, i = 1 - 4
Δnil_{t-i}, i = 1 - 4
$\Delta nafa_{t-i}$, i = 1 - 4
Δsa_{t-i}, i = 1 - 4

Tests of overidentifying restrictions:

Sargan (score) chi2(18) = 14.1958 (p = 0.7162)
Basmann chi2(18) = 7.47008 (p = 0.9855)

4. Conclusion

As Post Keynesians, we are conscious of the need to exercise caution in the use of econometrics to explain business investment behaviour. We think that it is counter-productive for Post Keynesians to retreat into empirical nihilism. We have explicitly adopted a Kaleckian approach in this paper as this appears to us to offer a course by which Post Keynesians may plot a hazardous voyage between the Scylla of theoretical integrity and the Charybdis of empirical testing. In this paper, we have attempted to examine the determinants on non-farm non-financial investment orders, as reported by the US Census Bureau in NAICS, and we then attempted to explain how these investment orders related to non-farm non-financial corporate investment expenditures.

New orders of capital non-defense goods are largely explained by four variables: 1) Cyclical variations in real GDP; 2) The interest rate spread between the Ten-Year Treasury Note Rate and Federal Funds Rate; 3) Net Cash Flow as modified by the net increase in financial liabilities and net acquisition of financial assets; and 4) The value of shipments of manufactured goods. The net increase in financial liabilities appears to be funding, in part, new investment orders, and the net acquisition of financial assets seems to be crowding out or substituting for new orders. Other financial variables, such as the debt-to-equity ratio, had no statistically significant effect on new orders. We attribute the lack of significance to the disparate levels of aggregation (the gearing ratio used was for a much larger sample of businesses than was used to generate investment orders). The wage share, during the period of 1992 to 2001, is statistically significant and inversely related to new orders, and is better than the cash flow variable in explaining new orders. During the period 2001 to 2010, no statistically significant relationship between new orders and the wage share is found. The test for the effects of military spending on new orders during the period of 2001 to 2010 revealed no statistically significant relationship. We show, using two-stage least squares, that the fitted values of new orders influence investment expenditures, and the impact of new orders on investment expenditures is altered by changes in contemporaneous economic conditions, as reflected in changes in the cyclical variations in output. The evidence suggests that contemporaneous changes in the interest rate spread have mild effects on the relationship between new orders and investment expenditures.

The results that we report in this paper, when taken in conjunction with the earlier results for the UK (Laramie, Mair and Miller, 2004), lead us to conclude that, on a behaviourist interpretation, Kalecki's investment theory provides a relevant 21st century explanation of investment volatility. To the best of our knowledge, ours are the only two studies that have recognised the importance of studying investment behaviour *ex ante* incorporating the behavioural and institutional influences that impact on business investment decision-making.

Appendix 1: Summary Statistics

Variable	Obs	Mean	Std. Dev.	Min	Max
I	76	.0680108	.0097155	.0475594	.085256
D	75	.0052239	.0008139	.0032192	.006756
P	76	.0723269	.0096786	.0520345	.0943206
c	76	-.0101991	.0263477	-.0809878	.0360491
s	76	.0161342	.0139979	-.009	.037
nil	76	.0420372	.0366392	-.0534217	.132459
nafa	76	.0426508	.0367002	-.0633431	.1330258
s	76	.0295416	.0022712	.0233804	.0330549
w	76	.6471342	.0174358	.6137	.68
d	76	.0467411	.0064668	.03692	.06011

Variable	Obs	Mean	Std. Dev.	Min	Max
ΔI.	75	.0002214	.0019291	-.0071994	.0030642
ΔD	74	-3.25e-06	.0002828	-.0008782	.0007263
ΔP	75	.0005316	.0035921	-.014004	.0106274
Δc	75	-.0004657	.0064084	-.0275054	.0104977
Δs	75	-.00008	.0051159	-.0108	.015
Δnil	75	-.0002867	.022125	-.0709683	.0526559
Δnafa	75	-.0001224	.0258837	-.1047796	.0602505
Δ2sa	74	-7.39e-06	.0007946	-.0036087	.0021967
Δw	75	-.0005707	.0052293	-.0146	.0104
Δc	75	-.0000569	.0012038	-.00322	.00322

References

Courvisanos, J. 1996. *Investment Cycles in Capitalist Economies: A Kaleckian Behavioural Contribution*, Cheltenham, Edward Elgar.

Downward, P. 2003. "Econometrics" in King, J. E. ed. *The Elgar Companion to Post Keynesian Economics*, Cheltenham, Edward Elgar.

Fazzari, S. M. and Mott, T. L. 1986–87. Investment theories of Kalecki and Keynes, *Journal of Post Keynesian Economics*, Vol. IX, No. 2, 171–187.

Gertler, R., Hubbard, R. Glenn, and Kashyap, Anil, "Interest Rate Spreads, Credit Constraints, and Investment Fluctuations: An Empirical Investigation," in Financial Markets and Financial Crises, ed. R. Glenn Hubbard, University of Chicago Press, 1991.

Kalecki, M. (1943), Political Aspects of Full Employment, *Political Quarterly*, pp. 347–356.

Kalecki, M. 1954. *Theory of Economic Dynamics*, London, Unwin University Books.

Kalecki, M. 1971/1968. Trend and the business cycle, *Selected Essays on the Dynamics of the Capitalist Economy*, Cambridge, Cambridge University Press.

Keynes, John Maynard 1936. *The General Theory of Employment, Interest and Money*, New York, Harbinger,

Laramie, A. J., Mair, D. and Miller, A.G. 2004. Kalecki's investment theory reconsidered, in Sadowski, Z. L. and Szeworski, A. (eds) *Kalecki's Economics Today*, London, Routledge.

Laramie, A. J., Mair, D. and Miller, A. G. 2007. 'Kalecki's investment theory: a critical realist approach', in Holt, R. P. F. and Pressman, S. (eds) *Empirical Studies in Post Keynesian Economics*, New York, M. E. Sharpe.

Laramie, A. J., Mair, D. 2010. "The Kalecki-Courvisanos Susceptibility Cycle: Does it Exist?" unpublished.

Loasby, B. J. (1967), "Long-Range Formal Planning in Perspective," *Journal of Management Studies*, 4, pp. 300–308.

Minsky, H. P. 1975. *John Maynard Keynes*, New York: Columbia University Press.

Minsky, H. P. 1982. *Can it Happen Again?*, Armonk, New York, M. E. Sharpe.

Shackle, G. L. S., 1970. Expectations, Enterprise and Profits: The Theory of the Firm, 2nd ed., Cambridge, Cambridge University Press.

White, G. 1999. 'Rethinking Kalecki on the Trend and Cycle', *Review of Political Economy*, Volume 11, Number 3, pp. 341–353.

Zarnowitz, Victor 1973, *Orders, Production and Investment – a Cyclical and Structural Analysis*, National Bureau of Economic Research, New York, Columbia University Press.

Koinon: Sozialwissenschaftliche interdisziplinäre Studien

Herausgeber: Savvas A. Katsikides and Evangelos Charos

Band 1 Karin Johanna Schneider. The Computerization of French Hospital Institutions. Social and Technical Implications for System Development. 1999.

Band 2 Kyriacos N. Demetriou: George Grote on Plato and Athenian Democracy. A Study in Classical Reception. 1999.

Band 3 Andreas Ieronymides: Verkehrsverhalten in Zypern. Der soziale Status als Einflußgröße. 2000.

Band 4 Michael Ornetzeder: Die Solaranlage. Soziale Genese einer zukunftsfähigen Technik. 2000.

Band 5 Hubert Eichmann: Medienlebensstile zwischen Informationselite und Unterhaltungsproletariat. Wissensungleichheiten durch die differentielle Nutzung von Printmedien, Fernsehen, Computer und Internet. 2000.

Band 6 Uwe Saint-Mont: Das Spiel der Interessen. Ein Essay über verblüffende Parallelen zwischen Politik, Wirtschaft, Soziologie und Biologie. 2002.

Band 7 Yiorghos Leventis: Cyprus: The Struggle for Self-Determination in the 1940s. Prelude to Deeper Crisis. 2002.

Band 8 Yiannos Charalambides: The Big Bet. Will the Turkish Accession to the EU Threaten the European Cohesion? 2010.

Band 9 Lambrianos Lambrianou: Ethnische Differenzierungsprozesse in der zypriotischen Gesellschaft bis zur Ausrufung der Republik Zypern (1960). 2011.

Band 10 Eleni Kalokairinou: From Meta-Ethics to Ethics. An Overview of R. M. Hare's Moral Philosophy. 2011.

Band 11 Evangelos N. Charos / Savvas Katsikides (eds.): Selected Essays in Kaleckian Economics. A Collection of Essays on Profits and Investment. 2018.

www.ingramcontent.com/pod-product-compliance
Ingram Content Group UK Ltd.
Pitfield, Milton Keynes, MK11 3LW, UK
UKHW041827100926
8556IPUK00002B/63

9 783631 678862